CW01402101

THE

PUBLICATIONS

OF THE

Lincoln Record Society

FOUNDED IN THE YEAR

1910

VOLUME 102

ISSN 0267–2634

THE COUNTRY JUSTICE
AND THE CASE OF
THE BLACKAMOOR'S HEAD

THE PRACTICE OF THE LAW
IN LINCOLNSHIRE, 1787–1838

PART I:

THE JUSTICE BOOKS OF THOMAS DIXON OF RIBY, 1787–1798

EDITED BY

B. J. DAVEY

PART II:

PAPERS IN THE CASE OF *THOROLD* v. *CATTON*, 1830–1838

EDITED BY

R. C. WHEELER

The Lincoln Record Society

The Boydell Press

First published 2012

A Lincoln Record Society Publication
published by The Boydell Press
an imprint of Boydell & Brewer Ltd
PO Box 9, Woodbridge, Suffolk IP12 3DF, UK
and of Boydell & Brewer Inc.
668 Mt Hope Avenue, Rochester, NY 14620–2731, USA
website: www.boydellandbrewer.com

ISBN 978–0–901503–94–7

A CIP catalogue record for this book is available
from the British Library

Details of other Lincoln Record Society volumes are available
from Boydell & Brewer Ltd

The publisher has no responsibility for the continued existence or accuracy of URLs for
external or third-party internet websites referred to in this book, and does not guarantee
that any content on such websites is, or will remain, accurate or appropriate.

Papers used by Boydell & Brewer Ltd are natural, recyclable products
made from wood grown in sustainable forests

FSC
www.fsc.org

MIX
Paper from
responsible sources
FSC® C013604

Printed and bound in Great Britain by
CPI Group (UK) Ltd, Croydon, CR0 4YY

CONTENTS

LIST OF ILLUSTRATIONS

PREFACE

The Society is most grateful to the respective depositors for permission to publish the documents printed in the two parts of this volume. Thanks are also due to the staff of Lincolnshire Archives for their ready assistance.

For permission to reproduce illustrations, acknowledgement is gratefully made to Lincolnshire County Council (Lincolnshire Archives and Lincoln Central Library), Lincoln Cathedral Library, R. C. Wheeler and Mrs M. Mottram.

Nicholas Bennett
Hon. General Editor

ABBREVIATIONS

CKS   Centre for Kentish Studies
LAO   Lincolnshire Archives
LRS   Lincoln Record Society
RO   Record Office
RS   Record Society

THE JUSTICE BOOKS OF THOMAS DIXON
OF RIBY, 1787–1798

EDITED BY

B. J. DAVEY

INTRODUCTION

The Justice Books of Thomas Dixon of Riby, 1787–1798

Thomas Dixon was the only Lincolnshire magistrate to leave records of his work 'out of sessions'. In three small 'Justice Books' he noted all those petty crimes and disputes brought to 'my house at Riby' between his appointment to the Bench in 1787 and his death in 1798. Unique for Lincolnshire, such records are rare nationally and only a handful have been published.[1] Dixon's books are brief. The first, hardback, predominantly contains summary convictions and commitments to the houses of correction during the early years of his magistracy. The other two are much smaller softback pocket-books, mainly formal records of 'Informations and Complaints' heard between

---

[1]   Lincolnshire Archives Office (LAO), Dixon 8/1/1–4. The most relevant published notebooks are: Alan F. Cirket (ed.), *Samuel Whitbread's Notebooks, 1810–11,1813–14* (Bedfordshire Historical RS 50, 1971); Elizabeth Silverthorne (ed.), *Deposition Book of Richard Wyatt, JP, 1767–1776* (Surrey RS 30, 1978); Elizabeth Crittall (ed.), *The Justicing Notebook of William Hunt 1744–1749* (Wiltshire RS 37, 1982); Michael McGarvie (ed.), *The King's Peace, The Justice's Notebooks of Thomas Horner of Mells, 1770–1777* (Frome, 1997); Gwenda Morgan and Peter Rushton (eds), *The Justicing Notebook (1750–64) of Edmund Tew, Rector of Boldon* (Surtees Society 205, 2000). There is a good list of unpublished sources in Douglas Hay, *Masters, Servants, and Magistrates in Britain and the Empire, 1562–1955* (Chapel Hill, 2004), 75n. Hay's list includes the notebooks of: Sir William Bromley (Warwicks RO, CR 103), part published in *Warwick County Records* 9 (1964); Sir Roger Hill (Bucks RO, D/W 97/8/8), extracts published in *Records of Buckinghamshire* 17:3 (1963), 182–188; Devereux Edgar (Suffolk RO, qS 347.96 and HA 247/5/4); Sir Thomas Ward (Warwicks RO, CR 162/688); Sir Gervase Clifton (Nottinghamshire Archives, M8050–51); The Reverend Henry Gorges Dobyns Yate (Hereford and Worcester RO, BB88/1); George Turner (Suffolk RO, HD 258/1). S. K. Sullivan, in 'Violence, local magistrates and the informal law 1700–1833: magistrates and mediation in Kent', in M. Adams, D. Barker and K. Poludniewski (eds), *Law and Public Policy: Taming the Unruly Horse?*, Australasian Law Teachers' Association, 62nd Annual ALTA Conference, University of Western Australia (2007), draws attention to the riches of magistrates' notebooks and papers in Kent: see Centre for Kentish Studies (CKS), TR 1564/1 (William Brockman, 1689–1701 and 1713–24); U442/045 (Paul D'Aranda, 1707–9); TR 1564/1 (James Brockman, 1725–67); U951/04 (Wyndham Knatchbull, 1734–47); U120/09 (notebook) and U120/011 (papers) (Edward Filmer, 1740–54); TR 1564/1 (Ralph Brockman, 1770–81); U2802/01 (A. Bradley, 1817–19); U951/05–06 (Edward Knatchbull, 1819–22 and 1830–35); U1482/01 (D. James, 1820–26); U2639/01 (Montagu Pennington, 1809–33); Bromley Records Office (BRO), U310/014 (William Emmett, 1711–37); U310/014 (G. Norman, 1792–1802).

1793 and 1798. In all there are entries concerning just over one hundred cases, most in Dixon's hand. The text below also includes information from: the local press, Lindsey Quarter Sessions minutes and rolls, calendars and accounts of the keepers of the houses of correction, parish officers' accounts and Dixon's other notebooks relating to his domestic and farming affairs. Although brief, Dixon's books are of interest, not only because of their rarity, but also because they appear to differ significantly from other known records. As such, they make a contribution to recent debates about magistrates and summary justice in the eighteenth century.

Summary Justice in the Eighteenth Century

Traditionally, magistrates have received a harsh press. It is almost obligatory to begin with Fielding's country justice who committed two men to the house of correction for cutting a twig: 'and with great lenity too; for if we had called it a young tree they would have been both hanged'.[2] Savagery was matched by injustice. The Hammonds' example was the Duke of Buckingham, who 'tried and convicted a man of coursing on his estate. The trial took place in the duke's kitchen: the witnesses were the duke's keepers.'[3]

Such anecdotes need to be placed in a wider context, for summary justice was only one part of the criminal law. The most serious offences were tried at Assizes. Twice every year, in March and July, the king's judges came to Lincoln. Escorted into the city by the sheriff and 'forty spearmen in blue uniforms', they were met by the leading gentry of the county who not only acted as the grand jury in the coming trials, but gathered for the social commotion of assize week, to manage county property, orchestrate coming elections, to dance, to gamble and to marry off sons and daughters.[4] The judicial business opened with the assize sermon in the cathedral, the robed judges then leading a procession across the bail to the castle. Those prisoners who had been held in 'The Pit', the notorious subterranean dungeon below the gaoler's house in the castle yard, were 'delivered' for swift trials. The proceedings ended with the black cap or the white gloves, and were often completed some days later by the grisly ritual of executions.

For the Victorians, looking back from their more ordered arrangements of police and reformatory prisons, eighteenth-century Assizes were part of 'the bloody code', the savage and chaotically ineffectual attempt to control an unruly age by arbitrary terror. In 1975 Douglas Hay challenged this view in a striking and still influential essay, the starting-point for much modern

2   Henry Fielding, *Joseph Andrews* (1742), quoted in John Rule, *Albion's People: English Society 1714–1815* (London, 1992), 227.
3   J. L. and Barbara Hammond, *The Village Labourer 1760–1832* (London, 1911), 14.
4   C. M. Lloyd (ed.), *Letters from John Wallace to Madam Whichcot*, LRS 66 (1973), 33.

discussion.[5] He argued that the eighteenth-century criminal law was in fact a sophisticated and powerful system for upholding the authority and therefore the property of the rich. The essential means by which it achieved this were first, the ceremony and theatre of Assizes; second, the widespread and selective use of reprieves which encouraged dependence on those with the influence to achieve them; and third, the hanging of an occasional lord to maintain the deeply held idea that, in England, all were equal before the law. As Hay put it:

> It was easy to claim equal justice for murderers of all classes, where a universal moral sanction was more likely to be found. ... The trick was to extend that communal sanction to a criminal law that was nine-tenths concerned with upholding a radical division of property.[6]

Such elements of the law created the ideology, the 'mind-forged manacles' which 'allowed the rulers of England to make the courts a selective instrument of class justice' by which, with very limited resources, the few governed the many.[7]

Although powerful and stimulating, Hay's thesis was not without difficulties. It was essentially an interpretation of assize proceedings. The problem with this was that fewer than twenty per cent, at most, of crimes and disputes were heard at Assizes. The remainder, the vast majority, were heard before local magistrates in Quarter Sessions. Studies of the copious records of these courts reveal a very different picture. Unlike Assizes, where property offences dominated the calendars, the most numerous cases tried by the magistrates in Sessions were assaults, with other inter-personal disputes like 'master and servant cases' also figuring largely. Further, in many cases the prosecutors were relatively poor, sometimes surprisingly poor: many were ill-treated servants and battered wives. In the eighteenth century these socially weaker and often illiterate people had to bring and conduct their prosecutions personally. That they did so was remarkable, and surely an indicator that they had confidence in the system. These and other features of Quarter Sessions led Peter King to conclude that, far from being an instrument of class justice, 'the criminal law may more fruitfully be described as a multi-use right within which various groups ... conflicted with, cooperated with and gained concessions from each other'.[8]

---

[5] D. Hay, 'Property, authority and the Criminal Law', in Douglas Hay *et al.*, *Albion's Fatal Tree: Crime and Society in Eighteenth-century England* (London, 1975), 17–63.

[6] *Ibid.*, 26.

[7] *Ibid.*, 48.

[8] Peter King, 'Decision makers and decision making in the English criminal law, 1750–1800', *Historical Journal* 27 (1984), 53. For the evidence of Lincolnshire (Lindsey) Quarter Sessions see B. J. Davey, *Rural Crime in the Eighteenth Century* (Hull, 1994).

Of course, such a conclusion was not compatible with traditional views of magistrates as local tyrants, and in two more recent important studies of summary justice King has argued for a much more complex picture of what happened in justices' parlours and at Petty Sessions. As part of his analysis he emphasises the great discretion which magistrates employed at initial hearings. Even in property offences Justice Samuel Whitbread of Bedfordshire 'clearly used his discretion in every case', exploring possibilities beyond simple conviction or committal for trial. William Hunt of Wiltshire went further, showing 'an even greater preference for informal settlement'.[9] As in the discussion of Quarter Sessions, King also demonstrates high 'plebeian usage' of the summary courts: 'Half of all cases heard by Whitbread ... involved either poor-law or master–servant disputes. In the former case, 83 per cent were instigated by ... paupers. In the latter case very nearly two-thirds were initiated by servants.'[10] Further, poorer prosecutors were adept at 'triangulation', managing their rulers by taking overseers and employers before the local magistrate.[11]

Certainly King warns us that 'At heart the eighteenth-century summary courts were not exclusively, or even primarily, mediation centres or arbitration tribunals ...' and when employers brought cases before local magistrates they did so within 'structures of social expectation which usually operated decidedly in their favour'.[12] However, he maintains his earlier view of the eighteenth-century criminal law as a 'use-right': if the summary courts were not 'neutral tribunals available to all' ... 'the spectrum of roles played by the summary courts ... meant that almost every social group could and did make strategic use of these judicial forums'.[13]

Hay has also given much attention to summary justice in recent years, and found little to challenge his view of the law as an instrument of class justice. He reminds us that 'in virtually all cases, magistrates were prosperous, or very wealthy' and that some of them were exceptionally harsh. He cites the Norfolk justice Thomas Hoseason who, in 1811, heard a case against one of his own employees, struck the man in the face, and sentenced him to a month in the house of correction, 'with twenty lashes'. For Hay, this is just one example of widespread 'oppressive magisterial activity of the most flagrant kind'.[14]

[9]   Peter King, *Crime, Justice and Discretion in England 1740–1820* (Oxford, 2000), 88.
[10]   Peter King, 'The summary courts and social relations in eighteenth-century England', *Past and Present* 183 (2004), 145.
[11]   *Ibid.*, 162.
[12]   *Ibid.*, 156.
[13]   *Ibid.*, 161.
[14]   Douglas Hay, 'Patronage, paternalism and welfare: masters, workers and magistrates in eighteenth-century England', *International Labor and Working Class History* 53 (1998), 29, 40–44.

A further important part of Hay's argument has been his use of the records of the houses of correction, showing that even where magistrates' notebooks are lacking, 'one thing we can count ... is how many men and women were committed to prison', and he finds multitudes there who must have been committed at summary hearings.[15]

Especially, Hay has explored the use of master and servant acts. This legislation was tightened in the eighteenth century so that by Dixon's time an erring servant could be sentenced, by a single justice sitting alone, to three months in the house of correction. Hay shows that it was extensively used, concluding that 'magisterial practice reinforced that social structure and the exploitation on which it was built'.[16] This latter point is of particular interest in the study of Dixon's notebooks because he appears to have spent much of his time hearing master and servant disputes. However, it is important to examine the context of his practice because in many respects he was not a typical magistrate.

Thomas Dixon (1729–1798)

In a county Bench dominated by substantial landowners and clergymen, Dixon was a successful tenant farmer, risen from local yeoman stock. Although he became wealthy enough to live the life of a landed gentleman, he preferred to be, and remained to the end of his life, a working farmer with deep roots and many connections in the local farming community. On the day he was sworn in as a JP, he made two entries in his account book:[17]

October 2 1787. Quallified at Gainsborough Sessions to Act as a Justice of the Peace in and for the Parts of Lindsey.
Sold to Mr William Richardson of Willerton when I was at Gainsborough Sessions 119 drape ews out of which there was fifty double gimbers and old ews sixty-nine, in all 119 at 17s 6d per head   £104 2s 6d

While he was proud to be a justice, there seems little doubt which of the day's business he considered more important and which, for him, really justified the sixty-mile round trip to Gainsborough.

Thomas Dixon was born in 1729, the only surviving child of William Dixon, a successful farmer who built up sizeable estates at Holton-le-Moor

---

15 *Ibid.*, 36; Douglas Hay, *Masters, Servants and Magistrates in Britain and the Empire, 1562–1955* (Chapel Hill, 2004), 95.
16 Hay, 'Patronage, paternalism', 44.
17 LAO, Dixon 4/1: Account Book of Thomas Dixon of Riby, 1755–98.

and elsewhere.[18] Young Thomas was educated locally, probably at Market Rasen, and in 1753 he took a holding of 670 acres of mainly grazing land at West Firsby. In 1758 he moved to Riby to occupy a mixed farm of 770 acres and here he remained for the rest of his life. He might have chosen otherwise. On the death of his father in 1781 he inherited 1750 acres in Holton-le-Moor, Thornton-le-Moor and Normanby-by-Spital, as well as properties in the Marsh around Skidbrooke. He built a substantial new house as the capital of these estates at Holton but sent his son William to live there. Thomas remained at Riby in a brick and apparently thatched farmhouse where his wife made do with only two maids and a boy. It has been described as 'a kindly if perhaps frugal household'.[19]

In 1755 Dixon had married Martha Walkden, daughter of a local clergyman. Her father, Thomas Walkden, seems to have acted as a 'useful ... stand-in vicar' and at one time or other in the eighteenth century was presented to several local livings by the aristocratic Pelham family. However, Mr Walkden lived on, and worked, a small farm at Great Limber, five miles from Riby. Thus Martha probably shared Dixon's preference for a relatively modest lifestyle. They had six surviving children whose careers are an interesting reflection of Thomas Dixon's preferences and ambitions. The eldest boy, William, was established as a farmer in the new house at Holton-le-Moor. He grew up to be a deeply religious, practical and parsimonious man with an almost consuming sense of personal responsibility for the local community. He played a leading role as a layman in the Church of England and founded the Caistor Society of Industry. This established a workhouse for the district and co-ordinated local organisations like friendly societies and the Caistor Matron Society, which encouraged Sunday schools. Although a wealthy man he 'studiously retained the habits and manners of a plain farmer'. Intensely serious, he sought to 'spread the light of the Gospel, and at the same time keep down the rates'. It is said that he had no great affection for his father, who charged him interest on the cost of the house at Holton, and that he was especially shocked and disappointed by his father's will, under which he was to inherit the house and main estate at Holton only after the death of his mother. The only surviving letter from Thomas Dixon to son William gives no trace of animosity. It is clearly a letter from a father to a son, giving practical instructions about the movement of sheep, but it begins 'Dear Son' and ends 'I am your affectionate father ... PS Remember me to your fireside.'[20]

Two younger sons were both given expensive university educations, were ordained and had livings purchased for them by their father. Thomas junior

---

[18] The following paragraphs on Dixon's life and family are *ex.inf.* Dr R. J. Olney, and from Lincolnshire Archives Committee, *Archivists' Report* 22 (1971), 18–26.

[19] T. W. Beastall, *The Agricultural Revolution in Lincolnshire* (History of Lincolnshire 8, 1978), 111.

[20] LAO, Dixon 7/5/19: Letter from Thomas Dixon to William Dixon (18 April 1794).

became Rector of Laceby (and later also a JP) and Richard was Rector of Claxby-with-Normanby. A daughter, Martha, died in 1784 at the age of twenty-one. The three surviving girls each received dowries of £3000 in money or land and all chose successful farmers or tradesmen for husbands. Rachel married a Gainsborough merchant, Jane a seed merchant from Brigg, and Ann a farmer who took over at Riby after Dixon's death. Thus the family certainly had and enjoyed wealth but for the most part they preferred a working, relatively frugal daily life and their connections and ambitions were local.

Although Thomas Dixon styled himself 'esquire' he certainly had no appetite for the cultivated inactivity of the landed gentry, or passion for their sports. He was always busy and his papers give the impression of a man who enjoyed the company of, and dealing with, other local farmers and businessmen, happier at Caistor market than he was in the drawing-room or on the hunting field. Apart from his own holding, he managed farms for two other landlords: he was Lincolnshire agent for T. F. Mackenzie who had properties at Somerby (near Gainsborough) and at Humberston, and in Riby he looked after the estate of his wealthy but not very practical neighbour, Marmaduke Tomline. Such tasks involved not only farming but a good deal of quasi-legal work in the buying, selling and administration of land.

Dixon also shared his neighbours' burden of filling the humble and troublesome parish offices. In a small village like Riby there were so few farmers that most of them had to take one of these offices each year, and Dixon was no exception. Almost every year between 1758 and 1787 he served as Churchwarden, Constable, Overseer of the Poor, or Surveyor of the Highways. In 1785 he wrote testily in the Parish Book: 'Thomas Dixon, Constable & Churchwarden, and out of pocket eleven shillings and one penny on account of being Surveyor of the Highway for the year 1784'.[21] Such wide experience of agricultural and parish affairs no doubt prepared him for his later more exalted public appointments as Land Tax Commissioner in 1769 and Justice of the Peace in 1787.

He also found time for wider business and political activities, especially those based at Caistor. In 1792 his name headed the list of ten 'Gentlemen, Land-Owners and others' who met at the George Inn to raise a subscription for 'the intended canal' from the river Ancholme to Caistor. Although the accounts and papers of this venture have been lost, the canal was built and the newspaper advertisements of its progress suggest that Dixon played a leading role.[22]

Every January he attended the Talbot Inn for the annual meeting of the Caistor Association for the Prosecution of Felons. In return for a subscription

---

21 LAO, Riby Par 7/1: Riby Parish Book, 1742–1856.
22 [*The Lincoln, Rutland and*] *Stamford Mercury*, 28 December 1792. See also Christopher Padley, 'Caistor Canal', *Lincolnshire History and Archaeology* 44 (2009), 5–22.

members received financial and other assistance in finding and prosecuting those who stole their property. These gatherings always attracted over one hundred members and there is a strong impression that the main business was the grand dinner ('on the table at two o'clock') rather than the election of officers and passing the treasurer's accounts. Indeed, the records of these associations suggest they were not very successful in apprehending felons but they were important social organisations which allowed local farmers and tradesmen to exchange views about crime and the causes of crime and especially to reinforce the obligation of neighbours to pursue and prosecute felons.[23]

In 1793 Dixon chaired a meeting at the George to insist on the application of the statute of Charles II's reign to the effect that 'the Winchester bushel only be used in the Sale of all Sorts of Grain' because 'the Customary Measure, when it differs from the Standard established by Law, is injurious to the Poor, and prejudicial to the Public'.[24]

Such concern for the poor appears to have been genuine, albeit partly stimulated by recent events in France. The French Revolution made a powerful impression on the propertied classes in Lincolnshire, including Dixon. In January 1793 over two hundred 'respectable persons' met at the Talbot to found the Caistor Constitutional Association which aimed to preserve the 'Liberty and Properties of His Majesty's Loyal Subjects against Republicans and Levellers' and 'those who disturb Society by seditious or treasonable Practices'. These ends were to be obtained by 'Vigilance and Activity in discovering and bringing to Justice' persons who published seditious writings, engaged in conspiracies, or attempted to 'excite disaffection'. It was also hoped to suppress riots and disorders, and, by 'the Distribution of Constitutional Writings' 'endeavour to undeceive' those who had been 'misled by ... delusive and inflammatory Suggestions'. A committee of twenty-five was elected to lead the association and Dixon was the first of those named.[25] It seems unlikely that he would have given his time to such an organisation unless he shared some of its probably exaggerated fears of dark-prowling 'treason and disaffection' subverting order and property in the area.

When war came, such fears increased. In 1794 a County Meeting was held in the Castle Yard at Lincoln to take steps for 'the internal defence ... and general protection of this Kingdom'. A subscription was raised to establish 'Volunteer companies ... especially near the coast' and 'to form Bodies of Cavalry ... to consist of the Gentlemen and Yeomanry'. The result was a fund of over £11,000 to support 'The Loyal Lincolnshire Yeomanry'. Dixon

---

[23] *Stamford Mercury*; LAO, 4DEG 2/4/1/1: Minutes of Resolutions of the Wragby Association for Prosecuting Felons, 1785; 4BM 5/5/1: Market Rasen New Association for the Prosecution of Felons, 1826.

[24] *Stamford Mercury*, 18 January 1793.

[25] *Ibid.*

was too old to serve but he did travel to Lincoln for the initial meeting and subscribed £20. It was not a huge sum compared with the £500 donated by the leading aristocrats of the county but it was comparable to subscriptions from other magistrates and enough to make him a member of the committee which directed the enterprise.[26]

Unfortunately there is little surviving evidence of Dixon's personality. There is a family story that he was habitually late, even for important meetings, and this is credible, given his demanding business life.[27] By the time he was appointed to the Bench he was fifty-nine and was thus in his sixties during his most active period as a magistrate. It is possible that he did not enjoy the best of health. The 1794 letter to his son begins 'I have been but indifferent lately' and he left a small notebook of 'receipts' for various ailments, collected from friends and relations.[28] Many are cures for animals but a good number deal with indigestion or stomach complaints, perhaps suggesting that he suffered from this sort of discomfort. His obituary notice in the county newspaper has only a brief, three-line statement: 'In him the poor have lost a good and real friend, and the neighbourhood an useful member.'[29] Allowing for the benevolence of an obituary, there may be something in the writer's selection and emphasis of Dixon's concern for the poor. If so, it is interesting because it appears to conflict with some aspects of his Justice Books.

Dixon thus emerges as a very hard-working, practical man with great knowledge and experience of the business and administrative affairs of his community. Above all, he was deeply embedded in that community. In the Caistor area, apart from numerous family contacts, he knew most of the gentry, farmers, tradesmen, parish officers, land agents, lawyers, clergy and many others who worked there. He knew them not merely as casual social acquaintances but as people he met regularly, at market, in vestry, through business negotiations, in the local societies and organisations. He traded with them, attended meetings with them, ran the parish and the district with them. This context was important. Dixon's wide experience ensured that he was a senior figure in his neighbourhood and it was above all his deep roots in that community which formed his approach to the administration of justice.

Dixon's Appointment to the Bench

In 1787 the Lord Lieutenant made a number of new appointments to the Bench and we are fortunate that some of his correspondence survives,

---

26   *Stamford Mercury*, 13 June 1794.
27   *Ex.inf.* Dr R. J. Olney.
28   LAO, Dixon 22/8/1: Pocket Book of Thomas Dixon, 1749–97.
29   *Stamford Mercury*, 14 September 1798.

shedding uncommon light on the process.[30] Lincolnshire magistrates were appointed by the Crown (in practice by the Lord Chancellor) on the recommendation of the Lord Lieutenant, the Duke of Ancaster, in his capacity as Custos Rotulorum, keeper of the rolls or records of the county. Ancaster was then in London so the process was managed by the Clerk of the Peace, Robert Chapman. Chapman wrote all the letters to the parties involved and passed replies, with comments and advice, on to Ancaster. There was no special motive for refreshing the Commission at that time, no fear of unrest nor even much concern about crime. However, rising population and new legislation meant Quarter Sessions were becoming longer and more arduous and a number of existing magistrates had died. The reason for the new appointments was simply to have enough justices to conduct 'the business of the county' which, it was claimed, would soon be 'entirely at a stand still for want of magistrates', in some areas at least.

Having decided on a new Commission, Ancaster's first step was to invite nominations from the aristocracy and leading gentlemen of the county. Dixon was proposed by Charles Anderson Pelham of Brocklesby, soon to be Baron Yarborough, owner of 50,000 acres and the dominant power in north Lincolnshire. Dr Olney points out that a tenant farmer would never have been considered for the Bench in the first half of the nineteenth century, and that Dixon may have been suggested to Pelham by a social intermediary like Revd Dr Parkinson of Ravendale, 'who seems, exceptionally, to have been at home both at Brocklesby and among his middle-class friends and relations'.[31] However, the fact that Pelham submitted nine names out of a county-wide list of only twenty-nine nominees perhaps reflects his concern at the shortage of magistrates in his area, and suggests that Dixon's known experience and active character may have been a recommendation.

Certainly the Lord Lieutenant hoped to recruit experience and hard work in 1787. The reason so much correspondence survives for this Commission is that the Duke of Ancaster had instructed the Clerk of the Peace to write to all gentlemen and clergy nominated to inform them that they would only be appointed if they agreed to 'sue out their *dedimus*' and begin to act immediately. He was trying to remedy a long-standing problem: many gentlemen wanted the honour of being 'in the Commission' but very few were prepared to act in rural Lincolnshire, 'so dull and so dirty' as one described it.[32] In mid-eighteenth-century Lindsey (the Part of Lincolnshire which stretched from Lincoln to the Humber and from the Trent to the sea) there were 197 magistrates. Of these, only between six and ten were active, regular attenders

---

[30] LAO, LQS/E/Justice of Peace/List of Magistrates. The following section is based on these documents and all quotations are taken from them.

[31] *Ex. inf.* Dr R. J. Olney.

[32] Sir Francis Hill, *Georgian Lincoln* (Cambridge, 1966), 94 n.3.

at Quarter Sessions.[33] Ancaster's demand that justices act was a severe jolt to this tradition and elicited some interesting responses. One nominee was blunt: he had 'no intention to act as a magistrate'; he was 'not apprised ... that putting my name into the commission would lay me under a necessity of acting'. At least he was clear and honest. The most popular strategy was to hedge, trying to ensure appointment without an absolute commitment to act: 'He intended to act whenever an opportunity offered of getting others to join him in his neighbourhood' but 'in the present circumstances' he 'did not suppose that he would sue out his *dedimus* immediately, therefore his name being inserted or not, must be left to the Duke to determine'. Some tried to bargain: 'I fear it will not be in my power to act unless his grace will nominate my Father also.' Some were flowery: 'It will afford me infinite satisfaction if I can be the instrument of producing so desirable an effect, but I am afraid, unless a proper colleague can be found, who will unite his endeavours with mine, that my friends here will be, in many instances, disappointed in the expectations they have formed.' One was resigned: 'The distress this part of the county has long been in from the want of magistrates made me apply to Mr Pelham ... and that application leaves me no alternative; though I am fully sensible of the inconveniences attending the duty of a magistrate.'

In the midst of these rather depressing replies, Dixon's was brief and businesslike:

> Sir,
> In answer to yours dated 22nd January last respecting my name being inserted in the Commission of the Peace for Lindsey; I can only say that I have no Objection to act, but perhaps may not immediately after the Commission is issued out.
>
> I am, Sir,
> Your Humble Servt.
> Dixon.
> Riby, Febry 3rd 1787

This was apparently enough to secure appointment, which tells us something else of significance: Dixon must also have been personally and socially acceptable to other members of the Bench. Not all candidates were. In the lists of nominees preserved in the Clerk's papers, several names have been struck through, rejected before being asked if they were prepared to act. There also seems to have been some sort of informal discussion of candidates amongst the existing magistrates and their views were made known to the Lord Lieutenant. After a meeting of Quarter Sessions in 1806, feeling was so strong that objections were put in writing to the Clerk of the Peace:

---

[33] Davey, *Rural Crime*, 59.

Sir,
When the magistrates last met at Kirton they were apprehensive that application for admission to the Bench might be made by persons with whom
they could not act. Aware that the rejection of men of that description from
whatever cause it might arise must be highly unpleasant as well to the Lord
Lieutenant as the magistrates it was then determined to request his grace
would have the goodness to admit no gentleman not mentioned in a list
then drawn up.

There followed a list of seven acceptable gentlemen. It seems likely that
Dixon had to pass a similar test of suitability in 1787 and was successful.
Given his cautious reply, he may also have been subject to further persuasion
to act because in October 1787 he travelled to Gainsborough Sessions to be
sworn in and immediately began his duties as a rural justice.

The Changing Pattern of Dixon's Records
and Activity as a Justice, 1787–1798

At first, Dixon seems to have intended to keep his promise to the Lord Lieutenant and for two years he attended Quarter Sessions. Each of the three
Parts of Lincolnshire (Holland, Kesteven and Lindsey) held its own Quarter
Sessions. Riby was in Lindsey which was so big that, in the eighteenth
century, each Sessions was adjourned to several towns. By 1787 the system
had been formalised and Sessions for the western division of Lindsey were
held alternately at Gainsborough and Caistor. After being sworn in, Dixon
never again made the long journey to Gainsborough Sessions but in 1788 he
travelled the six miles from Riby to Caistor for Epiphany and Midsummer
Sessions. In 1789 he was there for Epiphany but missed Midsummer, and
Epiphany 1791 was his last appearance at Quarter Sessions. His enthusiasm
for other gatherings of magistrates was similarly fragile. In March 1788 he
went to Lincoln for the meeting of justices from all three Parts to supervise
the county gaol. Once, in 1793, he served on the grand jury at Assizes.[34]

Of course, he may have been more active than the surviving evidence
suggests. Magistrates met regularly 'out of sessions', often in monthly meetings, to deal with administrative matters but also with other business if necessary. Although no formal records or press reports of these meetings have
survived in Lincolnshire, we know they took place and that Dixon attended
them. A relative by marriage, Robert Parkinson of Healing, kept a very brief
diary for 1794. On Wednesday 23 April, he wrote: 'A very fine warm spring
day. Went to Caistor to get the poor bill signed. Dined and drank tea with the

---

[34]   LAO, Lindsey Quarter Sessions Files and Minutes; *Stamford Mercury*, 15 March 1793.

Justices. Mr Thorold, Mr Dixon and Mr Empson there.'[35] Two other occasions have been found when Dixon acted with fellow magistrates on a Wednesday: in 1792 he signed a removal order with the Revd Amaziah Empson of Bonby and in 1797 he bound an apprentice with Marmaduke Alington of Swin-hope.[36] As these were Poor Law matters and the other magistrates came from the far side of Caistor, it seems very likely that they are glimpses of 'Monthly Meetings' at Caistor but how often Dixon attended, and what other business they dealt with, we do not know.

Thus the bulk of Dixon's books record matters dealt with summarily, out of sessions, 'in my house at Riby'. The main handbook for magistrates advised that in summary trials 'there must be a *record* of the whole proceedings' and, in certain respects, Dixon took this to heart.[37] His first 'Justice Book' was a substantial hardback, quite unlike the small, soft-covered notebooks he used for accounts, medicines and other jottings.[38] It was appropriate for the formal and serious matters it recorded. If asked, Dixon would probably have described it as his 'Mittimus Book', for most entries were copies of warrants to the Keeper of the House of Correction at Gainsborough, charging him to receive prisoners Dixon had committed, either after summary conviction or to await trial in the higher courts. In some ways such a formal record is less useful to us than the other surviving magistrates' books. William Hunt (Wiltshire) and Samuel Whitbread (Bedfordshire) both kept their records in a diary form, usually beginning 'Granted a warrant to ...'. They also noted the outcome of cases, including those when an informal settlement was made.[39] Dixon never did this. He simply kept careful copies of the warrants and other documents he issued or responded to. They were few enough, only seven or eight cases a year in his first two years, falling to just two in 1791 and five in 1792.

Dixon's declining activity is probably explained by changes made in the organisation of Quarter Sessions. In 1789 a magistrates' investigation reported that the House of Correction at Gainsborough was 'thoroughly insufficient' and in some parts 'so extremely offensive as to be scarcely supportable'. Indeed, it was declared to be 'so radically bad' that 'an entire new system should be proceeded upon'. Consequently it was decided to close Gainsborough and build a new house of correction, including a purpose-built courtroom, at Kirton-in-Lindsey. In future, Sessions for the western division would only be held at Kirton and the traditional meeting-places, Gainsborough and Caistor, would be abandoned. It was ordered that 'all the

---

[35] LAO, Dixon 16/14/4: Pocket Book of Robert Parkinson of Healing, 1794.
[36] 18 April 1792; 21 June 1797.
[37] Richard Burn, *The Justice of the Peace and Parish Officer* (London, 1837), i. 859.
[38] LAO, Dixon 8/1.
[39] Cirket, *Whitbread's Notebooks*; Crittall, *Justicing Notebook.*

books, Constables' staves, cushions, cloths, inkstands, and every other article hitherto kept at Caistor ... be removed to Kirton'.[40] This clearly affected, and probably irked, Dixon. The central incident of the family story referred to above that he was always late was his failure to turn up for the meeting which passed the Kirton scheme. Whether true or not, and it seems unlikely that Dixon's vote would have been enough to halt the changes, the enduring memory of the move to Kirton emphasises its significance for Dixon. He never again attended Quarter Sessions. Perhaps he used the irritation of the loss to Caistor as justification for a reduction in his activity. Most likely, it was just the physical distance (of seventeen miles) to Kirton which deterred him, although Dr Olney suggests that the social distance between the Caistor and Kirton Benches may also have been a factor.

Certainly he did very little during the three years after the move, recording only ten cases between 1790 and 1792. However, beginning in 1793, there was a significant increase in his activity and a change in the style of the records. His large formal 'Mittimus Book' has only three committals and no summary convictions after 1793. Instead, he now used small, soft-covered pocket-books, exactly like those he used for cures, farm notes and jottings of accounts.[41] Almost all the entries were 'Informations and Complaints', complaints by prosecutors that they had been wronged in some way; and if the notebooks were flimsy, the content was invariably formal and correct. Each entry was made in strict and prescribed form and signed personally by the prosecutor, the person bringing the complaint. Dixon recorded about fifteen such complaints each year between 1793 and 1798.

Unfortunately for us, he made no record of the outcomes of these cases. Initially more puzzling, only two, both property offences, led to a committal to the houses of correction, to further process in the higher courts or to an enrolled summary conviction. We can be sure of this. After 1787 the new Clerk of the Peace, Joseph Brackenbury, seems to have reformed and greatly improved the keeping of the Sessions Rolls.[42] By the 1790s the lists of summary convictions enrolled by magistrates were much more carefully and formally drawn up than in previous years. The calendars of prisoners in the Houses of Correction at Louth and Kirton are similarly complete and exact, written in large, careful hands and giving not only the names of prisoners, but dates, committing magistrates, crimes and sentences. It is true they are only lists of those in the prisons at the time of each Sessions and in theory it would have been possible for a prisoner to have been remanded and released, or even to have served a short sentence, between Sessions. However, in prac-

---

[40]   LAO, LQSM A/2/18, Lindsey Quarter Sessions Minutes, 14 July 1789 and 16 June 1791.

[41]   LAO, Dixon 8/2 and 3.

[42]   See, for example, LAO, LQS/F, Clerk's Memoranda Notebook, 1794–1825.

tice, no such prisoner could have escaped Brackenbury's methodical system because the keepers of the houses of correction also had to submit their accounts, detailing all prisoners they had maintained. As payment of their fees depended on these accounts, not only do they seem to have kept them very carefully but it is inconceivable that they would have omitted prisoners. The surgeons' accounts, full and precise for the same reason, also survive and most inmates seem to have needed medical attention at one time or another. If Dixon's accused do not appear in the calendars, keepers' accounts or surgeons' accounts, we can be confident they were not committed to the houses of correction.

There is slight evidence which might support the argument that Dixon referred most of his cases to Petty Sessions. These may have been invigorated after the Kirton reorganisation, when Dixon wrote in his Mittimus Book, 'His Majesty's Justices of the Peace in or near Louth intend to hold their meetings in the Town Hall of Louth on every Wednesday fortnight throughout the year, between the hours of 11am and 2pm. The first meeting to be held 13 June 1792.' If such sessions did take place and dealt with criminal rather than administrative matters, no records have survived and there are no traces of them in the press or elsewhere. However, it seems unlikely that Dixon would have referred cases there: Louth was fifteen miles away and in another petty sessional division. Further, if the offences were thought serious enough to go to Louth, we would expect that a few cases at least would appear in the Quarter Sessions rolls as summary convictions or committals to prison. There is no indication that any of Dixon's cases reached Sessions via Louth. Dixon would have been more likely to send offenders for trial at the much nearer Caistor Petty Sessions, which were in his own division and which we know he attended occasionally. However, the same argument holds: if none of the cases appears in the records of Quarter Sessions, it seems improbable that they were being prosecuted anywhere beyond Dixon's house at Riby. The explanation for Dixon's practice of not recording outcomes is discussed below.

We can speculate a little more confidently about the motives for Dixon's greater activity after January 1793. It is of course possible that the increase is more apparent than real: 'Information and Complaint' pocket-books for 1787–1792 may not have survived. However, Dixon's practice certainly changed at this time because his 'Mittimus Book' records only three summary convictions or committals after 1793. Thus the new pocket-books probably reflect a change in his methods and a real increase in his 'Justice of the Peace Business'. The cause was almost certainly political. War and revolution in Europe, especially the 'September Massacres' and the trial and execution of the king in France, spread an exaggerated terror in England that autumn and winter of 1792/3. On 1 December the government called out the militia and a fortnight later Parliament reopened with a king's speech which warned of 'a spirit of insubordination, tumult and disorder' and 'some fixed design against the constitution'.[43] It was such fears which led to the foundation of the Caistor Constitutional Association in January 1793. Dixon's place at the head of the committee list suggests he shared the anxieties of the moment and shared them sufficiently to act. It was probably a sense of obligation to the good government of his locality which led him to open his new pocket-books and make himself more available to his neighbours as a magistrate.

Dixon's Work as a Justice

Even for a man of Dixon's experience, the office of JP must have been daunting. He was alone. There was no other active justice within ten miles. He could thus expect, and soon received, a succession of complainants of all sorts at his door, often at irregular and perhaps inconvenient times. It is true that some of the complaints were trivial: it was relatively easy to fine a drunk 5s. However, some were not: many involved possible loss of liberty and a few carried the threat of transportation or death. Moreover the English, even the poor rural English, were a litigious lot with a tradition of using the courts going back many centuries and it was vital that any justice knew a good deal of law, and that in some detail. It was not only that he had to make rapid judgments on a wide range of cases, often involving knowledgeable prosecutors, witnesses and accused. There was always a fear that aggrieved parties might dispute the justice's decision in the higher court of King's Bench. Of course such action was rare and leading scholars have suggested that the threat was more apparent than real.[44] However, it was apparent to Dixon. On two occasions he copied judgments in King's Bench into his books, suggesting at least that he looked for such cases in the local newspaper and that he was aware of the possible consequences of error.

In such circumstances, many justices were helped by a clerk. It is not clear whether or not Dixon employed one but the evidence suggests that, if he did, it was only for a little clerical assistance. One or two of the longer 'Examinations' of witnesses were recorded by someone else but nearly all the other entries in Dixon's books are in his own firm, clear, black-ink hand. In the main he relied for advice on one of the many handbooks for justices. He chose the most popular and detailed, Richard Burn's *The Justice of the Peace and Parish Officer* (1774 edition), supported by a book of precedents.

---

[43] Charles Macfarlane and Thomas Thomson, *The Comprehensive History of England* (London, 1861), iv. 36.
[44] Douglas Hay, 'Dread of the Crown Office: The English Magistracy and King's Bench, 1740–1800', in Norma Landau (ed.), *Law, Crime and English Society, 1660–1830* (Cambridge, 2002).

Property Offences

Dixon seems to have taken a straightforward and consistent view of serious property offences. Confronted by the victim of a theft who named the probable offender, Dixon issued a warrant for the arrest of the accused and then, in eleven of the twelve such cases he heard, committed the alleged thief to prison to await trial by jury in a higher court. To which prison and to which court depended on the seriousness of the offence. Nine defendants were accused of stealing relatively trivial items, so were sent to the house of correction for trial at Quarter Sessions. Three suspects were committed to Lincoln Castle to be tried at Assizes. The consequences of any property trial could be serious: Mary Brown, who stole thirty yards of cloth, was transported for fourteen years. John Burton was no doubt relieved when the Grand Jury decided there was insufficient evidence to proceed with the case against him for theft of a shovel, but he had endured two months in prison awaiting trial – and two months in the old House of Correction at Gainsborough must have been a grim ordeal.

Dixon's practice in these cases was 'according to the book'. Burn advised that if there was a reasonable suspicion of guilt the accused should be sent for trial by jury: 'If a prisoner be expressly charged with felony upon oath, the justice cannot discharge him.' Further, he recommended that even 'if the justice finds upon examination that the prisoner is not guilty; yet the justice shall not discharge him, but he must either be bailed or committed; for it is not fit that a man once arrested and charged with felony, or suspicion thereof, should be delivered upon any man's discretion, without further trial'.[45] Dixon's persistent use of committal was therefore correct in law but was a markedly different choice of procedure from that of other magistrates who have left records and perhaps suggests a certain harshness in his approach.

He did have other options. Professor King has shown that it was common for magistrates to use a range of strategies to avoid the trouble, expense and possible social bitterness of trial in a higher court.[46] They might persuade the parties to come to some agreement, perhaps involving monetary compensation. Justice Edmund Tew of Durham marked 'most' of his allegations of theft 'agreed', 'made up' or 'compounded'.[47] The notebooks of the Wiltshire magistrate William Hunt (1744–1749) are the best source for this practice because they are informal records. Notes of property cases frequently end with '… they agreed it', '… I persuaded an agreement between them' or 'I ordered the sum of … to be paid by the offenders to the complainant for

---

[45] King, *Crime, Justice and Discretion*, quoting Burn, *Justice* (1766 edn), i. 337, 484.
[46] King, *Crime, Justice and Discretion*, Ch. 2.
[47] Gwenda Morgan and Peter Rushton, 'The magistrate, the community and the maintenance of an orderly society in eighteenth-century England', *Historical Research* 76 (2003), 74.

satisfaction'.[48] Hunt gives the impression of a magistrate who was trying to manage, to conciliate; and this was also the approach of Samuel Whitbread, the Bedfordshire justice whose similarly informal notebooks survive for 1810–1811 and 1813–1814. Of the twelve serious property offences he heard in these two years, only four were sent for trial in the higher courts; four were dismissed, as when, for example, he told the prosecutors the evidence 'Did not justify commitment'; five were settled by agreements such as the thief promising 'to satisfy' the victim and if the prosecutor 'was not satisfied' he was to return 'and a warrant would be granted'.[49] Whitbread was also careful to keep petty crimes in perspective and order out-of-court punishment. When someone stole six traps from him a neighbouring magistrate committed the thief to prison. However, on his way to prison the man was taken before Whitbread, who ordered the constable to give him 'six stripes' instead and then release him. This was his common practice during the autumn orchard-robbing season. Whitbread emphasised that the thieves were often only 'little boys' who were accordingly given 'four stripes' by the constable rather than a recorded summary conviction, let alone trial at Sessions.[50] Even the Surrey justice Richard Wyatt seems to have been more flexible than Dixon. His 'Deposition Book' is more comparable to Dixon's because it is a formal document rather than a diary and as such does not record informal settlements. However, he was careful to note that some statements were 'not sworn' or 'mark not made', which gave him more freedom to dismiss or manage the case than after a sworn accusation of felony. Further, when referring cases to the higher courts he made more use of recognizances, binding the accused to appear, rather than committing them to prison.[51]

This is part of the evidence that Dixon tended to harshness. The case of Simon Burnett only appears in Dixon's records because he took one of the witness statements.[52] The initial complaint was heard by a neighbouring magistrate, Revd William Thorold. Burnett was accused of stealing five ducks and was sent for trial at Quarter Sessions. However, Thorold did not commit him but only bound him to appear. Wyatt, dealing with a similar theft of five chickens, also bound the accused. This was not only usual practice but was sanctioned by Burn's instruction that those accused of felony must be 'bailed or committed'. It was Dixon's unswerving committals that were the exception. Thorold and Wyatt bailed those accused of stealing five fowls; when Robert Graves stole two geese, Dixon committed him to the house of correction. When John Tate stole some rabbits from a warren, not only did Dixon commit him but he sent him to Lincoln Castle for trial at Assizes,

48   Crittall, *Justicing Notebook*, nos 218, 283, 285.
49   Cirket, *Whitbread's Notebooks*, nos 59, 1037.
50   *Ibid.*, nos 427, 932, 939.
51   Silverthorne, *Deposition Book*, 18 (nos 92, 93); 37 (no. 204); 30 (no. 160).
52   27 March 1790.

rather than Quarter Sessions. It is perhaps not surprising that there is no record of the trial, probably implying that even the prosecutor thought this was too much and did not complete the case.[53]

It could be argued that Dixon's apparent severity is merely an illusion produced by the surviving documents. The first notebook is, after all, predominantly a 'Mittimus Book', mainly recording committals to prison, and thus could give an exaggerated view of the proportion of cases he dealt with in this way. Perhaps there were other, now lost, notebooks in which he recorded informal settlements or recognizances. This seems unlikely for three main reasons. First, if he did bind people to appear such recognizances would be listed in the Quarter Sessions records. None have been found. Secondly, the first notebook, although mainly a book of committals, does also contain informal jottings about court arrangements, constable's expenses, summary convictions and at least one recognizance in a bastardy case. There seems no reason why Dixon would not have entered recognizances and even informal settlements of property cases in this book. Thirdly, property offences formed a very small proportion of the cases in the surviving notebooks of the other justices, usually less than ten per cent. In Dixon's books, property offences made up fourteen per cent of cases, so it seems unlikely that many more were recorded elsewhere.

The more likely explanation is to be found in Dixon's background and in the prosecutors who brought property offences to him. Tew, Hunt, Whitbread and Wyatt were all Oxford-educated gentlemen of broad outlook and culture. Wyatt lived near London and drew his income mainly from rents. Whitbread was an MP and a national figure. These circumstances gave them a certain confidence, even detachment, in their dealings with the local farmers and tradesmen who brought complaints of theft before them. They were prepared to take them on, to sharply question their allegations, to suggest the offence did not amount to felony and to assert a natural authority to impose informal settlements. They also had the leisure and therefore time to negotiate such agreements, usually sitting daily in their 'Justice Rooms'. Dixon was more constrained. He was too busy to sit in a 'Justice Room' every morning. As a working farmer he heard cases when people caught him in, perhaps even taking complaints from colleagues when he met them at Caistor market. A commitment to prison was quicker than a negotiation over several days like those conducted by Whitbread. Dixon's entirely local education and his complete lack of any metropolitan, or even county, ambitions gave him a narrower outlook. As a hard-headed and very successful farmer, for many years involved in parish government, he shared and could not escape from the prejudices and outlook of the farmers and small businessmen who complained to him. Seven of the eleven prosecutors in the property cases

53 28 January 1791, John Tate.

Dixon heard were local farmers. He must have known them all and we can be certain that he knew at least three of them very well. One, Richard Walkden, was his wife's brother. William Torr was Dixon's close neighbour in Riby and shared parish offices with him. Philip Skipworth, who brought two of the prosecutions, lived only a couple of miles away in Aylesby and was a close colleague, Dixon sharing his special interest in sheep farming. The others were all wealthy farmers, very similar to Dixon, one styling himself, like Dixon, 'esquire'. They were all members of the Caistor Association for the Prosecution of Felons, and most of the Constitutional Association. Three of the other prosecutors were shopkeepers. One of them, Robert Swan of Caistor, was also well known to Dixon; he sat with him on the committee of the Caistor Constitutional Association and was a member of the Association for the Prosecution of Felons. Dixon's wife and daughters bought at least some of their clothes from him and he appears in Dixon's notebook of family remedies with a recipe for 'Elder Wine'.[54]

In this context, when his friends and close associates brought cases of theft to Dixon, he understood, and was part of, their mind-set and fears. He perhaps lacked confidence that his own knowledge of the law was sufficiently detailed to complicate matters. His instinct was not to negotiate, warn or arbitrate but to provide a swift and businesslike service for his neighbours and to work with them in the good governance of the district. He did not intend to be harsh or vindictive, but a commitment to the house of correction seemed prompt and straightforward to busy farmers and tradesmen and it was, of course, entirely and safely legal.

Summary Convictions

Magistrates were empowered to try some cases summarily, to hear and determine matters quickly and alone, without reference to a jury. Such cases were strictly defined by the relevant statutes and punishments were exactly limited. Burn made it clear that such summary justice was a serious matter because it was 'in restraint of the common law' and 'a tacit repeal of that famous clause in the Great Charter, that a man shall be tried by his equals'. Therefore, he advised, 'where this power is given to a justice of the peace by act of parliament, it must appear that he hath strictly pursued it; otherwise the common law will break in upon him, and level all his proceedings'.[55]

In practice, this meant that any summary conviction required a good deal of clerical work for the magistrate or his clerk. When Dixon summarily tried and (almost) convicted 'Yorkshire Tom' for poaching in 1796 he had to complete,

---

[54]   LAO, Dixon 22/8/1: Pocket Book of Thomas Dixon, 1749–97.
[55]   Burn, *Justice* (1837 edn), i. 858.

in full, correct, and legal form, the original 'Information and Complaint' of the prosecutor, in this case a gamekeeper; a summons or warrant to bring 'Yorkshire Tom' to Riby; a record of the summary conviction; and a warrant to commit him to the House of Correction at Kirton. He should also have preserved the 'Examinations' of the prosecutor, witnesses and the defendant, and the fact that they are missing may be one possible reason why this case was not brought to a conclusion. The documents listed were all prepared but the final details were not inserted and they were not signed by Dixon. Perhaps 'Tom' had just absconded. If he had been convicted, the record should have been enrolled at Quarter Sessions.[56]

Magistrates used summary convictions less than popular literature suggested: each year Whitbread recorded about twenty-eight, Hunt about ten and Wyatt only two. Dixon followed this pattern by summarily convicting just thirteen people in ten years. Like the other magistrates he followed the statutes, fining drunks 5s, those swearing profane oaths 1s for each oath, and he would have fined 'Yorkshire Tom' the standard £5 for poaching. He was a little more severe than Hunt on those convicted of stealing growing wood. Hunt's normal penalty was a small fine but Dixon fined Christopher Hobbins 40s and, in default of payment, sent him to the house of correction for one month, to be kept at hard labour and to be whipped before release. However, there was nothing exceptional about this: Whitbread and Wyatt both inflicted similar sentences.

The interesting feature of Dixon's summary convictions is what might be called his 'speciality'. Again, he was not alone in this: other magistrates had particular crimes which formed the majority of their summary convictions. Hunt's so favoured offence was wood theft, which made up about fifty per cent of his convictions. Approximately one-third of Whitbread's convictions were for 'traffic violations', mainly riding on the shafts of a waggon or not having draught horses properly under control. Partly this may have been due to the parish constables who, for some reason, preferred to take such prosecutions to Whitbread. Dixon's speciality was 'master and servant' cases, which accounted for six of his thirteen convictions. Not only was this emphasis quite different from that of other magistrates but Dixon's practice was unusual in two other respects. First, all the prosecutors were employers. Secondly, Dixon was exceptionally harsh in his judgments: five of the six servants convicted were sentenced to three months in the house of correction, the maximum allowed by law. Indeed Dixon's records of 'master and servant' cases appear so anomalous and form such a dominant part of his Justice Books, that they deserve more lengthy consideration.

---

[56] 22 January 1796. LAO, Dixon 8/4: Thomas Dixon's Papers as a JP.

Master and Servant Cases

In the eighteenth century servants were hired by the year, often at hiring fairs. Dixon and his neighbours usually went to the 'Statutes' in Keelby, a large open village about two miles from Riby, to recruit the people they needed to run their farms and homes. No doubt these fairs could sometimes be slightly forlorn. In November 1794 Parkinson wrote in his diary: 'A rime frost with a very cold day. Went to Keelby Statutes. Very shaby ones. Hired nobody.'[57] 'Shaby' they might have been, but they were formal occasions, supervised and recorded by the High Constable of the wapentake, and the contracts made there were binding.

Effectively, master–servant relations were governed by an Elizabethan statute of 1562. Although modified by subsequent legislation, its fundamentals endured and had become as much a part of English rural life as the Poor Law. The essential requirements were well known: the servant must work 'faithfully, diligently and obediently'; the master must maintain the servant (even in sickness) and pay wages. The annual contract could only be terminated by three months' notice. The law was so familiar because it was much used. In a hard world where both young female domestic servants and young male farm servants ('servants in husbandry') customarily 'lived in' with their employers, disputes were common and provided much work for the courts. In one respect the law was, and was perceived to be, unfair. If a master broke a contract with a servant, it was treated as a civil offence and he or she would be required to make restitution of unpaid wages, perhaps with compensation. If a servant broke a contract, it was treated as a criminal offence, punishable by imprisonment in the house of correction. This aspect of the law had been tightened in the eighteenth century, the maximum sentence being increased from one to three months.[58]

As Peter King has shown, this legislation could be employed for other purposes. Some magistrates used it in theft cases. It was much easier, and cheaper, for the prosecutor to summarily convict and punish a light-fingered servant as disobedient under the master and servant acts.[59] There is no evidence that Dixon used the legislation in this way. His common formula that the servant was 'guilty of divers misdemeanours, miscarriages and ill behaviour ... and particularly hath disobeyed his master's lawful commands' does not suggest it and is often qualified by additional details. In one case the misbehaviour is described as 'frequently running out of his master's house on the Sabbath Day as soon as dinner is over', in another 'giving his victuals to the dogs'.

---

[57]   LAO, Dixon 16/14/4: Pocket Book of Robert Parkinson of Healing, 1794 (12 January 1794).
[58]   See Hay, 'Patronage, paternalism', 27–45.
[59]   King, *Crime, Justice and Discretion*, 89.

For employers, the greatest problem was servants who absconded, especially in the few months after the hiring fairs of April and May. At Grimsby Petty Sessions in 1846:

> Several summonses were granted for servant lads and lasses who had in the previous week run away from their situations. The magistrates have generally a good many cases of this kind brought before them at this time of year. Silly fellows and love-sick maidens frequently, on changing their places, fancy, after they have been in their new houses a day or two, that they cannot settle there, and so without warning march off, generally before their masters are up in the morning, to the great inconvenience of the latter. A sharp reprimand and the payment of trifling costs generally serve, however, to make their services more palatable, and they mostly go back and serve their time.[60]

The rather light tone of the *Stamford Mercury* reflects the attitude of an early Victorian journalist. For a late eighteenth-century farmer, working long hours and depending on a few servants for essential tasks, an absconding servant was a serious and exasperating matter. One farm servant Dixon hired at May Day in 1785 'got married in grass mowing time and fled the farm at 3 a.m., leaving all the doors open in his haste'. The problem was not so much the doors but the fact that Dixon would have to find someone else to complete the vital hay mowing.[61]

Perhaps not surprisingly, many farmers were suspicious and at times intolerant of their servants. In some respects, Dixon appears to have been a good employer. In the 1790s he paid unskilled single labourers £15 5s a year with 2s 6d as a fastening penny. All were given a pair of boots and a greatcoat and sometimes also a hat and a pair of breeches. He lent one man 10s 6d 'for the Militia' and made him a gift of a Bible and a prayer book valued at 9s 6d. The servant who ran away in hay-making was being paid £11 a year. In 1779 he agreed that one labourer should have a house and garden and pig yard rent free, two loads of furze, a load of coal, and be allowed to keep one pig in the cratch yard. The man was guaranteed 'To find him constantly in work all the year round'.[62] The impression is that Dixon was generous to those who worked hard and, as he saw it, dealt fairly with him but he was impatient with those he thought idle. He kept notes on his servants in one of the account books, where the words 'dirty', 'impertinent', 'debauched', 'drunken', 'saucy' and 'went away' frequently appear. 'William Frow run away from his place on Thursday morning the first day of April 1774. He was a drunken, idle reprobate and debauched fellow, the worst servant I ever

60 *Stamford Mercury*, May 1846.
61 Beastall, *Agricultural Revolution*, 111, quoting LAO, Dixon 4/1, p.25.
62 *Ibid.*, and LAO, Dixon 4/1: case of Stephen Windley.

had.' 'William Robinson. He is the very worst boy I ever had in my life. A notorious lyer and a very idle boy.' 'Ann Coulson. A deceitful, lying, impudent jade as ever came into a house. Both the lasses are deceitful as the devil. They were up to everything that was bad.' 'Jane Blanchard. A lying impudent, saucy baggage as I ever had.'[63]

Such attitudes go some way to explaining Dixon's severity with servants when he became a JP – and he was very severe. In the two years after his appointment the first five servants who were brought before him for absconding or misbehaving were all sentenced to the maximum allowed, three months in the house of correction. None of the other magistrates who have left records approached this. In five years the only servant Hunt convicted was fined 5s; over nine years Wyatt sent his three to the house of correction for fourteen days. Whitbread tended to be harsher and convicted five servants in two years, but usually opted for the same term of fourteen days, although on two occasions he inflicted sentences of one month. Perhaps closest to Dixon was the Suffolk clerical magistrate George Turner, who was not averse to sending a girl to the house of correction for twenty-one days because she had slipped out of her master's house and been 'absent for the greater part of the night in a public house called the Chequers', but even he never inflicted sentences of three months on erring servants.[64] Even some of the prosecutors who hauled their servants before the new JP at Riby appear to have been shocked by the committals and thought them too much. Hewson Alcock 'pray'd the release' of his servant as soon as he heard he had been sent to the house of correction.[65] Three others sentenced to imprisonment do not appear in the house of correction calendars and we may guess that they were also released after intervention by the prosecutors. In spite of this mitigation Dixon was clearly establishing a reputation, making a statement to local servants and to his neighbouring farmers who brought the prosecutions.

If we can perhaps understand why Dixon was so harsh, it is more difficult to explain why master and servant cases comprised such an abnormally large proportion of the cases he heard. Master and servant disputes made up just over a quarter of George Turner's work, about twenty per cent of the total business dealt with by Wyatt, Whitbread and Tew, and eleven per cent of Hunt's caseload. Overall, such disputes amounted to forty-eight per cent of Dixon's work (and seventy per cent of his last two books), far ahead of his next largest categories, thefts at thirteen per cent and assaults at eleven per cent.

Their primacy is not the only anomaly in Dixon's records of employer–employee relationships. One of the significant findings of modern studies in

---

[63] LAO, Dixon 4/1, pp.25, 31, 33.

[64] Suffolk RO (Ipswich), HD 258/1 (Notebooks of George Turner), and B106/3/8.2 (Woodbridge Gaol Book, 28 September 1813: case of Rose Briggs).

[65] 2 November 1787.

the history of crime is how much ordinary, poorer people were prepared to use the courts. Master and servant cases play an important part in this argument because, as Professor King found in his study of the main surviving records of summary justice, 'in employee–employer disputes, most … were brought by servants or labourers'.[66] Even Douglas Hay, who argues that the master and servant laws were unjust and severely applied, acknowledges that almost half the prosecutions were initiated by servants.[67] The pattern in Lincolnshire was similar. At both Lindsey Quarter Sessions between 1740 and 1780 and Bradley Haverstoe (the rural hinterland of Grimsby) Petty Sessions between 1831 and 1849, just over one-third of the prosecutors in master and servant cases were servants.[68] In rural England, if a servant or labourer felt aggrieved, perhaps because his wages had not been paid or because he was being treated unfairly, he was quite prepared to take his case to a magistrate. This was no small matter. The possibly illiterate servant would have to plead his own case in an atmosphere dominated by his social superiors and in the knowledge that, if he failed, he would be bound to return to his employer's house to complete his contract. That so many weaker members of society were prepared to use the magistrates in this way must reflect not only the people's deep-rooted tradition of using this legislation but also their enduring confidence in the law, the courts and the justices.

The evidence in Dixon's books is radically different. In total he dealt with fifty-seven master and servant cases. Fifty-five of the prosecutors were masters. Forty-one were farmers, and again, many of them were not only similar to Dixon but were well known to him personally. Twenty-four were members of the Caistor Association for the Prosecution of Felons; one, William Ballans, was not only a farmer but also the landlord of the Talbot Inn, where the association met. Some of the most active prosecutors lived closest to Dixon. Jonathan Winship, prosecutor in four cases, farmed in Riby and shared the work of the vestry and parish offices with Dixon. William Richardson of Great Limber, with three prosecutions, was also an important tenant of the Pelham estate. Joseph Johnson, with seven prosecutions, farmed at Irby, a couple of miles along the main road from Riby. Several others, with two prosecutions each, lived in the closely neighbouring villages of Aylesby, Hatcliffe and Laceby. Another group with two or three prosecutions each lived in or near Caistor and had ready access to Dixon at Petty Sessions, on market days or at meetings of the various associations and business ventures he attended there.

---

[66] King, 'Summary courts and social relations', 148.

[67] Hay, 'Patronage, paternalism', 36.

[68] Davey, *Rural Crime*, 35; B. J. Davey, 'Crime and Community in the 1830s', in Dinah Tyszka, Keith Millar and Geoffrey Bryant (eds), *Land, People and Landscapes* (Lincoln, 1991), 144–156.

In trying to explain the dominance of master–servant cases and of employer prosecutors in Dixon's books, some possibilities can be rejected. It is very unlikely that Dixon was referring these cases to Petty Sessions, to other courts or to other magistrates for the reasons given above: not a single one of those accused by the 'Information and Complaints' appears in the full records of the houses of correction. From over forty accused in such cases we would expect at least one to have been sentenced to a term of imprisonment.[69] Similarly, none of the accused appears in the Quarter Sessions records. Furthermore, even if Dixon was sending the cases to other courts, that would not explain the predominance of master–servant disputes and employer prosecutors in his books.

It is also very unlikely that Dixon was settling these cases informally. The first five servants to come before him were all packed off to the house of correction for the maximum sentence allowed and although by 1793 Dixon had moderated the sentence to one month, it seems improbable that he took to arbitration in all the later cases. Moreover, the records are not informal. Although Dixon's second and third notebooks are small and quite possibly used in the course of his everyday travels and business, the records are precise, full and formal and must have taken some trouble. For each 'Information and Complaint' he carefully recorded the county where the complaint was made; the name, residence and occupation of the informer; that the information was given on oath; that the information was made before Dixon and that he was a justice 'in and for' the county where the offence had taken place; the dates of the information and the offence; the name, residence and occupation of the accused; and that the information was taken before 'T. Dixon'. Dixon always signed each one and insisted on a signature or mark by the informer.

Such precision and trouble would not have been necessary for informal arbitration, but only as the prelude to more formal procedure. That procedure was, almost certainly, the issue of a warrant for the arrest of the accused. In this Dixon was following the advice of Burn, albeit in an inflexible manner. The laws controlling servants had been steadily tightened in the eighteenth century and the Act of 1766 recited that 'it frequently happens' that servants 'do leave their respective services before the terms of their contract ... to the great disappointment and loss' of their employers. Consequently it emphasised that 'upon complaint ... made upon oath' to a magistrate 'such justice is hereby empowered to ... issue his warrant for the apprehending of every such' servant.[70] Usually such a warrant would be addressed to the parish constable and might be 'specific', ordering the servant to appear before a particular magistrate on a given day, or 'general', requiring the servant to

---

[69] Of the seventeen servants in George Turner's notebooks, three appear in the house of correction records: Suffolk RO (Ipswich), HD 258/1 and B106/3/8.1&2 (Woodbridge Gaol Books).

[70] Burn, *Justice* (1837 edn), v. 534.

appear before any magistrate sometime in the future. As there is no record of Dixon having anything further to do with these cases, it seems likely that he was issuing 'general' warrants and this conclusion is supported by one of the few arrest warrants which survives in Dixon's papers, dated 19 May 1788. It is a 'general' warrant, ordering the accused to be brought before 'me, or some other of his Majesty's Justices of the Peace' and not setting any date for the hearing.

This was, of course, the common practice of magistrates. Many of the entries in Hunt's journals begin 'Granted a warrant ...'. The difference is that in most of the other magistrates' books such warrants led to further proceedings and they were granted for a much wider range of offences than absconding or misbehaving servants. What seems to have happened here is that after the reorganisation of Quarter Sessions to Kirton, Dixon lost enthusiasm for his work as a JP. However, perhaps spurred by a sense of duty in the years of war and apparently threatened revolution, he found he could quickly and easily provide a useful service for his neighbours. If a farmer came to him at Riby, or perhaps met him in the course of business elsewhere, and complained that a servant had absconded, Dixon simply issued a warrant for the servant's arrest. The warrant was addressed to the constable but it would be given to the farmer lodging the 'Information and Complaint'. For a shilling, the employer was now armed with a powerful document. He would not need the constable to serve it. It would be enough just to let the servant know that he had a warrant for his arrest signed by Dixon. Faced with the prospect of at least one month in the house of correction, and probably three, most servants would surely have chosen to return to their employer or at least to have agreed some compromise. This simple procedure thus gave the employers exactly what they wanted in the rapidly restored services of their workers and saved Dixon the trouble of any further hearing or action. This explains the unusual predominance of master and servant cases and of employer prosecutors in Dixon's notebooks, and their formal nature. The last two small notebooks are most likely his warrant books, records of the warrants he issued, mainly to his close neighbours and colleagues.

Professor King's study of eighteenth-century pre-trial processes has drawn attention to the use of warrants in this way: 'Quite frequently the victim only had to get a warrant from the magistrate in order to obtain the required response.'[71] He notes that such procedures might be used even in property offences and that 'Hunt records at least eight occasions between 1744 and 1749 when he granted a warrant or summons for those accused of property appropriation to appear before him only to find that "the parties agreed it without a hearing".'[72] If we look beyond property offences at all the warrants

---

[71] King, *Crime, Justice and Discretion*, 104.
[72] *Ibid.*

that Hunt granted in those years, there were many occasions when a warrant was enough to bring the parties to agreement, although it is not always clear whether or not a hearing was required. However, for about one-third of the warrants he issued, no further process was recorded. In Wyatt's deposition book about one-sixth of the warrants did not result in any recorded hearing or action. No doubt in cases of assault or very petty theft these warrants were acting as a spur to arbitration, to the settlement of the argument or return of the property. In Northumberland, warrants and recognizances were also used in this way.[73]

The notebooks and papers of Edward Filmer, a Kent magistrate, contain many interesting examples of warrants and summonses acting as spurs to arbitration. Filmer excused a prosecutor who did not return a warrant because 'I have heard that Mr Took prevailed on him to make up the matter'; returned warrants were often endorsed with notes that masters and servants had 'made the matter up'.[74]

On some occasions, however, Filmer used warrants not just to bring the parties together but to insist that an action be taken. If a servant complained that his wages had not been paid, Filmer issued a summons to the employer 'to come before me … *unless … he forthwith pay* … the wages afore-said', and this was such a common practice that he had a stock of printed summonses with these words.[75] In Suffolk, Devereux Edgar used exactly the same procedure to settle wage disputes, instructing constables that they were 'To bring unless paid on sight hereof'.[76]

It was easy enough for these practices to drift and in one case Filmer used a summons to control a servant in exactly the same way as Dixon. Mary King was ordered to appear and answer the complaint of her master 'for not coming into service … according to her contract … unless she forthwith perform the same or give him satisfaction for not doing it'.[77]

However, the best example of how the procedure worked, and how masters used justices' warrants to control servants, is openly given in Burn. In his discussion of the law of settlement he offers the precedent of *Rex* v. *East Shefford*, 4 T.R. 804:

---

[73] Peter Rushton, 'The matter in variance: adolescents and domestic conflict in the pre-industrial economy of northeast England 1600–1800', *Journal of Social History* 25 (1991), 95.

[74] CKS, U120/09 (notebook) and U120/011 (papers), Edward Filmer, 1740–54.

[75] *Ibid.*, e.g. Thomas Fullager (21 September 1745), Francis How (13 October 1752). My italics.

[76] Suffolk RO (Ipswich), qS 347.96: The Devereux Edgar Notebook. (There is also a useful transcript by S. R. Schofield.) See, for example, Edgar Notebook, 17 March 1700, 19 May 1701, 27 October 1705.

[77] CKS, U120/011: Papers of Edward Filmer (4 October 1742).

The pauper was hired by Birch, for a year ... he went accordingly to his service, and continued there eight weeks, when he ran away, and was absent thirteen weeks ... Birch then apprehended him by a warrant; but in his way to a justice, asked him whether he would come back to his place or go to prison? and if he would come back, and go on in his place as he ought to do, he might. The pauper said, he would come back; and his master asked him then, what he should be willing to abate for the time he had been absent? The pauper said, he thought 1s. a week would not hurt him, which was agreed to; and the pauper returned into his service, and continued till the end of his year, when he received all his wages, except the 13s. which had been agreed to be deducted.[78]

Here are all the elements of Dixon's practice: the warrant put into the hands of the employer; the threat of prison; the servant compelled to agreement and compensation. Most magistrates used the warrant as a spur to arbitration in a wide variety of cases; occasionally they used it to compel or control. In his later notebooks Dixon slid well beyond this, hearing an unusual preponderance of master and servant cases and registering complaints almost exclusively from employers. In his hands, the warrant became not an encouragement to arbitration, but the instrument of a system of social control.

Dixon as a Magistrate

The evidence of Dixon's books could clearly be used to support Hay's view of summary justice, not only in the regular severity which they show but in the predominant use of the master and servant acts. These characteristics and the one-sided employment of warrants might well sustain Hay's description of the 'immiseration, despair and powerlessness' of the rural poor and his assertion 'that in the late eighteenth and early nineteenth centuries ... agricultural laborers may have been experiencing a far harsher use of master and servant legislation than was evident in industrial areas'.[79]

However, important qualifications need to be made. The first is that Dixon's books can still support King's view that there was room for much discretion and flexibility in eighteenth-century summary justice. The fact that very few employees took their cases to Dixon shows that they were exercising their discretion: they did not find Dixon a sympathetic magistrate, so they went elsewhere. Further, the evidence may be incomplete. There may have been employers who were not granted warrants because Dixon dismissed their cases. It is not probable, but it is possible.

The most important qualification is that Dixon's books are a chance survival of brief records left by a lesser magistrate. Just because they are the only books we have for Lincolnshire, it would be unwise to conclude

---

[78] Burn, *Justice* (1831 edn), iv. 386–387.
[79] Hay, 'Patronage, paternalism', 44.

that all magistrates in the county were like this. Indeed, the fragmentary evidence we have is to the contrary. One of the most prominent eighteenth-century Lincolnshire magistrates was Thomas Whichcot of Harpswell (active 1740–1774) and he had a genuine reputation as a champion of the rights of the poor:

> ... when Sir Cecil Wray made his park at Fillingham and enclosed it with a wall, he obstructed a right of way ... to the great Lincoln road. Mr Whichcot once a year used to order his coach and four, and, attended by a lot of labourers, used to drive up to the park wall, (and) pull it down.... Sir Cecil then built it up, and the next year old Whichcot did the same, up to the time of his death, when no-one else was patriotic enough to keep up the right.[80]

In the Quarter Sessions rolls there is some evidence that Whichcot was, like Devereux Edgar, popular with servants who wished to claim unpaid wages and that he was quick to uphold the rights of employees. In one case he summoned the farmer to appear 'this afternoon'.[81]

Similarly, by the early nineteenth century the copious records of Bradley Haverstoe Petty Sessions (courts held in Grimsby to serve the surrounding villages) show a magistracy more formal, more detached and very concerned to appear as impartial arbitrators. Consequently, they were much used by the poor. One-third of the prosecutors might be characterised as poorer people, not only victims of assaults, but servants demanding wages or better treatment and paupers demanding relief from reluctant overseers.[82]

These magistrates were different from Dixon. Like Hunt and Whitbread, Whichcot was Oxford-educated and an MP. The magistrates in Bradley Haverstoe reflected the prejudices of Lord Brownlow, Lord Lieutenant of Lincolnshire from 1809 to 1852. He regarded anyone with a landed estate of under 2000 acres as a 'yeoman' and therefore unfitted for the Bench. Further, he thought 'defective education' a bar to appointment. He would really have preferred to restrict the Commission to the 'county gentry', members of the old-established families, true 'gentlemen' of good education and large estates. A clergyman commenting on the suitability of Thomas Dixon's grandson, T. J. Dixon, and his neighbour George Skipworth as possible magistrates felt it necessary to explain that 'Their education has not fitted them completely

---

[80]   Sir Lewis Namier and John Brooke (eds), *The History of Parliament: The Commons 1754–90* (3 vols, London, 1964), iii. 629.
[81]   LAO, Lindsey Quarter Sessions Files A161 Midsummer 1768; Davey, *Rural Crime*, 35.
[82]   LAO, Bradley Haverstoe Petty Sessions; Davey, 'Crime and Community'.

for magisterial duties but they would not disagreeably oppose their more experienced brethren.'[83]

Quaint though we may find Brownlow's ideas, in many ways Dixon exemplifies his concerns. His harshness did not come from personal cruelty or even insensitivity. One scholar who has studied Dixon's farming records describes his household as 'kindly but frugal'[84] and there is much evidence to support such a view. Dixon was a hard-working, self-made man and he worked into old age; he continued to run his farm, rather than let it out and retire to the life of a landed gentleman. While he built a new house for his son in which the occupant was assumed to keep a liveried male servant, Dixon remained in the farmhouse at Riby, where his wife managed with two maids and a boy. He was correct in his dealings with his family, in the estates he left his eldest son and in the education and livings he provided for his younger boys, while the dowries bestowed on his daughters were enough to require selling some of the estates. Again, it perhaps says much about the family that the three girls all married working farmers and merchants rather than landed gentry.[85]

Thus his harshness as a magistrate is best explained by a certain narrowness of education, of vision, and above all, of leisure. Dixon was one of those magistrates of slightly lower social status who were being elevated to the Bench at the end of the eighteenth century.[86] Such candidates were often chosen because they were men of business who would be active and effective magistrates. Perhaps the main reason that Dixon did not assume the role of mediator in all the petty disputes which were brought before him was that he was just too busy: it was quicker and simpler to sentence or commit. Certainly, too, he was deeply embedded in the local community of farmers and tradesmen. He lacked the detachment of a true landed gentleman, separate and independent enough to treat farmers and servants equally. Dixon was too involved in running the farms, governing his parish, meeting and trading with his neighbours, to escape from their mentality. In the 1790s, when he (rather quickly) became disillusioned with the long journeys and tedious proceedings of Quarter Sessions meetings, he found a method of acting which was even quicker and more flexible than committing or sentencing: he issued warrants to his neighbours which enabled them to control their servants. This use of warrants, not just as spurs to mediation but as a means of control, is perhaps the most significant feature of Dixon's books.

At present we do not have a clear picture of how widespread this use of warrants was but any investigation would need to examine another linked issue: the role of parish constables. In Dixon's case it looks as though he

[83] LAO, 4 BNL boxes 1–3; R. J. Olney, *Rural Society and County Government in Nineteenth Century Lincolnshire* (History of Lincolnshire 10, 1979), 44, 97–101.
[84] Beastall, *Agricultural Revolution*, 111.
[85] *Ex. inf.* Dr R. J. Olney.
[86] King, *Crime, Justice and Discretion*, 165.

was giving the warrants to the employers and there is nothing in the Riby constables' accounts to suggest otherwise.[87] However, most other magistrates addressed warrants to the parish constables, who could then be much more effective. One of George Turner's cases is a good example. He recorded an 'Information and Complaint' in an assault case in exactly the same way as Dixon, but then made an additional note to the constable:

> Mr Turner will thank the Constable of Cretingham to go to Abraham Osborn of his parish and inform him and his wife that if they do not conduct themselves more peaceably towards their neighbours and particularly towards Samuel Kettle and his wife they will be severely punished.[88]

In Kent, Wyndham Knatchbull noted that he had granted a warrant but 'the woman told me she deliver'd it to the Constable, and that he never executed it, but persuaded her contrary to her own inclination to make up with the man'.[89]

Such cases remind us that there may have been much more than a simple legal process behind all those claims in constables' accounts for 'Serving a warrant'. Although the Victorian reformers liked to portray them as bumbling part-timers, totally inadequate as 'police', a parish constable armed with a warrant may in fact have been an active and powerful agent in his community.

Table 1: Summary Caseloads: Dixon and Three Other Rural Justices

	Tew (Tyne &Wear) 1750–1764	Whitbread (Beds) 1810–1814	Hunt (Wilts) 1744–1749	Total Others	Dixon 1787–1798
Property offences	6	20	42	15	13
Interpersonal violence	43	12	29	31	11
Poor Law	4	32	12	13	17
Master–servant disputes	27	17	6	21	48
Social/economic regulation	21	19	11	19	12

The classification used here and figures for other justices are from Peter King, 'The Summary Courts and Social Relations in Eighteenth-Century England', *Past and Present* 183 (2004), 125–172.

The figures are percentages.

---

[87] LAO, Riby Par 7/1: 'Riby Parish Book, Commencing 1742'.
[88] Suffolk RO (Ipswich), HO 258/13, 1522/13.
[89] CKS, U951 0.3: Account of Warrants issued by Wyndham Knatchbull, 1734–44.

Editorial Note and Conventions

Dixon's 'Justice Books' include one hard-cover and two small soft-cover volumes, together with a packet of documents concerning the arrest of 'Yorkshire Tom' for poaching. Further information has been added from: other notebooks kept by Dixon, Lindsey Quarter Sessions files and minutes, the records of the houses of correction, local parish officers' accounts, private diaries and *The Lincoln, Rutland and Stamford Mercury.*

In the text, entries from Dixon's 'Justice Books' are in larger type; entries from all other documents are in smaller type and editorial comments are italic. All entries have been arranged chronologically. Explanatory headings and days of the week have been added. Generally, original spelling has been retained. Capitals have been modernised.

Acknowledgements

My thanks are due to the staff of Lincolnshire Archives, the Suffolk Record Office (Ipswich Branch) and the Centre for Kentish Studies.

I am especially grateful to Dr Richard Olney who generously shared his knowledge of the Dixon family and made many helpful suggestions.

The work has been encouraged and supported by: Rex Russell, Dinah Tyszka, Mr R. and Mrs T. Davey, and Professor Peter King. Dr Nicholas Bennett was a supportive editor. Mrs Heather Holt read the proofs and improved the text. I thank them all.

The views expressed in the introduction and any errors which remain are entirely my own.

THE JUSTICE BOOKS OF THOMAS DIXON OF RIBY, 1787–1798

Tuesday 2 and Wednesday 3 October 1787. Attended first Quarter Sessions at Gainsborough.

Richard Ellison, Pemberton Milnes and Thomas Dixon severally took and subscribed the oath prescribed by the Statute of 18 Geo.2.Ch.20 before they acted as Justices of the Peace for the said Parts.[1]

From Dixon's Account Book.

October 2 1787 Quallified at Gainsborough Sessions to Act as a Justice of the Peace in and for the Parts of Lindsey.

NB Begun to Act as a Commissioner of the Land Tax in the year 1769.

October 2 1787 Sold to Mr William Richardson of Willerton when I was at Gainsborough Sessions 119 drape ews out of which there was 50 double gimbers and old ews 69 in all 119 at 17s 6d pr head £104 2s 6d.[2]

Friday 2 November 1787. Warrant to discharge Thomas Ashley from the House of Correction at Gainsborough.

No 9. Lincolnshire Lindsey. To the Keeper of the House of Correction at Gainsborough in the said Parts.

These are to authorize and require you on sight hereof to discharge out of your custody in the said House of Correction Thomas Ashley who stands committed for three months from the second day of this instant November for swearing at his master Hewson Alcock of Healing in the parts aforesaid and giving his victuals to the dogs, if the said Thomas Ashley is not charged in your custody on any other account the said Hewson Alcock having pray'd his release and discharge.

Given under Our Hands and Seals the Second Day of November in the year of Our Lord One Thousand Seven Hundred and Eighty Seven. William Thorold. Thomas Dixon.[3]

---

[1] LAO, LQSM A/2/16, Lindsey Quarter Sessions Minutes, Epiphany 1787–Epiphany 1788.
[2] LAO, Dixon 4/1, Account Book of Thomas Dixon, 1755–98.
[3] LAO, Dixon Notebook 1, p. 9.

Friday and Saturday 28 and 29 January 1788. Quarter Sessions.
Thomas Dixon attended Epiphany Quarter Sessions at Caistor.[4]

Monday 28 February 1788. Warrant to discharge Samuel Bilton or Belton from the House of Correction at Louth.
No. 8. Lincolnshire Lindsey. To the Keeper of the House of Correction at Louth in the said Parts.
Whereas Samuel Bilton otherwise Belton is and stands committed by us unto your custody for neglecting and refusing to perform a certain order in bastardy made by us for paying the weekly sum of one shilling towards the support of a female bastard child born of the body of Ann Shepherd single woman in the parish of Great Limber in the said Parts whereof he was adjudged the putative father and also the further sum of one pound ten shillings the expenses incurred by the said parish respecting the same. And whereas due proof having been made before us that the said recited order has since been complied with to the satisfaction of the overseers of the parish of Great Limber aforesaid. These are therefore to command you the said Keeper of the said House of Correction immediately upon sight hereof to discharge out of your custody in the said House of Correction the said Samuel Bilton otherwise Belton if he shall not stand committed for or on any other account. Given under Our hands and seals the twenty eight Day of February 1788. William Thorold, Thomas Dixon.[5]
Samuel Bilton or Belton does not appear in any of the records of the houses of correction. Perhaps he was released immediately after committal like Thomas Ashley, above.

Tuesday 25 March 1788. Special Sessions at Lincoln Castle.
Justices of the Peace from the three Parts of Lincolnshire met to govern the County Gaol. Dixon attended this session which discontinued 'the allowance which hath lately been made to Mr Isaac Wood, Keeper of His Majesty's Gaol the Castle of Lincoln in lieu of the profits lately derived from the Sale of Liquors in the Gaol', and instead ordered 'an additional Salary of forty six pounds per annum ought to be made to the Gaoler's present salary'. It was also agreed that the salary of the prison surgeon, Mr Parnell, be increased by £5. He had asked for £10.[6]

4   LAO, LQSM A/2/16, LQS Minutes.
5   LAO, Dixon Notebook 1, p.8.
6   LAO, LQSM A/2/16, LQS Minutes, Epiphany 1788, p.79.

Monday 19 May 1788. Warrant for Pound Breach.

Lincolnshire. Lindsey. To the Constable of *Habrough* in the said *Parts* and all other his Majesty's Officers of the Peace whom it doth and may concern

Forasmuch as *William Sharpe of Habrough in the said Parts Common Pinder* hath this day made Information and Complaint upon oath before me *Thomas Dixon* one of his Majesty's Justices of the Peace in and for the said Parts, *that Thomas Hall* of *Habrough aforesaid Labourer on this eighteenth instant May rescued about thirty five Geese from the said William Sharpe who were driving them out of the Cow Pasture to the Common Pound.*

These are therefore to command you, in his said Majesty's name, forthwith to apprehend and bring before me, or some other of his Majesty's Justices of the Peace for the said Parts, the body of the said *Thomas Hall* to answer unto the said complaint, and to be further dealt with according to law. Herein fail you not. Given under my hand and seal the *nineteenth* day of *May* in the year of our Lord one thousand seven hundred and *Eighty eight*.

Thomas Dixon

Endorsed A warrant […] or pound breach.[7]

Saturday 21 June 1788. Committal of Disobedient Servant to the House of Correction at Louth.

No 7. Lincolnshire Lindsey. To the Constable of Rothwell in the said Parts and to the Keeper of the House of Correction at Louth in the Said Parts

Whereas Information and Complaint hath been made upon oath before me Thomas Dixon one of His Majesty's Justices of the Peace in and for the said Parts that Rebecca Green late of Irby in the said Parts was hired to serve Joseph Johnson of Irby aforesaid as a servant in husbandry, a few days after May Day last to May Day following seventeen hundred eighty nine, hath in the said service been guilty of several misdemeanours and particularly in neglecting her work and refusing to obey the reasonable commands of the said Joseph Johnson her master and has also absented herself from her said master's service.

And whereas in pursuance of the statute in that case made and provided I have duly examined the proofs and allegations of both the said parties touching the matter of the said complaint and upon due consideration had thereof, have adjudged and determined that she the said Rebecca Green

---

7   LAO, Dixon 21/3/3/2.

hath in her service as aforesaid been guilty of divers misdemeanours and particularly in neglecting her work and refusing to obey her said master's reasonable commands and also absenting herself from her said master's service as aforesaid.

These are therefore to command you the said Constable forthwith to convey the said Rebecca Green to the said House of Correction at Louth aforesaid and to deliver her to the Keeper thereof, together with this warrant. And I do hereby command you the said Keeper to receive the said Rebecca Green into your custody in the said House of Correction there to remain and be corrected, and held to hard labour for the space of three months from the date hereof. And for your so doing this shall be your sufficient warrant.

Given under my hand and seal the twenty first day of June in the year of Our Lord one thousand seven hundred and eighty eight.[8]

There is no record of Rebecca Green's committal in the records of the House of Correction, nor in the Quarter Sessions files and minutes. She was probably released immediately, as in the case of Thomas Ashley, above.

June 1788. Record of a Case in the Court of King's Bench.

June 1788. Saturday was determined in the Court of King's Bench a case of considerable importance to parishes. It came before the court upon a motion to quash an order of Sessions. The circumstances of the case were as Follow: A female servant having hired herself for the year, gave notice to quit at the end of the year. Her mistress, however, in consequence of impertinent behaviour, dismissed her eight days before the expiration of the year, at the same time paid her wages up to the end of the term. The question was 'Whether this servitude gained a Settlement?' which the court determined in favour of the settlement.[9]

This entry is not in Dixon's hand, but perhaps it is evidence that he was sensitive to the role of King's Bench in correcting magistrates who erred.

[8]   LAO, Dixon Notebook 1, p.7.
[9]   LAO, Dixon 8/1, Notebook 1, p.1 from end.

Tuesday and Wednesday 15 and 16 July 1788. Midsummer Quarter Sessions at Caistor.

Election of Chief Constable. Mr Scutt Gibbeson of Haxey, Innholder, and Mr Thomas Gervase of Epworth, Schoolmaster, having offered themselves as candidates for the office of Chief Constable for one of the divisions of the wapentake of Manley in the said Parts in the room of Mr George Coggan who has resigned the said office, His Majesty's Justices of the Peace for the said parts in Court assembled voted as follows

For Scutt Gibbeson	for Thomas Gervase
Sir Cecil Wray Baronet	Cornelius Stovin
Alan Johnson	Richard Ellison
John Harrison	Henry Hutton
William Allenby	Thomas Dixon
William Johnson	George Uppleby
Richard Ryther Popplewell Steer	Robert Well, DD, Clerk
Marmaduke Allington, Clerk	William Thorold, Clerk
	Caley Illingworth, Clerk
	Amaziah Empson, Clerk

And the said Thomas Gervase was thereupon declared duly elected and was sworn Chief Constable

Wednesday business was the routine administration of most Quarter Sessions, including bounties for hemp and flax, and fees for the Keeper of the House of Correction at Gainsborough, the Clerk of the Peace and the County Treasurer, Mr Richard Clitherow.[10]

Friday 25 July 1788. The Indictment of John Burton for Theft of a Shovel.

Friday 25 July 1788. Information and Complaint of the Accuser.

Lincolnshire Lindsey. The Information and Complaint of William Torr of Riby in the said Parts, grazier, taken on oath before me Thomas Dixon one of His Majesty's Justices of the Peace for the said Parts the twenty fifth day of July one thousand seven hundred and eighty eight.

The above named informant on his oath saith that on Wednesday last the twenty third day of this instant he discovered a steel shovel his property to be wanted and having a suspicion that the same had been stolen and

[10] LAO, LQSM A/2/17, LQS Minutes, Midsummer 1788, pp.24, 29.

his suspicion falling on John Burton of Riby aforesaid carpenter he went to his house where he found the same and this informant believes and suspects that the same was stolen and taken from out of his garden by the said John Burton the same being there to his recollection two days before he discovered the same to have been taken away. William Torr
Taken and sign'd before me, T. Dixon

Tuesday 30 July 1788. Accuser Bound to Prosecute John Burton at the next Quarter Sessions.

Wm Torr of Riby in £20. To prefer a Bill of Indictment against John Burton joiner at the next General Quarter Sessions of the Peace to be held at Gainsborough in and for these Parts on suspicion of stealing from him a steel shovel his property and also to give evidence to the Grand Jurors and to the jury who shall pass upon the trial of the said John Burton and not depart without leave of the court. Are you content.

In Margin:

Warrant	1s 0d
Information	1s 0d
For ye depositions of every witness taken in Writing	1s 0d
Recognizance	2s 0d
Warrant Commitment	1s 0d
	6s 0d

Tuesday 30 July. John Burton Committed to the House of Correction at Gainsborough to await trial at the next Quarter Session.

John Burton of Riby Committed to the House of Correction at Gainsborough the 30th day of July on a violent suspicion of stealing a steel shovel the property of William Torr of Riby. Committed by me, T. Dixon.

Lincolnshire Lindsey. To the Constable of the Parish of Riby and also to the Keeper of the House of Correction at Gainsborough in the said Parts. Forasmuch as John Burton of Riby aforesaid carpenter is now brought before me Thomas Dixon one of His Majesty's Justices of the Peace in and for the said Parts charged on the oath of William Torr of Riby aforesaid grazier on a violent suspicion of having stolen from him in the night of the twenty second day of this instant in the parish of Riby aforesaid a steel shovel the property of him the said William Torr.

These are therefore to command you the said Constable in His Majesty's name forthwith to convey the said John Burton to the House of Correction at Gainsborough in the said parts and you the said Keeper are hereby required to receive the said John Burton into your custody in the said House of Correction and him there safely to keep until he shall thence be delivered by due course of law and therein fail you not.

Given under my hand and seal the thirtieth day of July in the year of Our Lord one thousand seven hundred and eighty eight.

John Burton in the House of Correction at Gainsborough.

Lindsey Quarter Sessions File, Michaelmas 1788, Gainsborough.
A Calendar of All the Prisoners Confined in the House of Correction at Gainsborough in the parts of Lindsey in the County of Lincoln for What, When, and by Whom Committed in order to take their Trialls at the next general Quarter Sessions of the Peace.

John Burton committed the 30th of July charged on the oath of Wm Torr of Riby grazier on violent suspicion of having stolen from him on Tuesday night the twenty second day of this instant or earley on Wednesday morning in the Parish of Riby aforesaid a steel shovel the property of him the said William Torr. Justice Thos. Dixon.

Lindsey Quarter Sessions File, Epiphany 1789, Spilsby.
A Bill of Allowance for Prisoners
To Maintaining John Burton from the 30th of July to 7th of October 10 weeks
17s 6d

Tuesday 7 October 1788. John Burton's Trial at Gainsborough Quarter Sessions.

Recognizances. Thomas Dixon. William Torr of Riby Grazier in £20 for his appearance at this Sessions to prosecute and give evidence against John Burton late of Riby aforesaid joiner for feloniously stealing one steel shovel the property of the said Wm Torr. Discharged.

Indictments. John Burton late of Riby carpenter for petty larceny. No Bill. Delivered by Proclamation.
William Torr appeared to prosecute and give evidence against Burton, but the Grand Jury found there was insufficient evidence to proceed. Burton was therefore discharged, after two months in the House of Correction. The House of Correction at Gainsborough was described in a magistrates' report as: thoroughly insufficient, … eleven persons were crowded together in this small Day

Room, which is dark close smoky and so extremely offensive as to be scarcely supportable, and ... the appearance of the prisoners was forlorn desperate and abandoned and for some time past their conduct had been so refractory as to give serious alarm and apprehension to the Gaoler, a sensible discreet man and worthy the confidence of the magistrates, and who from the unprovided and insufficient state of the House, confesses himself unable to restrain employ or keep the prisoners in order. There is not any water, no places for bathing washing or cleaning the prisoners in the courts, no places for solitary confinement and no provisions for the sick, the diseased, or the filthy.

Your committee have viewed with great concern so large a number of their fellow creatures thus confined together, in a place injurious to their health (the effects of which were generally apparent and upon one in particular was so strongly depicted as to give most sensible pain to the feelings) and daily growing more profligate and abandoned from idleness and vicious conversation, so that instead of reformation by hard labour, an idle disposition is established; instead of improvement by a separation from bad company, vice and profligacy are increased and confirmed, and the commitments of offenders instead of producing punishment and amendment become a gratification to the hardened sinner by feeding him in idleness and bad society; and the ruin of the young offenders by exposing them to debauched conversation and bad company.

The present Establishment (if so it can be called) is so radically bad as in the contemplation of this committee ... an entire new system should be proceeded upon.[11]

Friday 1 August 1788. Committal of Two Labourers for Abandoning Harvest Work.

Joseph Stotherd of Hatcliffe, labourer, committed to the House of Correction at Louth for 3 months for deserting from William Baldwin's service which he the said Joseph Stotherd had agreed to continue with him during the harvist seasons at the same prices he paid to the rest of his labourers. Committed the 1st day of August 1788 by me T. Dixon.

Edward Smith a strolling labourer committed to the House of Correction at Louth for 3 months for deserting from William Balding's service which he the said Edward Smith had agreed to continue and work for him during the harvist seasons at the same prices he gave to the rest of his labourers. Committed the 1st day of August 1788 by me T. Dixon.[12]

---

[11]   LAO, Dixon 8/1, Dixon Notebook 2; LQSM A/2/18, LQS Minutes, Midsummer 1789; LQS File A/1/242, and LQSM A/2/17, LQS Minutes, Michaelmas 1788, Gainsborough; and LQS File A/1/243, Epiphany 1789.
[12]   LAO, Dixon 8/1, Notebook 1, p.5.

The Records of the House of Correction at Louth include:

A List of the Prisoners Confin'd in Louth House of Correction October 1, 1788 Edward Smith Aged 24 Years & Joseph Stotherd aged 40 years for leaving their work. Committed by T Dixon August 1st 1788 for three Months Imprisonment Each.

Allowance for Prisoners from Sept 1st to the 10th of October following
Joseph Stothard and Edward Smith 40 Days each   £1 0s 0d
(A list of seven prisoners for) Occasional Expenses when spinning *includes* Edward Smith Joseph Stothard
The Surgeon's bill
September 26th A pot of ointment (Smith)   2d
Fees Oct 24th Joseph Stodherd and Edward Smith Discharged   13s 4d[13]

Wednesday 10 September 1788. Summary Conviction of Christopher Hobbins.

Christopher Hobbins of Keelby labourer committed to the House of Correction at Gainsborough the tenth day of September 1788 for one month and kept to hard labour and also to be whipt within the last week of the said month for cutting up several oak and ash trees in a certain wood in Roxton in the parish of Immingham. Committed by me T. Dixon.

No 4. Lincolnshire Lindsey. To the Constable of the parish of Keelby and also to the Keeper of the House of Correction at Gainsborough in the said Parts.

Whereas Thomas East of Habrough in the said Parts carpenter on the eight day of this instant did make oath before me Thomas Dixon One of His Majesty's Justices of the Peace in and for the said Parts that on the same day he saw Christopher Hobbins of Keelby aforesaid labourer cut up several young oaks and ash's growing from the old stools and other trees growing in a certain wood in Roxton in the parish of Immingham in the Parts aforesaid the property of Charles Anderson Pelham Esq.

And the said Christopher Hobbins being now brought before me is convicted on the oath of William Everitt of Kernington in the said Parts carpenter of cutting and spoiling the said wood, and ordered to pay the penalty of forty shillings for the use of the said Thomas East the informer

---

[13]   LAO, LQS File A/1/242, Michaelmas 1788, Louth.

and the said Charles Anderson Pelham the proprietor and also the further sum of six shillings the charges previous to and attending the said conviction

And said several sums or either of them or any part of them not being paid immediately by the said Christopher Hobbins as by the Statute in that case made and is required. I do hereby require you the said Constable of Keelby aforesaid to convey the said Christopher Hobbins to the House of Correction at Gainsborough aforesaid and I do also hereby require you the said Keeper of the House of Correction to receive the said Christopher Hobbins into your custody in the said House of Correction and him there keep to hard labour for the space of one month now next ensuing, and you the said Keeper are also hereby ordered within the last week of the said Month to whip the said Christopher Hobbins in your said House of Correction and for your so doing this shall be your sufficient warrant.

Given under my Hand and Seal the tenth day of September One Thousand Seven hundred and Eighty eight. T. Dixon.
This summary conviction was enrolled at Quarter Sessions.

Michaelmas Quarter Sessions 1788.
Accounts of the Keeper of the House of Correction at Gainsborough include:
To Maintaining Christopher Hobbins from the 10th September to the 7th October, 4 weeks at 1s 3d: 7s.[14]

Saturday 20 September 1788. Mary Brown Committed for Trial at Assizes.
Mary Brown the wife of Thomas Brown of Great Limber labourer committed to Lincoln Castle the 20th day of September 1788 for felloniously stealing taking and carrying away divers goods out of the shop of Robert Swan's of Castor being his property.

No 5. Lincolnshire Lindsey. To the Constable of Castor in the said Parts of the said County to the Keeper of His Majesty's Gaol in the Castle of Lincoln in the said Parts of the said County.

Whereas Mary Brown the wife of Thomas Brown of Great Limber in the

---

[14] LAO, Dixon 8/1, Notebook 1, pp.2–3; LQSM A/2/17; LQS Files A/1/243, Michaelmas 1788, Gainsborough.

said Parts is now before me Thomas Dixon Esq. one of His Majesty's Justices of the Peace in and for the said Parts and County charged upon oath with felloniously stealing taking and carrying away ten yards and three quarters of an ell wide lelique chintz, also twenty two yards and a half of black callimanco out of the shop of Mr Robert Swan at Castor aforesaid.

These are therefore to require you the said Constable in His Majesty's name forthwith to convey and deliver into the custody of the Keeper of the said Gaol the body of the said Mary Brown, and you the said Keeper are hereby commanded to receive the said Mary Brown into your custody in the said gaol untill the next General Gaol Delivery for the said county. Herein fail not. Given under my hand and seal this twentieth day of September one thousand seven hundred and eighty eight.[15]

Mary Brown was convicted at Lincoln Assizes, Lent 1789, and sentenced to fourteen years' transportation. The gaoler, William Lumby, took her to Blackwall on 5 February 1791, from where she embarked on the Mary Ann *for New South Wales.*[16]

Wednesday 15 October 1788. Conviction of Robert Rollison for Profane Swearing.

October 15th 1788. Robt Rollisson of Rothwell blacksmith was this day convicted before me Thos Dixon one of His Majesty's Justices of the Peace in and for the Parts of Lindsey on the Information on Oath and Witness of John Barton of Castor taylor for profane cursing and swearing and paid the penalty of two shillings being the first offence of which he has been convicted. T. Dixon.[17]

Friday and Saturday 16 and 17 January 1789. Epiphany Quarter Sessions at Caistor.

Dixon attended the sessions.

A vagrant's pass was enrolled, signed by Henry Hutton and Thomas Dixon esquires, allowing Mary Shepherd to pass from the Bail of Lincoln to Ireland. Mary Shepherd had been 'brought before the court in the custody

---

15 LAO, Dixon 8/1, Notebook 1, pp.5–7.
16 C. L. Anderson, *Lincolnshire Links with Australia 1788–1840* (Gainsborough, 1988), 16.
17 LAO, Dixon 8/1, Notebook 1, p.7.

of the Keeper of the House of Correction' and discharged. As a Lincoln magistrate Hutton often dealt with the vagrants who gathered around the Castle. It appears that he had committed Mary Shepherd, 'a rogue and vagabond found wandering and begging in the Bail of Lincoln', to the House of Correction, and Dixon simply provided the necessary second signature on the pass at Quarter Sessions. However, Dixon also signed the warrant ordering the Constable to convey Shepherd on the first part of her journey from Lincoln to Ireland.[18]

Monday 26 January 1789. Committal and Trial of Wright Emmerson for Theft from a Shop in Caistor.

Monday 26 January. Wright Emmerson Committed to the House of Correction at Gainsborough.

Wright Emmerson committed to the House of Correction at Gainsborough on Monday the 26th day of January 1789 on a violent suspicion of felloniously taking and carrying away a square butter basket half a ream of wrighting paper 3 butter cloths and one hoping sack being the property of William Coleman of Owersby shopkeeper in the parts of Lindsey (*in margin*) upon the oath of James Taylor.

William Coleman bound by recognizance to prefer a bill of indictment and give evidence against Wright Emerson at the next General Quarter Sessions of the Peace holden at Gainsborough in £30 James Taylor to give evidence in £20 at the next General Quarter Sessions at Gainsborough aforesaid.[19]

Monday 26 January. Statements taken by Dixon.

26 January 1789. Information and Complaint of William Coleman taken before Thomas Dixon esq.

On Saturday last 24 January 1789 being at the market at Caistor where he had purchased sundry articles he went down to the house of James Taylor known by the sign of the Plough in Caistor where he usually innes about three of the clock in the afternoon and going into the kitchen he there set down his market basket in which were contained half a ream of writing paper, three linen butter cloths and a large hempen sack marked WC; that having occasion to go into the town again he left his basket in the kitchen which is in the room in which the customers of the house usually leave their marketings; and returning about a quarter of an

[18]   LAO, LQSM A/2/17; LQS Files A/1/243, Epiphany 1789, Caistor.
[19]   LAO, Dixon 8/1, Notebook 1, p.7.

hour afterwards the basket with the articles above specified were taken away and could not be found. Upon which William Coleman went home and about six of the clock in the evening of the same day the above named innkeeper James Taylor came to this informant's house at Owersby aforesaid and informed him that he had found the things upon a man he had taken into custody and desired he would go with him to Caistor to challenge his property which he accordingly did, and going into the house of said James Taylor he found a person called Wright Emmerson under confinement and his, this informant's, basket in the same room and upon examining into it he found not only the particulars above mentioned but also a quantity of flour in a linen bag which did not belong to this informant who was then and is now certain of the said basket and other things being his property. William Coleman

Taken and signed before me Thomas Dixon

Examination of James Taylor of Caistor victualler before Thomas Dixon esq., 26 January 1789.

He keeps a public house in Caistor known by the sign of the Plough and that William Coleman of Owersby shopkeeper who usually makes use of his house informed him between the hours of three and four in the afternoon of the 24th instant that his market basket in which was half a ream of writing paper a hempen sack and three butter cloths had been taken out of the kitchen where he had left it a little time before upon which this examinant searched the house and rode about the ends of the town in order to discover if possible any person having about them the things that were missing but not seeing any such he returned home and soon afterwards one Wright Emmerson of North Kelsey labourer came into the house and from having his boots exceedingly dirty and being absent from the company he had been with in the house about the time the things were supposed to be taken away this examinant suspected him to be the person who had stolen the same and therefore determined to watch him on his return home. That the said Wright Emmerson did not leave the house till he found the said William Coleman had gone home when he went on the road leading to Owersby. This examinant then got into a close adjoining the road and laid himself down under the hedge to prevent being discovered; that the said Wright Emmerson soon afterwards came to the hedgeside and looking round him, this examinant saw him clear the snow away with his foot and take up a sack and put it under his arm and then take up a square market basket; that seeing one John Todds in an adjoining garden he went towards him and desired him to come to him; he then jumped over the hedge and seized the said Wright Emmerson by the collar of his coat; and said John Todds coming and taking the basket this examinant led his prisoner to his house and desiring his companion to reach him the basket, the prisoner took a pint bottle out of it in which was about a gill of rum, and which he said was his, and that he had given seven pence for the liquor and this examinant upon examining into the basket found half a ream of paper and some butter cloths and some flour in a hempen bag. That leaving the prisoner to the charge of some people who were in the house he took his horse and rode to the house of William Coleman at Owersby and meeting with him at home he desired him to come back with him to Caistor to challenge the things he had lost which he accordingly did, and upon the basket and other articles being shown him, he said he was certain they were all his, except the flour and the bag that contained it.

Friday 24 and Saturday 25 April 1789. Trial of Wright Emmerson, Easter Quarter Sessions at Gainsborough.

The Sessions were held at the house of Francis Riley, innholder (on Friday), and in the town hall (on Saturday). Thomas Dixon did not attend.
Indictments. Wright Emmerson late of North Kelsey Labourer for Grand Larceny.
True Bill. William Coleman and James Taylor sworn in court.
Plea Not Guilty. Jury say Guilty.
To be transported for seven years to some place beyond the seas.

The Prosecutor's Claim for Expenses.

The King against Wright Emmerson on the Prosecution of William Coleman
To William Coleman and two Witnesses for their Trouble and Expences attending the prosecution against Wright Emmerson for felony and for orders

	£3	3s	0d
January			
Journey to Caistor to own my property and expenses		2	4
Time Trouble		1	6
Paid for Horsehire 6 miles		2	0
To my journey to Riby Self and Witness			
Time trouble and expences at 3s 10d each		7	8
To horsehire for two horses 6 miles at 4d per each		4	0
Paid for Examination, recognizance etc		7	0
April			
Journey to Gainsborough to prosecute Emmerson			
Self and two witnesses time trouble and expenses			
for 3 days at 3s 10d per day each		11	6
To horsehire for one horse 20 miles at 4d per mile		6	8
To horsehire for 26 miles at 4d per mile for two horses		17	4
Paid for indictment		3	0
Gainsborough Easter Sessions	3	3	0

Allowed by the court Rd Ellison

Wright Emmerson's Imprisonment and Transportation.

Calendar of the House of Correction at Gainsborough includes:
Wright Emmerson committed 26 January by Thomas Dixon
Wright Emmerson to be transported for seven years to some place beyond the seas.

Accounts of the Keeper of the House of Correction at Gainsborough include:
Maintaining Wright Emmerson from 24 April to 28 April and on April 28 conveying Wright Emmerson to Lincoln Gaol to go beyond the seas for the term of seven years   18s

Transport Order. Whereas at this present Sessions Wright Emmerson hath been convicted of felony for which he is liable by the laws of this realm to be transported. It is therefore ordered by this court that the said Wright Emmerson be transported as soon as conveniently may be to some place beyond the seas for the term of seven years to be computed from the time of his conviction as aforesaid pursuant to the late Act of Parliament. And it is also ordered by this court that Sir Cecil Wray Baronet Lawrence Monck John Harrison Richard Ellison Junior Benjamin Bromhead and Henry Hutton Esquires Robert Wells Doctor in Divinity and Caley Illingworth Clerk His Majesty's Justices of the Peace for the said parts or any two of them be and they are hereby nominated and appointed to contract with any person or persons for the transportation of the said Wright Emmerson as above mentioned and to cause such security to be taken as the statutes in that case made and provided direct to be taken by order of court. And also to order the said Wright Emmerson to be delivered pursuant to such contract to the person or persons contracting for him or to his or their assigns.[20]
(Emmerson was not transported. He escaped from prison on 13 October 1789 and remained at large until 20 July 1797.)[21]

March 1789. Two Vagrants' Passes.

Isle of Ely To Wit. These are to desire you and every of you to permit and suffer the bearer hereof Abraham Ellis, Eleanor his Wife, and three children peaceably and quietly to pass unto Scarborough in the county of York they not staying above eight hours in any place (except in case of sickness or during the night time of any day) without ant lett, hindrance or molestation whatsoever they demeaning themselves orderly and not

---

[20] LAO, LQS File A/1/244, Easter 1789, Gainsborough; LQSM A/2/18, Easter 1789, Gainsborough.
[21] Anderson, *Lincolnshire Links with Australia 1788–1840*, 16.

exceeding the space of forty days from the date hereof, to accomplish their said Journey.

Given under my Hand and Seal Thomas Sheepshead being one of His Majesty's Justices of the Peace in and for the said Isle the sixteenth day of March in the 29th Year of the reign of Our Sovereign Lord George the third by the grace of God of Great Britain France and Ireland King defender of the Faith and in the Year of Our Lord 1789.

To all Justices of the Peace, Mayors, Sheriffs, Bailiffs, Constables, and all other his Majesty's Officers whom this may concern.[22]

From Montague Paxton JP of Mark Hall, Latton, Essex
To all Constables, Overseers and others
Whereas Alexander Paxton and his wife appear to me to be in a very indigent miserable state and are desirous to return to their own parish of Beverley in the county of York, these are to desire you to permit them to pass through your different parishes peaceably and to give them the necessary assistance.[23]

Tuesday 12 May 1789. Summary Conviction for Drunkenness at Keelby.

Lincolnshire Lindsey. Be it remembered that Thomas Starke of the parish of Keelby in the said parts labourer was this twelfth day of May one thousand seven hundred and eighty nine convicted before me Thomas Dixon one of His Majesty's Justices of the Peace in and for the said Parts upon the oath of Thomas Sommerscales of the parish of Keelby farmer for being drunk on Sunday the tenth day of this instant May in the said parish of Keelby aforesaid and he paid the penalty of five shillings being the first offence of which he has been convicted.[24]

Wednesday 10 June 1789. Two Summary Convictions for Drunkenness at Laceby.

Lincolnshire Lindsey. Be it remembered that Robt Wallis of the Parish of Aylesby in the said parts labourer was this tenth day of June one thousand

---

22   LAO, Dixon 8/1, Notebook 1, p.13.
23   LAO, Dixon 8/1, Notebook 1, p.13.
24   LAO, Dixon 8/1, Notebook 1, p.13.

seven hundred and eighty nine convicted before me Thomas Dixon one of His Majesty's Justices of the Peace in and for the said Parts upon the oath of William Davy of the parish of Laceby labourer in the said parts, for being drunk on Sunday the seventh day of this instant June in the parish of Laceby aforesaid and he paid the penalty of five shillings, according to the direction of the statutes in such case made being the first offence of which he has been convicted. T. Dixon.

Lincolnshire Lindsey. Be it remembered that George Rannard of the parish of Stallingborough in the said parts labourer was this tenth day of June one thousand seven hundred and eighty nine, convicted before me Thomas Dixon one of His Majesty's Justices of the Peace in and for the said Parts, upon the oath of William Davy of the parish of Laceby in the said parts labourer, for being drunk on Sunday the seventh day of this instant June in the parish of Laceby aforesaid and he paid the penalty of five shillings according to the direction of the statutes in such case made, being the first offence of which he has been convicted. T. Dixon.[25]

Monday 3 August 1789. Committal of Father of Bastard Child.

July 25th 1789 A Warrant of Apprehension from William Thorold, clerk, one of His Majesty's Justices of the Peace in and for the Parts of Lindsey to take Thomas Thissleton of Beelsby labourer for begetting a male bastard child on the body of Sarah Dawson of Beelsby, widow, of which child she was delivered on the 16th day of June last past, and that on Monday the 3rd day of August last past the said Thomas Thissleton was brought before me Thomas Dixon one of His Majesty's Justices of the Peace in and for the Parts aforesaid and refused to give security to indemnify the said parish and hath also refused to enter into a recognizance with sufficient surety, upon condition to appear at the next General Quarter Sessions and perform such order or orders as shall be made in pursuance of an Act passed in the eighteenth year of the reign of her late Majesty Queen Elizabeth concerning bastards begotten and born out of lawful matrimony.

Upon which refusal I committed the said Thomas Thissleton to the House of Correction at Gainsborough.[26]

---

[25] LAO, Dixon 8/1, Notebook 1, pp.13–15.
[26] LAO, Dixon 8/1, Notebook 1, pp.14, 15.

Monday 10 August 1789. Committal of a Servant for Deserting Service.

August 10th 1789 Joseph Cooke committed to the House of Correction at Gainsborough for three months for not fulfilling his contract as hired to Philip Skipworth about a fortnight before May Day last to serve him for a year till 1790 at £7 10s 0d for the year, and refused and still refuses to perform the said service according to agreement made at the time.[27]

Tuesday 10 November 1789. Committal and Trial of Robert Graves for Theft of Geese at Great Limber.

Tuesday 10 November 1789. Graves Committed to the House of Correction.

Robert Graves in the parish of Keelby labourer committed the House of Correction at Gainsborough on a violent suspicion of killing two geese in the poultry house of Richard Walkden of Great Limber farmer about eleven o'clock at night on [*Tuesday deleted*] Monday the 9th day of November 1789 they being the property of the said Richard Walkden. Committed on Tuesday the 10th day November 1789 to the House of Correction at Gainsborough.

Tuesday 10 November. Statements of Witnesses.
John Everitt, Serving Man.

Information and Complaint of John Everitt serving man in behalf of his master Richard Walkden of Great Limber … farmer taken on oath before me Thomas Dixon one of his Majesty's Justices of the Peace for the said parts the tenth day of November one thousand seven hundred and eighty nine.

The above named informant on his oath saith about eleven o'clock on Monday night being the ninth instant November he heard his master's goose and ducks make a great noise and suspecting that the fox was got amongst them he got out of bed and went into the out house and there found Robert Graves of Keelby labourer laid down in the house and two geese just killed beside him and this informant hath great cause to suspect and doth suspect that the aforesaid Robert Graves did kill the two geese with an intent to steal and carry them away.
John Heveritt
Taken before me, T. Dixon

William Stothard, Shepherd.

The Examination of William Stothard Shepherd to Richard Walkden of Great

---

27   LAO, Dixon 8/1, Notebook 1, p.17.

Limber in the said Parts farmer taken on oath before me Thomas Dixon one of his Majesty's Justices of the Peace in and for the said Parts, Tuesday 10 November 1789.

The above named examinant on his oath saith that about ten o'clock at night he went to bed and about eleven on Monday night the ninth instant November he heard his master's geese making a great noise in their house and he came down immediately and thought that the fox had got amongst them; and in going into the house he found Robert Graves of Keelby labourer laid down in the house and two geese just killed beside him, and this examinant hath great cause to suspect and doth suspect that the aforesaid Robert Graves did kill the two geese with an intent to steal and carry them away.
William Stothard
Taken before me, T. Dixon

Witnesses Bound to Appear at Quarter Sessions.
T Dixon Esq. John Evritt of Great Limber Servant in £20 for his appearance at this Sessions to prosecute and give evidence against Robert Graves of Keelby labourer for killing two geese the property of one Richard Walkden. Discharged.

William Stothard of Great Limber shepherd in £10 for his appearance at this Sessions to give evidence against Robert Graves as above. Discharged.

Trial of Robert Graves at Quarter Sessions, Michaelmas, 1789, Gainsborough Indictment.
Robert Graves late of Keelby labourer for petty larceny.
True Bill. John Everitt and William Stothard sworn in court.

Trial.
Plea Not Guilty Jury say Guilty.
To be publickly whipt at Caistor aforesaid from the Court House there round the Market Place up to Mr Haddesley's house and back again and then discharged.

Prosecutor's Costs.
Expences
To Richard Walkden for the use of himself and three witnesses for their trouble and expences in prosecuting Robert Graves for felony

£1   6s   4d

Additional charges King against Robert Greaves indictment for felony

Paid Clerk of Peace for drawing indictment	2s	0d
Two witnesses attending Caistor Sessions two days	3s	0d

One witness attending Caistor Sessions one day	1s	6d
Expences two witnesses at Caistor Sessions 2 days	9s	4d
Expences of one witness at ditto 1 day	2s	4d
Horsehire 3 horses from Limber to Caistor 5 miles	5s	0d
Caistor Epiphany Sessions 1790	£1 3s	10d

Allowed this bill by the court R. Ellison.[28]

4 January 1790. Summary Conviction for Hedge Breaking.

Hannah Wells the wife of Thomas Wells of Laceby labourer convicted upon the oath of Christopher Bell of Laceby aforesaid grazier for tearing and breaking down the hedges of the said Christopher Bell in the parish of Laceby aforesaid and is to pay to the said Christopher Bell for satisfaction and charges the sum of ten shillings on or before the first day of April 1790. January 4th 1790.

Convicted before me Thomas Dixon of Riby one of His Majesty's Justices of the Peace in and for the said Parts of Lindsey in the county of Lincoln. T Dixon.[29]

This conviction was not enrolled at Quarter Sessions.

Friday 15 and Saturday 16 January 1790. Quarter Sessions at Caistor.

Thomas Dixon attended this Sessions. He signed two Removal Orders and an indictment of a parish for the state of its roads.

Saturday 16 January 1790. Removal of the Family of Thomas Stark.

Removal Order.

16 January 1790 Removal Order signed by Andrew Empson and Thomas Dixon esquires, two of His Majesty's Justices of the Peace in and for the said Parts, upon complaint of Overseers of Nettleton, for Elizabeth, wife of Thomas Stark, John, four and a half years, Frances, two years, and Mary, five weeks; ordered removed to Great Grimsby.

Appeal Against the Removal. Easter Sessions at Gainsborough, 16 April 1790.

And whereas the Inhabitants of the said parish of Great Grimsby have appealed

---

[28] LAO, Dixon 8/1, Notebook 1, p.19; LQS Files A/1/246 Michaelmas 1789, A/1/247 Epiphany 1790, Caistor; LQSM A/2/17 Michaelmas 1789, A/2/18 Epiphany 1790.
[29] LAO, Dixon 8/1, Notebook 1, p.19.

to this court against the said order of Removal, ordered (after a full hearing of all the parties on the merits of the said appeal) that the said order of Removal be and the same is hereby quashed, And that the churchwardens and Overseers of the Poor of the parish of Nettleton aforesaid or some or one of them do forthwith pay or cause to be paid unto the Churchwardens and Overseers of the Poor of the parish of Great Grimsby aforesaid or some or one of them the sum of five pounds and tenpence towards their costs and charges sustained in this cause. Mr George Babb for the Appellants. Mr John Trevor for the Removants.

Mr Babb, for the appellants, placed in evidence an indenture dated 1 December 1770 binding Thomas Stark apprentice to William Drant of Waltham, cordwainer. This would have given Stark and his family settlement in Waltham, not Grimsby. Dixon was not present at this Sessions.[30]

Saturday 27 March 1790. Prosecution of Simon Burnett for Theft of Ducks.

The initial complaint in this case had been made before another justice, William Thorold, on 1 February 1790. Thomas Harneiss of Laceby had accused Simon Burnett, fisherman, of Immingham, of stealing five ducks, valued at 10d, from him. Thorold had bound them and a witness, Thomas Stark of Laceby, to appear at the next Quarter Sessions.

Saturday 27 March 1790. Information of Thomas Chapman taken before Thomas Dixon.

[*Damaged*]
The Information of Thomas Chapman late of Hallington [...] Taylor [...] 27 March 1790 [...] saw him take five or six ducks or more and that he the said Simon Burnett afterwards put them into a sack and went off with them but that he did not see this informant nor did this informant speak or discover himself to him.
Thomas Chapman.
Signed and sworn before me Thomas Dixon.

Easter Sessions, 1790. Gainsborough. Trial of Simon Burnett.

Simon Burnett late of Immingham fisherman for petty larceny.
A True Bill.
Plea Not Guilty, Jury say Guilty.
To be recommitted to the House of Correction at Louth aforesaid there to remain

---

[30] LAO, LQS Files A/1/247, Epiphany 1790, Caistor, A/1/248, Easter, Gainsborough; LQSM A/2/19, Easter, Gainsborough.

one calendar month and publickly whipt from the south east corner of the church there and back again on the market day next preceding his discharge.

Expenses: To Thomas Harneis Esquire for himself and witnesses for their trouble and expences in prosecuting Simon Burnett for felony   £8   7s   1d[31]

28 January 1791. John Tate Committed for Trial at Assizes for Theft of Rabbits.

Lincolnshire Lindsey. To the Constable of North Kelsey in the said parts and County and to the Keeper of his Majesty's Gaol in the Castle of Lincoln in the said parts of the said County

Whereas John Tate of North Kelsey in the said parts cordwainer is now before me Thomas Dixon one of His Majesty's Justices of the Peace in and for the said Parts, charged upon the oath of John Kirkby of Croxby in ye said parts warrener that on Saturday the twenty second day of this instant January he the aforesaid John Tate did willfully and wrongfully in the night time enter the warren of Richard Goulton of Croxby in the said Parts aforesaid and take therefrom a certain number of conies commonly called rabbets.

These are therefore to require you the said Constable in his Majesty's name forthwith to convey and deliver into the custody of the Keeper of the said Gaol the body of the said John Tate and you the said Keeper are hereby commanded to receive the said John Tate into your custody in the said Gaol untill the next General Gaol Delivery for the said county, herein fail not.

Given under my hand and seal this twenty eight day of January one thousand seven hundred and ninety one.[32]

A Note on Records of Fines.

A bill, containing a great number of sheets, has lately been filed in the Court of Exchequer, against several Justices of the Peace, to compel them to render an account to the government of a number of fines they have received upon the prosecution of penal actions; but of which no account has been given for twelve Years.[33]

---

[31] LAO, LQS File A/1/248, Easter 1790, Gainsborough; LQSM A/2/19, Easter 1790, Louth.

[32] LAO, Dixon 8/1, Notebook 1, p.10.

[33] LAO, Dixon 8/1, Notebook 1, p.11.

1791. Reorganisation of Quarter Sessions.

Sessions

First Whole Week after Epiphany – at Spilsby and Castor

First whole Week after Easter – at Louth and Gainsborough

First whole Week after Thomas a Becket – at Spilsby and Castor

First whole Week after Michaelmas – at Gainsborough and Louth

Lincolnshire Lindsey. Notice is hereby given that the General Quarter Sessions of the Peace for Gainsborough and Castor subdivision of the Parts of Lindsey, in the county of Lincoln, which have usually been held at Gainsborough and Castor, in the said Parts, will, for the future, be held at Kirton, in the said parts; – and that the several General Quarter Sessions of the Peace to be hereafter held for the same subdivision; and for Louth and Spilsby of the said Parts, will be holden at the times and places following (viz.)

Every Midsummer, at Kirton aforesaid on Thursday in the first week after the Translation of St Thomas the Martyr, and (by adjournment) at Spilsby, on Tuesday in the week following.

Every Michaelmas, at Kirton aforesaid, on Thursday in the first week after the Feast of St Michael, and (by adjournment) at Louth, on Tuesday in the week following.

Every Epiphany, at Spilsby, on Thursday in the first week after the Epiphany, and (by adjournment) at Kirton aforesaid, on Tuesday in the week following.

Every Easter, at Louth, on Thursday in the first week after the Clause of Easter, and (by adjournment) at Kirton aforesaid, on Tuesday in the week following.

The General Quarter Sessions of the Peace for the Parts of Lindsey in the county of Lincoln will be held at the times and places following viz: at Spilsby, on Friday the thirteenth (instead of Thursday the twelfth) day of January 1792; and at Kirton, on Tuesday the seventeenth day of the same January 1792 at nine o'clock in the forenoon of each of the said dayes. The Grand Jury at Kirton Sessions will be called over and sworn precisely at eleven o'clock in the forenoon.

Brackenbury, Clerk of the Peace.

*Dixon's notes and copies of an announcement by the Clerk of the Peace
record a major reorganisation of Quarter Sessions, centred around the
opening of a new house of correction and courtroom at Kirton Lindsey. At
the Easter Sessions that year it was resolved that, until the new building
was ready, magistrates would meet 'at the house of Sarah Dunn, widow'
in Kirton, and, further, it was 'Ordered that the Statutes at Large and all
the books, Constables' staves, cushions, cloths, inkstands, and every other
article hitherto kept at Caistor in the said parts for the use of Caistor
Sessions be removed to Kirton'.[34]*

December 1791. Allowing Constable's Expenses for Committal of a Vagrant to the House of Correction at Gainsborough.

To Thomas Stark Constable of Laceby October 1791. For Conveying
David Gosling a vagabond to Gainsborough House of Correction.

Lincolnshire Lindsey. December 1791. Allowed by me one of His Majesty's Justices of the Peace in and for the said Parts, and the same is to
be paid by the Treasurer of the Same Parts for which this shall be his
sufficient warrant.

Lincolnshire Lindsey. Allowed by me One of His Majesty's Justices of the
Peace in and for the said Parts, and the Chief Constable of the wapentake
or the Treasurer for the same parts are required to discharge the same.

*This entry may be linked to one of the magistrates' periodic drives against
vagrancy. This time, they seem to have been blaming Hull:*
Ordered that George Uppleby esquire and The Reverend Amaziah Empson Clerk
two of His Majesty's Justices of the Peace for the said parts be requested to take
upon themselves the trouble to give immediate directions for the erection of a
warning table at Barton waterside intimating that all vagrants who shall enter this
Division without a legal pass will be immediately apprehended and dealt with
according to law – And to cause a whipping post to be set up there to give effect
to such warning table.

Ordered that the Clerk of the Peace do write to the Mayor of the town of King-
ston upon Hull with information of the great grievance which this Division
labours under in consequence of a practice of the Constables or other inferior

---

[34] LAO, Dixon 8/1, Notebook 1, pp.11, 21, 22; LQSM A/2/19, Easter 1791, Gainsborough.

officers in that town to encourage and frequently to bribe vagrants to enter into this Division;

Also to state that many vagrants do come with passes signed by the magistrates without having the requisites of the Act of Parliament;

To request that the Mayor will please to make inquiry into such proceeding, and to express the hope of the magistrates of this Division that he will as far as possible put a stop to it and concur in the useful labour of preventing an offence so injurious to society,

And further to suggest that the great burthen thrown upon this Division will oblige the magistrates to apply to the proper courts for a remedy against such evil unless the same be speedily prevented.[35]

30 May 1792. Future Arrangements for Petty Sessions.
Notice. His Majesty's Justices of the Peace in or near Louth intend to hold their meetings in the Town Hall of Louth on every Wednesday fortnight throughout the year, between the hours of 11am and 2pm. The first meeting to be held 13 June 1792. Dated 30 May 1792.[36]

Wednesday 18 April 1792. Order to Remove an Irish Family from Waltham.
On complaint of Overseers of Waltham, Martha Handling, wife of Robert Handling, an Irishman who has gained no lawful settlement in England with three children named Elizabeth, James and Thomas, Elizabeth aged about 4 years and an half, James aged about 2 years and seven months, Thomas aged about one year and a quarter, came lately to dwell in the parish of Waltham removed to Louth.
Removal Order dated 18 April 1792 by A. Empson and T. Dixon

Tuesday 17 July 1792. Removal Order Quashed on Appeal.
Louth Appellants and Waltham Removants. Whereas by virtue of an order under the hands and seals of Thomas Dixon Esquire and Amaziah Empson Clerk two of His Majesty's Justices of the Peace for the said Parts and one of them of the quorum bearing date the eighteenth day of April last past Martha Handling (Wife of Robert Handling an Irishman) with three children named Elizabeth James and Thomas, Elizabeth aged about four years and an half, James aged about two years

---

35 LAO, Dixon 8/1, Notebook 1, p.23; LQSM A/2/22, Michaelmas 1791, Kirton.
36 LAO, Dixon 8/1, Notebook 1, inside front cover.

and seven months and Thomas aged about one year and a quarter were removed from the parish of Waltham in the said Parts to the town of Louth in the said parts as the place of their last legal Settlement,

And whereas the inhabitants of the town of Louth aforesaid have appealed to this court against the said order of Removal ordered, by and with the consent of the Removants, that the said order of removal be and the same is hereby quashed, And that the Churchwardens and Overseers of the Poor of the parish of Waltham aforesaid or some or one of them do forthwith pay or cause to be paid unto the Churchwardens or Overseers of the Poor of the said town of Louth or some or one of them the sum of eighteen pounds for and towards the maintenance of the said Martha Handling and her said three children from the time of their Removal to this day and for and towards their costs and charges sustained in this cause. Mr Willis for the appellants.[37]

Saturday 28 April 1792. Father of a Bastard Child Bound to Appear at Quarter Sessions.

Recognizance. Stephen Cam of Owersby serving man and William Thorp of Owersby grazier personally came before me Thomas Dixon One of his Majesty's Justices of the Peace in and for the said Parts bound and acknowledged themselves bound in £40 and £20 respectively that Stephen Cam appear at the next General Quarter Sessions of the Peace for the said Parts to give security for begetting a bastard child on body of Elizabeth Armstrong of Owersby, single-woman.

Taken and acknowledged before me Thomas Dixon.
Stephen Camm appeared at Midsummer Sessions.[38]

Friday 11 May 1792. Committal of John Mayfield for Leaving His Wife and Family Chargeable to the Parish of Riby.
Calendar of Prisoners in House of Correction, Kirton.

John Mayfield committed May 11th, a rogue and vagabond having absconded and left his wife and family chargeable to the parish of Riby. Committed by Wm Thorold, clerk, and Thomas Dixon esq.

Accounts of the Overseer of the Poor for Riby, showing the cost of Mayfield's committal, and of maintaining his family.
Disbursements of the Overseer 1791–1792

Febry 24th Pd John Mayfield wife 10s 6d for 7 weeks collection   10s 6d
Pd to Do. for child close 10s 6d   10s 6d

37 LAO, LQS File A/1/257; LQSM A/2/20, Midsummer 1792, Kirton.
38 LAO, LQS File A/1/257; LQSM A/2/20, Midsummer 1792, Kirton.

Overseer of the Poor's Disbursements 1792–1793

Given Mayfield's wife towards her laying in	9s	0d
My trouble and expence going to Louth and from thence to Grimblethorpe to take Mayfield	11s	4d
Pd for a Warrant 1s Do for an Examination	2s	0d
Three journeys to Croxby and one to Stalinbro'	5s	6d
Pd the Stalinbro' Constable for his trouble and expences	11s	0d
A journey to Grimsby	1s	6d
Pd E Farrow for bringing Mayfield to Riby	2s	0d
For a Commitment	1s	0d
Pd Thos Clayton for going to Kirton	1s	6d
Pd Two horses going to Kirton	5s	0d
Pd E Farrow for his trouble and expences going to Kirton House of Correction	11s	1d
Pd Mayfield's wife collection 13 at 1/6 pr week	19s	6d

Thos Skipworth Disbursements of the Overseer from Easter 1793 to 1794

Pd to M. Mayfield 6 weeks collection at 2s 6d pr w.	15s	6d
Pd her for 4 at 1s	4s	0d
Pd for blankets for her child	2s	0d
Pd to the nurse for her attendance	8s	0d
Pd to the midwife for her	3s	0d
Pd Thos Acrill for a pair of shoes for M Mayfield	4s	6d
M Mayfield coals portage and toll	13s	4d

Wm Torr Disbursements of the Overseer of the Poor from Easter 1794 to Easter 1795

Pd for ¾ qtrs of coals for Mayfield's wife port and leading		16s	0d
Pd for Do. house rent £1 1s load of furze and leading 5s	£1	6s	0d

The Overseer of the Poor Disbursements from Easter 1795 to 1796

My team fetching Mayfield's wife	2s	6d

The Overseer of the Poor's Disbursements from Easter 1797 to Easter 1798

Pd for 3 chald. of coals for Mary Mayfield	15s[39]

[39] LAO, LQS Files A/1/257, Midsummer 1792, Kirton; Riby Par/7/1, Riby Parish Book, 1742–1856.

Tuesday 11 September 1792. Committal of Father of Bastard Child.
William Leaning of Audleby in the Parish of Caistor serving man to
Abraham Horne committed upon the oath of Ann Smith of Riby single
woman with having begotten her with child. Committed for want of sure-
ties by me, T. Dixon.[40]
*Leaning does not appear in the records of Quarter Sessions or the House
of Correction.*

**Wednesday 12 September 1792. Committal of Absconding Servant
from Aylesby.**
Mary Robinson of Grasby, singlewoman, committed to the House of
Correction at Kirton ... for departing from the service of Richard Ostler
of Aylesby, grazier. Committed for three months by Revd William Thorold.[41]

**Wednesday 12 September 1792. Note of Committal of Thomas
Grant for Leaving His Wife and Family Chargeable to Riby.**
Revd Mr Thorold committed Thos. Grant of Riby, labourer, to the House
of Correction at Kirton in the Parts of Lindsey for absconding from, and
leaving his wife and family chargeable to, the parish of Riby in the said
Parts.

Tuesday 22 January 1793. Grant Appeared at Quarter Sessions.
Ordered that Thomas Grant brought before this court in the custody of the
Keeper of the said Bridewell for leaving his wife and family be and he is hereby
discharged.

Cost of Maintaining Grant's Family.
Riby Overseer's Disbursements 1792–1793

Pd For advertising Thos Grant	£1	3s	6d
Pd for the old woman at Mucton	£4	4s	0d
Pd Grant's wife 12 weeks collection at 2/6 pr wk	£1	10s	0d
To one mett of coals for Ann Grant		1s	6d

40 LAO, Dixon 8/1, Notebook 1, p.24.
41 LAO, Dixon 8/1, Notebook 1, p.24.

Wm Torr Disbursements of the Overseer of the Poor from Easter 1794 to Easter 1795

Pd Ann Grant 50 weeks collection at 3s per week	£7	10s	0d
Pd for Do 1 chald of coales 16s port and leading the same 4s	£1	0s	

Riby Overseer of the Poor Disbursements from Easter 1795 to 1796

Pd Ann Grant 51 wks at 3s per wk	£7	13s

Riby Overseers of the Poor Disbursements from Easter 1796 to Easter 1797

Pd Ann Grant at 3s 6d for 55 weeks	£9	12s	6d
Pd for 1 strike of rye for Ann Grant 4s and nurse attending her		5s	

Riby Overseer of the Poor's Disbursements from Easter 1797 to Easter 1798

Pd Ann Grant 3s for 51 wks	£7	13s	
Pd For one strike of bread corn for Ann Grant		3s	9d[42]

Saturday 22 December 1792. Riot and Theft at Caistor.
Information and Complaint of the Prosecutor.

The Information and Complaint of William Addison of Barton upon Humber in the said Parts higler taken on oath before me Thomas Dixon one of His Majesty's Justices of the Peace for the said Parts the twenty second day of December 1793.

The above named informant on his oath saith that Geoffrey Gunby, Joseph Johnson and Timothy Morley of Nettleton, labourers, between the hours of eleven and twelve o'clock in the forenoon of the eighth day of December instant came into the house of John Varlow of Caistor in the said Parts victualler and unlawfully did take from this informant one goose, twenty pair of giblets and six pounds of butter the property of this informant which he this informant had on the said eighth day of December bought in the open market at Caistor aforesaid. William Addison X his mark
Taken before me the 22nd Day of December 1792 T. Dixon

Statement of Witness.

The Examination of John Varlow of Caistor in the said parts victualler taken on his oath before me Thos Dixon esq. one of His Majesty's Justices of the Peace for the said parts this 22nd December 1792.

---

[42] LAO. Dixon 8/1, Notebook 1 p.24; LQSM A/2/21, Epiphany 1793, Kirton; Riby Par/7/1, Riby Parish Book, 1742–1856.

This examinant on his oath saith that on Saturday the eighth instant Joseph Johnson, Timothy Morley and Geoffrey Gonby, labourers, of Nettleton between eleven and twelve of the clock of the same day in the forenoon were in the house of this examinant and behaving in a riotous manner and that Timothy Morley aforesaid had one pound of butter in his hand.
Signed John Varlow
Taken before me the 22nd Day of December 1792 T. Dixon.

Prosecutor and Witness Bound to Appear at Quarter Sessions.

Recognizances T. Dixon esq.
William Addison of Barton higler in £40 for his appearance at this Sessions to prosecute and give evidence against Geoffrey Gunby, Joseph Johnson and Timothy Morley late of Nettleton labourers for stealing one goose, twenty pair of giblets and six pounds of butter the property of the said William Addison.

John Varlow of Caistor in £20 for his appearance at this Sessions to give evidence against the said Geoffrey Gunby Joseph Johnson and Timothy Morley.

22 January 1793. Trial of the Accused at Kirton Quarter Sessions. Indictment.

Indictment of Geoffrey Gunby, late of Nettleton, labourer, Joseph Johnson, late of the same place, labourer, and Timothy Morley late of the same place, labourer, together with diverse other evil disposed persons to the number of five and more on 22 December 1792 at Caistor did unlawfully and riotously assemble and gather together to disturb the peace, and there assembled and gathered together one goose fifteen pair of goose giblets and six pounds weight of Butter belonging to William Addison higler then and there being in a certain dwelling house of John Varlow victualler of Caistor did unlawfully riotously and riotously did take and carry away.

William Addison John Varlow, George Gridham, Thomas Watmough sworn in Court.
True Bill
Pleas Not Guilty. Jury Say Guilty.

Geoffrey Gunby fined 5s and to be recommitted to the said bridewell and there kept to hard labour in a solitary cell twelve calendar months.
Joseph Johnson fined 1s and to be recommitted to the said bridewell and there kept to hard labour in a solitary cell one calendar month.
And Timothy Morley fined one shilling and to be recommitted to the said bridewell and there kept to hard labour in a solitary cell six calendar months, and untill payment of their respective fines.

Prosecutor's Expenses.

Account of the expences of William Addison and his witnesses in prosecuting Jefferey Gunby, Timothy Morley, and Joseph Johnson for a riot at a general Quarter Sessions of the Peace holden at Kirton in and for the said parts before Richard Ellison esquire Chairman and William Rd Wilson esq. and others His Majesties Justices of the Peace in and for the said Parts, this 23rd Day of January 1793

To my Horsehire (including keeping) from Caistor to Kirton it being 18 miles at 4d per Mile is		6s	0d
To my 3 witnesses horsehire for 18 miles at 4d per ditto is		18s	0d
To my expences at Kirton for 3 days at 2s 4d per day is		7s	0d
To my witnesses expences for 3 days each at ditto is	£1	1s	0d
To myself 3 days attendance at the Sessions at 1s 6d		4s	6d
To my 3 witnesses attendance 3 days each at do		13s	6d
Pd for drawing up the Bill of Indictment and a Counsell employed on the business as per bill	£4	18s	2d
	£7	8s	2d

Kirton Epiphany Sessions 1793 Allowed by the Court
Rd Ellison Chairman

Prisoners in the House of Correction.
Epiphany Sessions, January 1793. Calendar of Prisoners in the House of Correction at Kirton includes:

Timothy Morley, Joseph Johnson, Geoffrey Gunby committed 22 December 1792 by T. Dixon esq.
Easter Sessions, April 1793.
Calendar of House of Correction Kirton
Geoffrey Gunby, Timothy Morley Remain under sentence

Accounts of the Keeper of the House of Correction at Kirton.

For Maintaining Joseph Johnson from 22nd January to Feb 19th one month		7s	0d
To Maintaining Geoffrey Gunby from January 22nd to April 16th 12 Weeks	£1	1s	0d
To Maintaining Timothy Morley from January 22nd to April 16th 12 Weeks	£1	1s	0d
Additional expence for maintaining prisoners when ill 3d per day each Timothy Morley 3 Days			9d

Midsummer Sessions, July 1793.
Accounts of the Keeper of the House of Correction at Kirton.
To Maintaining Geoffrey Gunby from April 16 to 19 inst
13 weeks 4 days   £1   3s   9d
Timothy Morley April 16th to July 9th 12 weeks   £1   1s   0d

Michaelmas Sessions, October 1793
Accounts of the Keeper of the House of Correction at Kirton.
July 19 to Oct 11 12 weeks Geoffrey Gunby   £1   1s   0d[43]

Winter 1793. Fear of Revolution.
10 December 1792. Caistor Constitutional Association.
The inaugural meeting of this association, one of many in the county, was held at Caistor on 10 December 1792 and attended by 'near two hundred respectable persons'. Thomas Dixon was not only present but elected to the committee. The aims of the association were:

'That we will, by the distribution of constitutional writings, and by every effort of calm reasoning, endeavour to undeceive and inform such persons as may have been misled by the delusive and inflammatory suggestions of evil-designing men, who seek to excite a general spirit of restlessness and discontent ...'

Tom Paine 'Executed'.
6 January 1793. The Account of Prisoners Confined in the Louth House of Correction submitted to Epiphany Sessions includes, at the end of the usual list of prisoners:
Tom Paine, discharged and publickly executed on the Market Hill amidst the acclamations of thousands.

Saturday 12 January 1793. The Price of Bread.
On Saturday 12 January 1793 Thomas Dixon chaired a meeting at Caistor which resolved:
That the standard measure Winchester Bushel be enforced, as the customary measure is injurious to the poor.
Enforcing existing market legislation was still the standard reaction of magistrates to times of hardship. Perhaps this concern was related to the case of Gunby, Johnson and Morley for theft of food at Caistor on 22

---

[43] LAO, LQS Files A/1/259, Epiphany 1793, Kirton; A/1/260, Easter 1793, Kirton; A/1/261, Midsummer 1793, Kirton.

December 1792, recorded above. Although the files suggest it was just a drunken spree, it may have been part of a more serious food riot.[44]

Tuesday 1 January 1793. Father of a Bastard Child Bound to Appear at Quarter Sessions.

John Harrison of Laceby shopkeeper bound in £40 George Harrison yeoman of Great Grimsby in £20 for John Harrison's appearance at the next General Quarter Sessions of the Peace holden at Kirton in the Parts of Lindsey and also to abide and perform such order or orders as shall be made touching a child or children unlawfully begotten on the body of Hannah Grant of the parish of Laceby singlewoman.

Taken and acknowledged before me T. Dixon   Are You Content

The recognizance is enrolled in the Quarter Sessions files and gives a little more information than Dixon recorded in his notebook:

Recognizance taken before Thomas Dixon esq. 1st January 1793. John Harrison of Laceby grocer and George Harrison of Great Grimsby yeoman, bound in £40 and £20 on condition that John Harrison appear at Kirton and obey the orders of the court concerning bastards begotten and born out of wedlock upon complaint of the churchwarden and overseer of the poor of the parish of Ludborough for begetting a child on the body of Hannah Grant, singlewoman, likely to be chargeable to Ludborough.[45]

Notes of Forms of Summonses at the End of Dixon's Second Notebook.

Notes, from their position in the notebooks, made in January 1793.

You are also to Summon A. B. Labourer of North Kelsey aforesaid to Appear at the same time and give Evidence concerning the above Complaint.

You are to Summon I. F. and C. D. Labourers to appear at the same time to give such Evidence upon Oath as they know to be true touching the Premises.[46]

---

44 LAO, LQS File A/1/259, Epiphany 1793, Spilsby; *The Lincoln, Rutland and Stamford Mercury*, 18 and 26 January 1793.
45 LAO, Dixon 8/2, Notebook 2, end pp.1–2; LQS File A/1/259, Epiphany 1793, Kirton.
46 LAO, Dixon 8/2, Notebook 2, end page 5.

Monday 7 January 1793. Information and Complaint. Absconding Servant at Laceby.
Information and Complaint of Christopher Bell of Laceby, grazier, against Alice Smith, servant, for leaving his service without permission – hired a little after May Day.

Sunday 13 February 1793. Misbehaving Servant at Stallingborough.
Information and Complaint of Thomas Mumby of Stallingborough, farmer, against Charles Wass that he hath neglected his master's business, behaved with much insolence and otherwise ill conducted himself by frequently running out of his master's house on the Sabbath Day as soon as dinner is over.[47]

Monday 11 March 1793. Father of a Bastard Child Bound to Appear at Quarter Sessions.
Lincolnshire Lindsey. Thomass Burkinshaw of North Killingholm farmer bound in £40 and John Burkhill of North Killingholm yeoman in £20 for Thomass Burkinshaw's appearance at the next General Quarter Sessions of the Peace to be holden at Kirton and also to abide and perform such order or orders as shall be made touching a child or children unlawfully begotten on the body of Ann Smith single woman of the parish of North Killingholm.
Taken and acknowledged before me, T. Dixon.   Are You Content

This recognizance was enrolled at Quarter Sessions. The action was initiated by the Churchwarden and Overseers of the Poor of North Killingholme.[48]

Thursday 14 March 1793. Lincoln Assizes.
On Thursday 14 March Thomas Dixon attended the Lent Assizes at Lincoln and served on the Grand Jury.[49]

Saturday 23 March 1793. Committal of a Servant for Ill Behaviour.
Committed Leonard Beecroft, servant in husbandry to Mr William

---

[47] *Ibid.*
[48] LAO, Dixon 8/2, Notebook 2, end page 2; LQS File A/1/260, Easter 1793, Kirton.
[49] *The Lincoln, Rutland and Stamford Mercury*, 15 March 1793.

Holgate of Thoresway ['*Farmer*' *deleted*] to the House of Correction at Kirton for the Space of one month from the above date for being guilty of divers misdemeanors miscarriages and ill behaviour towards him the said William Holgate and particularly hath disobeyed his lawful commands.[50]

Monday 8 April 1793. Information and Complaint. Absconding Servant.

Lincolnshire Lindsey. The Information and Complaint of Mark Aistropp of Tealby, labourer, taken oath before me Thomas Dixon One of His Majesty's Justices of the Peace in and for the said Parts the 8th Day of April 1793

That a few days before Old Candlemas last he Agreed with Christopher Howson to serve him from the 13th Day of February last to May Day seventeen hundred and ninety three at 13s 6d per week when he was at home, and 1s 0d per week more when he could not sleep at home.

And on or about the twenty sixth day of March last he departed from his master's service without his permission for so doing.
Taken before me, T. Dixon.   Signed, Mark Astrop.[51]

Tuesday 7 May 1793. Incomplete Information and Complaint.

Lincolnshire Lindsey. The Information and Complaint of Elizabeth Fulforthworth of Laceby in the said Parts widow on oath before me Thomas Dixon One of His Majesty's Justices of the Peace in and for the said Parts this seventh day of May 1793
That on the ... [*record ends*].[52]

Tuesday 7 May 1793. Information and Complaint. Servant Breach of Contract.

Lincolnshire Lindsey. The Information and Complaint of Mr Paul Hackett of Wailsby farmer taken on oath before me Thomas Dixon One of His Majesty's Justices of the Peace in and for the said Parts this seventh day of May 1793 that on Thursday the twenty eight day of March last he hired Ann Phillipson late of Great Limber but now of Stallingborough to serve

50 LAO, Dixon 8/2, Notebook 2, end p.1.
51 LAO, Dixon 8/2, Notebook 2, front p.1.
52 LAO, Dixon 8/2, Notebook 2, front p.2.

him for one year from the twelfth day of May this instant and that she has returned her earnest money and still refuses coming to her said service according to agreement.

Taken before me, T. Dixon.

Signed, Paul Hackett.[53]

Wednesday 1 August 1793. Information and Complaint. Absconding Servant.

Lincolnshire Lindsey. The Information and Complaint of John Parsons of Great Limber in the said Parts brickmaker taken on oath before me Thomas Dixon One of His Majesty's Justices of the Peace in and for the said Parts this first day of August 1793.

That a few days before old May Day last he agreed with John Prat of Great Limber, labourer, to serve him from Old May Day last to Old Michaelmas or the season at the making of bricks at 3s 3d per thousand and on Monday last he absconded from his master's service without his permissions for so doing.

Taken before me, T. Dixon.

Signed, John Parsons.[54]

Thursday 2 August 1793. Information and Complaint. Absconding Servant.

Lincolnshire Lindsey. The Information and Complaint of Martin Frankish of Barnoldby le Wold, farmer, taken on oath before me Thomas Dixon One of His Majesty's Justices of the Peace in and for the said Parts this second day of August seventeen hundred and ninety three.

Who on his oath saith that at the meeting held at Keelby for the retaining of servants he hired Thomas Catley from May Day last for one year to May Day one thousand seven hundred and ninety four at certain wages and that last night or early this morning he departed from his service without his master's permission for so doing.

Taken before me, T. Dixon.

Signed, Martin Frankish.[55]

---

[53] *Ibid.*, front p.5.
[54] *Ibid.*, front p.9.
[55] LAO, Dixon 8/2, Notebook 2, front p.10.

Tuesday 7 August 1793. Information and Complaint. Absconding Servant.

Lincolnshire Lindsey. The Information and Complaint of Thomas Watmough of Caistor in the said parts brickmaker taken on oath before me Thomas Dixon One of his Majesty's Justices of the Peace in and for the said Parts this seventh day of August 1793.

That on the twentieth day of April last he agreed with William Brown late of South Kelsey in the Parts aforesaid, labourer, to serve him from the 29th April last 'till old Michaelmas or the season, for tempering of clay at 1s 0d pr thousand and when by day 2s 6d per day, and that on Monday morning the 5th instant August he absconded from his said master's service without his permission for so doing.

Taken before me, T. Dixon.

Signed, Thomas Watmough.

Lindsey Quarter Sessions Minutes reveal a William Brown imprisoned in the House of Correction and whipped for vagrancy. As the usual sentence for an absconding servant was a maximum of three months it seems unlikely that this is the same William Brown, but the possibility warrants including the record:

Ordered that William Brown brought before this court in the custody of the Keeper of the said bridewell for vagrancy be immediately publickly whipt at Kirton aforesaid and recommitted to the said bridewell 'till the next General Quarter Sessions of the peace to be holden in and for the said parts.[56]

Tuesday 7 August 1793. Information and Complaint. Absconding Servant.

Lincolnshire Lindsey. The Information and Complaint of Thomas Mundy of Castor in the Parts aforesaid, wheelwright, taken on oath before me Thomas Dixon One of his Majesty's Justices of the Peace in and for the said Parts this seventh day of August 1793.

That on the latter end of April last he agreed with James Hainsworth of Castor, sawier, to serve him [*'as a Sawyer' deleted*] so long as he wanted

---

[56] LAO, Dixon 8/2, Notebook 2, front p.13; LQSM A/2/21, Michaelmas 1793, Kirton.

him at 4s 6d by the hundred. He entered upon his work stay'd only one day and then absconded without the consent of his master.
Taken before me, T. Dixon.
Signed, Thomas Mundy.[57]

Sunday 19 August 1793. Absconding Servant at North Kelsey.
Information and Complaint of Christopher Ayscough of North Kelsey, farmer, against Ellen Chapman hired at Market Rasen for the year at £3 10s. Absconded 14 August.[58]

Monday 3 September 1793. Information and Complaint.
Absconding Servant.
Lincolnshire Lindsey. The Information and Complaint of William Ballans of Caistor in the said Parts, inn keeper, taken on oath before me Thomas Dixon One of his Majesty's Justices of the Peace in and for the said Parts this third day of September 1793.

That he hired Sarah Kenning a few weeks after May Day last to May Day next 1794 and yesterday in the afternoon she absconded from his service without his leave for so doing.
Taken before me, T. Dixon.
Signed, William Ballans.
Ballans was landlord of the Talbot Inn in Caistor. He was a tenant of nearly one hundred acres of land in Caistor and of smaller plots in Cabourn and Nettleton. In 1795 he employed a lawyer to appeal against his assessment for the poor rate. The appeal was dismissed.[59]

Monday 10 September 1793. Committal and Trial of Christopher Hobbins for Theft of Iron.
Although Dixon was the committing magistrate, this case does not appear in his notebooks, probably because Hobbins confessed. If he voluntarily went with the prosecutor to Dixon's house, there would be no need to

---

[57] LAO, Dixon 8/2, Notebook 2, front p.14.
[58] LAO, Dixon 8/1, Notebook 1.
[59] LAO, Dixon 8/2, Notebook 2, front p.18. The last line of the record reads 'with his leave for so doing' which is assumed to be an error here. *The Lincoln, Rutland and Stamford Mercury*, 4 December 1795; LAO, LQSM A/2/19, A/2/20, Midsummer and Michaelmas 1790.

issue a warrant for his arrest, so no entry would be made in Dixon's books. Documents here are from Quarter Sessions and the press.

Monday 10 September 1793. Accusation and Committal.
Christopher Hobbins committed to the House of Correction at Kirton on September 10th charged on the oath of Thomas Everitt of Keelby, farmer, on a strong suspicion of having stolen from him at different times within the last six months a quantity of iron from the ploughs and gates of him the said Thomas Everitt.
Committed by Thomas Dixon Esq.

Confession.
The voluntary confession of Christopher Hobbins made before me Thomas Dixon one of His Majesty's Justices of the Peace for the said Parts this 10th of September 1793,
Who saith that a quantity of iron secreted within some banks in the parish of Keelby in the said Parts had been stolen by him at different times from the ploughs, waggon, and gates of Thomas Everitt of Keelby aforesaid.
The mark of Christopher Hobbins.
Taken and signed before me, Thomas Dixon.

Friday 14 September 1793. Prosecutor and Witnesses Bound to Appear at Quarter Sessions.
Recognizances
T. Dixon Esq. Thomas Everitt of Keelby, farmer bound in £20 for his appearance at Sessions to prosecute and give evidence against Christopher Hobbins late of Keelby aforesaid, labourer, for feloniously taking and carrying away a certain quantity of iron the property of him the said Thomas Everitt.
William Stephenson of Keelby, blacksmith, bound in £20 for his appearance at Sessions to give evidence against the said Christopher Hobbins as above.

Trial of Christopher Hobbins at Michaelmas Sessions at Kirton.
Indictment.
Christopher Hobbins late of Keelby, labourer, for stealing on 10 September1793 forty pounds weight of iron value 10d, the property of Thomas Everitt.
Thomas Everitt and William Stephenson sworn in court.
True Bill
Plea not guilty. Jury say guilty.

Sentence.
Christopher Hobbins convicted of Petty Larceny. To be recommitted to the bridewell at Kirton and there confined in a solitary cell twelve calendar months.

Hobbins in the House of Correction at Kirton.
Keeper of the House of Correction's bill Michaelmas 1793
Maintaining Christopher Hobbins from September 10 to 16 October
4 weeks and 4 days   8s   0d

Death of Christopher Hobbins.
Account of Keeper of the House of Correction at Kirton, Midsummer 1794.
Additional Maintenance for prisoners when ill
Christopher Hobbins 11 weeks   19s   9d

George Foster's Bill (Medical).
May 4. The Mixture Christopher Hobbins   2s   0d

Expenses of funeral of Christopher Hobbins, who died 5 May.
Laying him out   2s   0d
Flannill for ditto   3s   0d
Paid for carrying him to the grave   4s   0d
Burying fees   3s 6d[60]

Monday 19 November 1793. Information and Complaint. Assault.
Lincolnshire Lindsey. The Information and Complaint of Jane Bray the
wife of John Bray of Laceby in the said Parts, taylor.

Who on oath saith that on Sunday last about eleven or twelve o'clock in
the forenoon Edward Smith in the parish of Laceby, baker, did assault
and ill treat her the said Jane Bray in her own yard at Laceby aforesaid
against his Majesty's Peace.
Taken before me the nineteenth day of November 1793, T. Dixon.

Jane Bray, her Mark.
Witness, William Richal.[61]

Monday 28 November 1793. Information and Complaint.
Absconding Servant.
Lincolnshire Lindsey. The Information and Complaint of Benjamin Bark-

[60] LAO, LQS Files A/1/262, Michaelmas 1793; A/1/265, Midsummer 1794; LQSM
A/2/21, Michaelmas 1793; *The Lincoln, Rutland and Stamford Mercury*, 18 October 1793.
[61] LAO, Dixon 8/2, Notebook 2, p.21.

worth of Nettleton in the said Parts, farmer, taken on oath before me, Thomas Dixon, one of His Majesty's Justices of the Peace in and for the said Parts this twenty eight day of November 1793.

That a few dayes before old May Day he hired William Mumby at a meeting at Brigg for the retaining of servants for one year at £3 0s 0d wage, and that on Monday last he absconded from his service without his master's permission for so doing.
Taken before me, T. Dixon.
Signed, Benjamin Barkworth.[62]

Sunday 20 January 1794. Information and Complaint. Master Refuses to Pay Wages.

The Information and Complaint of Samuel Roberts of Castor, brickmaker, taken on his oath before me, Thomas Dixon, one of His Majesty's Justices of the Peace in and for the said Parts this 20th day of January 1794.

Who on his oath saith that about a fortnight before Michaelmas last he agreed with Thomas Watmough of Castor aforesaid, brickmaker, to make bricks and take care of them while they was ready to put into the killen at 2s 4d per thousand and that the said Thomas Watmough has refused and still refuses paying him his wages according to agreement.
Taken before me, T. Dixon.
Samuel Roberts X his mark.[63]

Monday 24 March 1794. Information and Complaint. Absconding Servant.

Lincolnshire Lindsey. The Information and Complaint of Benjamin Barkworth of Nettleton in the said Parts, farmer, taken on his oath before me, Thomas Dixon, one of His Majesty's Justices of the Peace in and for the said Parts this twenty fourth day of March 1794.

That about a month after Christmas last he agreed with William Parker of Nettleton in the Parts aforesaid, labourer, to thrash all his corn he had, Oates at 8d per quarter, pease and beans 10d per quarter, and barley at

---

[62] *Ibid.*, p.22.
[63] *Ibid.*, p.25.

1s 0d per quarter, and on Saturday the 22nd instant he departed from his work without his master's leave for so doing.
Taken before me, T. Dixon.
Signed, Benjamin Barkworth.[64]

Tuesday 1 April 1794. Information and Complaint. Absconding Servants.

Lincolnshire Lindsey. The Information and Complaint of John Bratton of Rothwell in the said Parts, farmer, taken on his oath before me, Thomas Dixon, one of his Majesty's Justices of the Peace in and for the said Parts this first day of April 1794.

That about three weeks or a month since he agreed with William Stanley and John Howsam of Nettleton in the Parts aforesaid, labourers, to paire about fourteen acres of land at 15s 0d per acre and to begin a week before old Lady Day or a week after, and on Friday last in the afternoon they begun to paire and in the evening they departed from their work without the permission of their master for so doing and have not returned since.
Taken before me, T. Dixon.   Signed, John Bratton.[65]

Monday 14 April 1794. Pound Breach at Nettleton.

Lincolnshire Lindsey. The Information and Complaint of John Cole-beck of Nettleton in the said Parts, labourer, taken on his oath before me Thomas Dixon one of his Majesty's Justices of the Peace in and for the said Parts the fourteenth day of April 1794.

That on Sunday morning last the 13th instant he, along with Edmund Gibbon and Charles Watters, impounded two mares the property of Collison, butcher, and [illeg.] the property of Thomas Thomlinson of Castor, cordwainer, and about 10 o'clock of the said morning Thomas Thomlinson came to the Pound in the Parish of Nettleton and broke the said pound and with his nephew broke the said pound and rescued the horses droving the horses out and took them away.
Taken before me, T. Dixon.   Signed, John Coelebek.[66]

---

64 *Ibid.*, p.26.
65 *Ibid.*, p.29.
66 *Ibid.*, p.33.

Thursday 1 May 1794. Special Sessions at Brigg.

We Thomas Dixon esquire and A. Empson clerk, two of His Majesty's Justices of the Peace for the said Parts at a Special Sessions held at Brigg in the said Parts on the first day of May 1794, having upon view found that a certain highway lying between Broughton and Manby in the said Parts of the length of one mile and twenty two yards and particularly described in the plan hereunto annexed may be turned so as to make the same more commodious to the Public; and having viewed a course, proposed for the new highway in lieu thereof through the lands and grounds of Charles Anderson Pelham esquire and the honourable Thomas Shirley of the length of one mile and seventy yards particularly described in the plan hereunto annexed and having received evidence of the consent of the said Charles Anderson Pelham esquire and the honourable Thomas Shirley to the said highway being made through their lands herein before described by writing under their hands and seals, we do hereby order that the said Highway be turned through the lands aforesaid.

Given under our hands and seals the day and year above written

Thomas Dixon, Amaziah Empson.

Signed and sealed agreement by Charles Anderson Pelham and Thomas Shirley attached.[67]

Tuesday 6 May 1794. Assault at Audleby.

Lincolnshire Lindsey. The Information and Complaint of Joseph Shaw of Audleby in the parish of Castor in the said parts taken on his oath before me Thomas Dixon one of His Majesty's Justices of the Peace in and for the said Parts this sixth day of May 1794.

That this present morning John Russels of Audleby aforesaid serving man to Samuel Arnne of Audleby aforesaid did violently assault and otherwise ill treat him the said Joseph Shaw in breach of His Majesty's Peace.

Taken before me, T. Dixon.

Joseph Shaw X his mark.

You are to sumon John Heaton of Audleby serving man to appear at the same time to give such evidence as he knows to be true touching the above complaint.[68]

Monday 19 May 1794. Absconding Servant at Rothwell.

Lincolnshire Lindsey. The Information and Complaint of George Mills of Rothwell in the said Parts, farmer, taken on his oath before me Thomas

---

[67] LAO, LQS Files A/1/264, Epiphany 1794.
[68] LAO, Dixon 8/2, Notebook 2, p.37.

Dixon one of His Majesty's Justices of the Peace in and for the said Parts this nineteenth day of May 1794.

Who on his oath saith that Mary Green [*'of Rothwell' deleted*] who was hired to serve him for one year from the twelfth day of this instant did on the evening of Saturday last abscond from and leave his service without his consent.
Taken before me [*record ends*].[69]

Friday 30 May 1794. Removal of Michael Good from Great Coates to South Killingholme and Appeal.

Removal Order *30 May 1794, signed by Thomas Dixon and Wm Thorold. Complaint of the parish of Great Coates that Michael Good is liable to become chargeable to the parish of Great Coates. Michael Good was therefore examined before the said justices as to his settlement and ordered to be removed to South Killingholme.*

Appeal by South Killingholme at Midsummer and Michaelmas Sessions 1794.
Kirton Midsummer Sessions, Friday 18 July 1794.
South Killingholme Appellants and Great Coats Removants. Whereas by virtue of an order under the hands and seals of William Thorold clerk and Thomas Dixon esquire two of His Majesty's Justices of the Peace in and for the said Parts, and one of them quorum, bearing the date the thirtieth day of May last past Michael Good was removed from the parish of Great Coats in the said Parts to the parish of South Killingholme in the said Parts as the place of his last legal Settlement,

And whereas the inhabitants of the said parish of South Killingholme have appealed to this court against the said order of Removal,

Ordered (on account of the pauper being unable to attend) that the hearing of the merits of the said appeal be and the same is hereby respited to the next General Quarter Sessions of the Peace to be holden in and for the said Parts.

Kirton Michaelmas Sessions, Friday 10 October 1794.
Ordered (after a full hearing of all the parties on the merits of the said appeal) that the said order of Removal be and the same is hereby quashed with £20 costs.

[69] *Ibid.*, p.38.

Mr Clarke and Mr Anstruther for the appellants
Mr Ayscough and Mr Milnes for the removants.

Costs

The Churchwardens & Overseers of South Killingholme To Richard Nicholson.
Yourselves against the Churchwardens of Great Coates upon an appeal touching
the settlement of Michael Wood, Kirton Midsummer Sessions 1794.

Several attendances upon you conferring and advising with you about the pauper's legal place of settlement retained on your behalf for the Sessions and other trouble	10s	6d
Copy Order of Removal	2s	0d
Paid Counsel moving to lodge appeal and to have the same respited till next sessions	10s	6d
My fee attending Counsel and Court	10s	6d
Paid Court fees	14s	0d
October		
Attending to examine the pauper to take instructions for brief	6s	8d
Drawing Brief 2 sheets of Paper	13s	4d
Two fair copies thereof	13s	4d
Subpoena	2s	6d
Two Ticketts	2s	0d
Drawing notice of appeal being entered and trying the same at the next Sessions and three fair copies	6s	8d
Clerk's journey to Great Coates to deliver the above notices to the Churchwardens and Overseers of the poor there, horsehire expenses etc.	13s	4d

Kirton Michaelmas Sessions	£2	2s	0d
Pd Mr Clerk with his Brief		2s	6d
Attending him		3s	4d
Paid Mr Anstruther with Brief	£1	1s	0d
	£8	4s	2d
His Clerk		2s	6d
Attending him etc		3s	4d
My journey to this sessions to attend the trial of this appeal, when the Order was quashed with costs, Two days from home	£2	2s	0d

Horse hire and expences	£1	1s	0d
Paid Court Fee		10s	0s
Paid for the pauper's board and lodging 23 weeks at 5s per week	£5	15s	0d

Paid the Doctor's Bill	£4	4s	0d
Three witnesses journey to this Sessions,			
2 days from home	£3	0s	0d
	£25	12s	0d

Kirton Michaelmas Sessions 1794
Twenty Pounds is allowed by the Court Rd Ellison, Chairman.[70]

Tuesday 3 June 1794. Assault at Stallingborough.

Lincolnshire Lindsey. The Information and Complaint of Robert Smith, shopkeeper, of Stallingborough in the parts aforesaid taken on his oath before me Thomas Dixon One of His Majesty's Justices of the Peace in and for the said Parts this third Day of June 1794.

That on Saturday the 31st day of May last Mark Newton of Stallingborough in the said Parts did violently assault and otherwise ill treat him the said Robert Smith in the parish of Stallingborough in breach of his Majesty's peace.
Taken before me, T. Dixon.
Signed, Robert Smith.
You are to S[…] [record ends].[71]

Friday 6 June 1794. Absconding Servant at Aylesby.

Lincolnshire Lindsey. The Information and Complaint of Mr Philip Skipworth of Aylesby in the said Parts, grazier, taken on his oath before me Thomas Dixon One of his Majesty's Justices of the Peace in and for the said Parts the 6th June 1794.
That James Lader who was hired to serve him for one year from the twelfth day of May last hath neglected coming to his service according to the agreement made with his said Master.
Taken before me, T. Dixon.
Signed, Philip Skipworth.[72]

Monday 9 June 1794. Absconding Servant at Keelby.

Lincolnshire Lindsey. The Information and Complaint of Mr Thomas Holgate of Keelby Grange in the said Parts, farmer, taken on his oath

---

70   LAO, LQS File A/1/266, Midsummer 1794, Kirton; LQSM A/2/21, Michaelmas 1794, Kirton.
71   LAO, Dixon 8/2, Notebook 2, p.41.
72   Ibid., p.42.

before me Thomas Dixon One of His Majesty's Justices of the Peace in and for the said Parts this ninth day of June 1794.

That Elizabeth Barton who was hired to serve him for one year from the twelfth day of May last did [*'about twelve o'clock last' deleted*] night abscond from and leave his service without his consent.
Taken before me, T. Dixon.
Signed, Thomas Holgate.[73]

Saturday 7 June 1794. Meeting at Lincoln Castle to Raise Volunteer Infantry and Yeomanry.

On Saturday 7 June 1794 'A General Meeting of the Nobility, Gentry, Clergy and Freeholders of the County, held at the Castle of Lincoln … to take into Consideration the best Means of carrying into Effect the Plans recommended by the Government, and sanctioned by Parliament, for the internal Defence of this County, and for the general Protection of the Kingdom' resolved to raise volunteer infantry and yeomanry forces, supported by subscription and organised by a County Committee. Thomas Dixon attended this meeting and subscribed £20, a sum large enough for him to be a member of the General Committee of Expenditure.[74]

[n.d.] Absconding Servant at Habrough.

Lincolnshire Lindsey. The Information and Complaint of John Bowers of Habrough in the said Parts, farmer, taken on his oath before me Thomas Dixon one of His Majesty's Justices of the Peace in and for the said Parts.

That William Kemp, who was hired on the 24th of May last [*date altered, not certain*] to serve him to May Day seventeen hundred and ninety five did in the morning of Tuesday last abscond from and leave his service without his consent.
Taken before me, T. Dixon.
Signed, John Bowers.[75]

---

[73] *Ibid.*, p.47.
[74] *Lincolnshire, Rutland and Stamford Mercury*, 13 June 1794. See also R. J. Olney, *Rural Society and County Government in Nineteenth Century Lincolnshire* (Lincoln, 1979), 20; Rex Russell, *Sedition – Insurrection – and Invasion? French Revolution in Lincolnshire History* (Lincoln, 1997).
[75] LAO, Dixon 8/2, Notebook 2, p.51.

Monday 23 June 1794. Absconding Servant at Nettleton.

Lincolnshire Lindsey. The Information and Complaint of Mr John Codd of Nettleton in the said Parts, farmer, taken on his oath before me Thomas Dixon one of His Majesty's Justices of the Peace in and for the said Parts this 23rd day of June 1794.

That Francis Taylor who was hired on the 7th of June last to serve 'till May Day seventeen hundred and ninety five has been guilty of several misdemeanours and miscarriages and particularly for absenting himself from his said master's service and also disobeying the lawful commands of his said master.

Taken before me, T. Dixon.

Signed, John Codd.[76]

Monday 1 September 1794. Disobedient Servant at Searby.

Lincolnshire Lindsey. The Information and Complaint of John Clark of Searby in the said Parts, farmer, taken on his oath before me Thomas Dixon one of His Majesty's Justices of the Peace in and for the said Parts this first day of September 1794.

That Joseph Harrison who was hired the day after Old May Day 1794 to serve him till May Day 1795 and that he has been guilty of several misdemeanours and miscarriages and particularly in disobeying his master's lawful commands.

Taken before me, T. Dixon.

John Clark X his mark.[77]

Thursday 16 October 1794. Absconding Servant at Roxton.

Lincolnshire Lindsey. The Information and Complaint of Mr William Marris of Roxton in the said Parts, farmer, taken on oath before me Thomas Dixon one of His Majesty's Justices of the Peace in and for the said Parts this sixteenth day of October 1794.

That on Friday last the 10th instant October he agreed with William Moody of Keelby in the Parts aforesaid, labourer, to work for him during all the wheat saed time at 1s 6d per day and that this morning of the sixteenth

---

[76] *Ibid.*, p.52.

[77] *Ibid.*, p.55.

instant he departed from his said master's service without his permission for so doing.
Taken before me, T. Dixon.
Signed, William Marris.[78]

Thursday 30 October 1794. Absconding Servant at Cabourn.

Lincolnshire Lindsey. The Information and Complaint of Richard Ellerby of Cabourn in the said Parts, farmer, taken on oath before me Thomas Dixon one of His Majesty's Justices of the Peace in and for the said Parts the thirtieth day of October 1794.

That on Tuesday last he agreed with Andrew Daddy the younger to thrash him ten quarters of barley at 1s 4d pr quarter. He entered on his work on Tuesday last and on Wednesday morning the nineteenth instant October he departed from his said master's service without his permission for so doing.
Taken before me, T. Dixon.
Signed, Richard Ellerby.[79]

Tuesday 30 December 1794. Assault at Waltham.

Lincolnshire Lindsey. The Information and Complaint of Isaiah Suttoby of the parish of Waltham in the said Parts taken on his oath before me Thomas Dixon one of His Majesty's Justices of the Peace in and for the said Parts this 30th day of December 1794.

That on Sunday the 21st instant Richard Surfleet of the parish of Waltham in the Parts aforesaid did violently assault and otherwise ill-treat the above said Isaiah Suttoby in the parish of Waltham in breach of His Majesty's Peace.
Taken before me, T. Dixon.
Isaiah Suttoby X his mark.[80]

February 1795. Assault at Swallow.

Lincolnshire Lindsey. The Information and Complaint of John Atkinson

---

[78] *Ibid.*, p.56.
[79] *Ibid.*, p.59.
[80] *Ibid.*, p.60.

of Swallow in the said Parts, servant, taken on oath before me Thomas Dixon one of His Majesty's Justices of the Peace in and for the said Parts.

That on Sunday last the 1st day of this instant February Thomas Wright of Swallow in the said Parts, serving man did violently assault and otherwise ill treat him the said John Atkinson in breach of His Majesty's Peace.
John Atkinson X his mark.
[*The usual 'Taken before me, T. Dixon' is missing.*][81]

Thursday 26 February 1795. Absconding Servant at Immingham.

Lincolnshire Lindsey. The Information and Complaint of Mr Robert Marshall of Immingham in the said Parts, grazier, taken on oath before me Thomas Dixon one of His Majesty's Justices of the Peace in and for the said Parts this twenty-sixth day of February 1795.

That Edward Kendall whom he hired as a labourer to serve him in husbandry for one year from May Day last at certain wages has this present morning absented himself from his said master's service without his permission for so doing.
Taken before me, T. Dixon.
Signed, Robert Marshall.[82]

Monday 9 March 1795. Pass for a Sick Militiaman.
Surgeon's Certificate.
This is to certify that Joseph Clark is at present troubled with a severe rheumatic affection of his knee and thigh which renders him unable to march.
Signed, Samuel Turner, surgeon.

Dixon's Pass.
Lincolnshire Lindsey. Permit the bearer hereof Joseph Clark, Private in the East York Regiment of Militia, to pass from Castor in the county of Lincoln and on the nineteenth of this instant March 1795 to join his battalion and company, he behaving as becometh a soldier and being detained by a severe affection of the rheumatism as appears by the above certificate.

---

[81]   *Ibid.*, p.63.
[82]   *Ibid.*, p.67.

Given under my hand at Riby the ninth day of March 1795. T. Dixon, one of His Majesty's Justices of the Peace in and for the said Parts. Hitching in Hertfordshire, furlow given by Major Garforth.[83]

Monday 9 March 1795. Assault at Laceby.

Lincolnshire Lindsey. The Information and Complaint of John Odling of Laceby in the said Parts, butcher, taken on his oath before me Thomas Dixon one of His Majesty's Justices of the Peace in and for the said Parts this ninth day of March 1795.

That on Sunday the 8th instant William Haith of Tetney in the said Parts, blacksmith, and Henry Collidge, late servant in husbandry to Richard Burnett of Tetney aforesaid did violently assault and otherwise ill treat him the said John Odling in the parish of Laceby in breach of His Majesty's Peace.
Taken before me, T. Dixon.
Signed, John Odling.[84]

Monday 23 March 1795. Absconding Servant at Irby.

Lincolnshire Lindsey. The Information and Complaint of Mr Joseph Johnson of Irby, farmer, taken on oath before me Thomas Dixon one of His Majesty's Justices of the Peace in and for the said Parts the 23rd day of March 1795.

That he agreed with John Plasket of Irby in the said Parts, labourer, to plough for him and to give him 6d pr ?Yeake and two meals, breakfast and dinner, and to go into the barn to thrash about 5 o'clock in the morning and to go to plough about seven and leave about 2 o'clock and then go into the barn about 3 o'clock, and on Wednesday the 18th he departed from his said master's service without his permission for so doing.
Taken before me, T. Dixon.
Signed, Josh Johnson.[85]

Saturday 25 April 1795. Assault at Beelsby.

Lincolnshire Lindsey. The Information and Complaint of James Wallace

---

83 LAO, Dixon 8/3, Notebook 3, p.32 (horizontal).
84 LAO, Dixon 8/2 Notebook 2, p.30.
85 *Ibid.*, p.71.

of Beelsby in the said Parts, labourer, taken oath before me Thomas Dixon one of His Majesty's Justices of the Peace in and for the said Parts this 25th day of April 1795.

That Henry Haith of Beelsby aforesaid, shepherd, did on Thursday the 23rd instant violently assault and otherwise ill treat him the said James Wallace in the Parish of Beelsby in breach of his Majestyes peace.
Taken before me, T. Dixon.
Signed, James Wallis.

John Ward living with Mr Skipworth at Beelsby said he wou'd not speak as an evidence in [*'support' deleted*] an assent against James Wallis of Beelsby, labourer.[86]

Thursday 19 May 1795. Absconding Servant at Irby.
Lincolnshire Lindsey. The Information and Complaint of Richard Clayton of Irby in the said Parts, farmer, taken on oath before me Thomas Dixon one of His Majesty's Justices of the Peace in and for the said Parts the 19th day of May 1795.

That William Burleigh hired himself for one year to May Day next, that this morning he departed from his said master's service without his permission for so doing.
Taken before me, T. Dixon.
Signed, Richard Clayton.[87]

Thursday 19 May 1795. Absconding Servant at Irby.
Lincolnshire Lindsey. The Information and Complaint of Mr Josh Johnson of Irby in the said Parts, farmer, taken on oath before me Thomas Dixon one of His Majesty's Justices of the Peace in and for the said Parts this nineteenth day of May 1795.

That at a meeting held at Keelby for the retaining of servants four days before May Day last he hired Sarah Bailey to serve him for the year to May Day next and that she has refused coming to her said service according to the agreement made with her his said master.

86 *Ibid.*, p.68.
87 *Ibid.*, p.72.

Taken before me, T. Dixon.
Signed, Josh Johnson.[88]

Monday 25 May 1795. Pound Breach at South Kelsey.

Lincolnshire Lindsey. The Information and Complaint of William Wilson of South Kelsey Saint Nicholas, Common Pinder, taken on oath before me Thomas Dixon One of His Majesty's Justices of the Peace in and for the said Parts the 25th day of May 1795.

That on Friday last the 22nd day of this instant Thomas Smith of the parish of North Kelsey, farmer, did rescue three old geese and about 20 goslings from the common pound in the parish of South Kelsey St Nicholas aforesaid contrary to law.
Taken before me, T. Dixon.
William Wilson X his mark.[89]

Sunday 28 May 1795. Sabbath Breaking at Riby.

William Young, servant to Mr Jonathan Winship, and William Manders, servant to Mr J. Winship, was both of them playing at Pitch Hole on Sunday the 28th day of May in the afternoon upon the Stocks Hill at Riby upon my own view, Thomas Dixon.

Inside back cover in pencil 'NB complaints generally brought upon Mondays.'[90]

Wednesday 1 June 1795. Assault at Laceby.

Lincolnshire Lindsey. The Information and Complaint of Thomas Chapman of Laceby in the said Parts taken on his oath before me Thomas Dixon one of His Majesty's Justices of the Peace in and for the said Parts this first day of June this instant 1795.

That about seven o'clock last night William Petch the elder of Laceby, drover, did violently assault and otherwise ill treat him the said Thomas

---

88 *Ibid.*, p.74.
89 *Ibid.*, p.76.
90 LAO, Dixon 8/3, Notebook 3. p.34.

Chapman in John Shearsmith's house at Laceby aforesaid in breach of His Majesty's Peace.
Taken before me. T. Dixon.
Signed, Thomas Chapman.[91]

Wednesday 1 June 1795. Assault at Laceby.

Lincolnshire Lindsey. The Information and Complaint of Thomas Chapman of Laceby in the said Parts taken on his oath before me Thomas Dixon one of His Majesty's Justices of the Peace in and for the said Parts this first day of June this instant 1795.

That about seven o'clock last night William Petch the younger of Laceby, drover, did violently assault and otherwise ill treat him the said Thomas Chapman in John Shearsmith's house at Laceby aforesaid in breach of His Majesty's Peace.
Taken before me, T. Dixon.
Signed, Thomas Chapman.[92]

Thursday 2 June 1795. Absconding Servant at Healing.

Lincolnshire Lindsey. The Information and Complaint of Mr John Birkett of Healing, farmer, taken on his oath before me Thomas Dixon one of His Majesty's Justices of the Peace in and for the said Parts this second day of June 1795.

That Mary Button whom he hired at Keelby Statutes a few days before May Day last for one year did on Tuesday the 26th Day of May last depart from her said master's service without his permission for so doing.
Taken before me, T. Dixon.
Signed, John Birket.[93]

Monday 11 July 1795. Committal of Absconding Servant at South Kelsey.

Benjamin Dixon of South Kelsey, servant to William Stothard, farmer, was committed upon the oath of the said William Stothard to the House of Correction at Kirton in the Parts of Lindsey and County of Lincoln for the

91 LAO, Dixon 8/2, Notebook 2, p.79.
92 *Ibid.*, p.80.
93 *Ibid.*, p.83.

space of 3 Months for committing divers misdemeanours and particularly in absenting himself from his said master's service without his permission for so doing. T. Dixon.[94]

Saturday 3 September 1795. Absconding Harvest Worker at Riby.

Lincolnshire Lindsey. The Information and Complaint of Mr Jonathan Winship of Riby, farmer, taken on oath before me Thomas Dixon one of His Majesty's Justices of the Peace in and for the said Parts this third day of September 1795.

That on or about the seventh day of July last he agreed with John Cordock of Keelby, labourer, to work with him during hay and harvist at such prices as the majority of the farmers at Riby gave, and on [*'Thursday' deleted*] this present morning the 3d instant he absconded from his service without his said master's permission for so doing.

Taken before me, T. Dixon.   Signed, Jonathan Winship.[95]

Thursday 15 September 1795. Absconding Servant at Stallingborough.

Lincolnshire Lindsey. The Information and Complaint of Nathaniel Taylor of Stallingborough in the said Parts, farmer, taken on his oath before me Thomas Dixon one of His Majesty's Justices of the Peace in and for the said Parts this fifteenth day of September 1795.

That Benjamin Mackril whom he hired a few dayes before May Day last to serve for one year did on Wednesday the eighth day of July last depart from his service without ['with' *assumed error*] the permission of his said master for so doing.

Taken before me, T. Dixon.

Signed, Nathaniel Taylor.[96]

Sunday 16 October 1795. Assault at North Kelsey.

Lincolnshire Lindsey. The Information and Complaint of Thomas Smith of North Kelsey in the said Parts, farmer, taken on oath before me Thomas

---

[94] *Ibid.*

[95] *Ibid.*, p.84.

[96] LAO, Dixon 8/2, Notebook 2, p.48.

Dixon one of His Majesty's Justices of the Peace in and for the said Parts this sixteenth day of October 1795.

That John Barnard of North Kelsey, farmer, did this morning violently assault and otherwise ill treat within the parish of North Kelsey him the said Thomas Smith in breach of His Majesty's Peace.
Taken before me, T. Dixon
Signed, Thomas Smith.
Thomas Osgodby and George Birkett, farmers, of North Kelsey, witnesses.[97]

January 1796. Proceedings Against 'Yorkshire Tom' for Poaching.
These documents are in a separate file.[98] The Information and Complaint and the Summons are complete, but the Summary Conviction and the Warrant for Committal to the House of Correction are not completed or signed. This may be because the accused did not answer the summons, because the prosecutor decided not to proceed, because the case was settled by arbitration, or because these are copies of documents enrolled elsewhere. As Yorkshire Tom does not appear in the House of Correction records and the conviction is not enrolled at Quarter Sessions, the most likely explanation is that he did not answer the summons.

Friday 22 January 1796. Gamekeeper's Information and Complaint.
Lincolnshire Lindsey. The Information and Complaint of William Russell, game-keeper to the Right Honourable Charles Lord Yarborough of Brocklesby in the said Parts, made before me Thomas Dixon esquire and one of His Majesty's Justices of the Peace in and for the said Parts the twenty second day of January in the year of our Lord 1796.

Who saith that on the seventeenth day of this instant being the Lords Day commonly called Sunday a person whose name is to this informant unknown but who is commonly called or known by the name of Yorkshire Tom and hath resided at Great Limber in the Parts aforesaid for one year last past and upwards did use two greyhounds in the parish of Great Limber aforesaid belonging to Thomas Marris and George Nelson Farmers there and therewith did kill one hare against the statute in that case made and provided.
Signed, William Russell

[97] *Ibid.*, p.6.
[98] LAO, Dixon 8/4, Thomas Dixon's Papers as a JP.

Taken before me, T. Dixon. [*This document is signed by Dixon, but not in his hand.*]

Friday January 22. Summons to Bring 'Yorkshire Tom' Before Thomas Dixon.

The summons is a printed form. Dixon signed and sealed the document, but the words inserted, shown below in italics, are not in his hand.

No 32 R.B. Summons. To the Constable of *Gt Limber in the said Parts.*

Whereas Information and Complaint has been made before me *Thomas Dixon Esq* One of his Majesty's Justices of the Peace in and for the said Parts that *a Man of the name of Yorkshire Tom now residing at Great Limber* aforesaid *Labourer* on the *Seventeenth Day of January instant being the Lords day commonly called Sunday at the parish of Great Limber* aforesaid, did keep and use *two certain Greyhounds and therewith did kill and take one Hare,* he the said *Yorkshire* [*'Thomas' deleted*] *Tom* not being qualified by the Laws of this Realm so to do: These are therefore to require you forthwith to summon the said *Person so called Yorkshire Tom* to appear before me at *my House in Riby* in the Parts on *Wednesday next* the *twenty seventh* Day of *this instant* at the Hour of *twelve* in the *fore*noon of the same Day, to answer to the said Information and Complaint, and to be further dealt with according to Law. And be you then there to certify what you shall have done in the Execution thereof. Given under my Hand and Seal the *twenty second* Day of *January* in the Year of our Lord One Thousand Seven Hundred and *Ninety Six.*

Summary Conviction.

There are two copies of this document, one in Dixon's hand and one which appears to have been copied by a clerk. In both documents the blanks have not been completed and neither of them is signed by Dixon.

Summary Conviction Be it Remembered that on the ___ day of January in the year of our Lord seven hundred and Ninety Six a certain Person residing at Great Limber in the said Parts who followeth the occupation of Labourer and who is commonly called or known by the name of Yorkshire Tom his real name being unknown is convicted before me Thomas Dixon Esquire one of his Majesty's Justices of the Peace for the said Parts of having in the daytime of Sunday the seventeenth day of this instant at Great Limber aforesaid with and by the means of two Greyhounds killed one Hare against the Statute in that case made and provided And I do adjudge him to pay and forfeit for the said offence (the same being the first) the sum of ___ Pounds Given under my Hand and Seal the Day and Year aforesaid

[*Sealed but not signed by TD*]

Committal to the House of Correction at Kirton.

Again, there are two copies of this document, one in Dixon's hand and one copied

by a clerk. In both documents the blanks have not been filled in and neither is signed by Dixon.

To the Constable of Great Limber and also to the Keeper of the House of Correction at Kirton both in the said Parts.

Whereas a certain Person residing at Great Limber in the said Parts by occupation a Labourer whose real name is not known but who is there commonly called or known by the name of 'Yorkshire Tom' was on this day of January duly convicted before me Thomas Dixon Esquire One of his Majesty's Justices of the Peace in and for the said Parts upon the oath of Christopher Quickfall of Great Limber aforesaid Serving Man of having in the day time of Sunday the seventeenth day of this instant with and by means of two greyhounds killed one hare in the Parish of Great Limber aforesaid and for the said offence the same being the first I did convict him in the penalty of   Pounds and whereas it duly appears to me as well on the oath of the said Constable of Great Limber as otherwise that the said Person so convicted is not a housekeeper nor possessed of any known or visible property whereon to levy the said Penalty These are therefore to require you the Constable of Great Limber aforesaid to convey the said offender so only known as aforesaid by the name of Yorkshire Tom to the said House of Correction at Kirton aforesaid and deliver him to the Keeper thereof together with this Precept And you the said Keeper are hereby commanded to receive into your custody in the said House of Correction the said Offender so convicted and called or known as aforesaid and him there safely to keep for the space of   months without bail or mainprize and for your so doing this shall be your sufficient Warrant Given under my Hand and Seal the   day of January 1796

Wednesday 23 March 1796. Absconding Farm Servant at Aylesby.

Lincolnshire Lindsey. The Information and Complaint of Mr Richard Ostler of Aylesby, farmer, taken on his oath before me Thomas Dixon one of His Majesty's Justices of the Peace in and for the said Parts this 23rd day of March 1796.

That about a fortnight since he agreed with John Armstrong of Laceby, labourer, to assist him in thrashing out a stack of wheat and the said John Armstrong was to have three shillings per quarter for thrashing it and on Friday the 10th day of this instant he absented himself from his service without his master's permission for so doing.

Taken before me, T. Dixon
Signed, Richard Ostler.[99]

---

99   LAO, Dixon 8/3, Notebook 3, p.1.

Friday 1 April 1796. Committal of the Father of a Bastard Child at Goxhill.

April the 1st 1796. Committed John Cawton, servant man, to the House of Correction at Kirton on the oath of Bridget Paddison, single woman, for begetting a child or children on the body of Bridget Paddison.

April the 1st 1796. John Cawton of Barton in the parish of Saint Peters. Bridget Paddison of the parish of Goxhill, single woman.[100]

April 1796. Pauper's Pass Granted by a Yorkshire Magistrate.

Tadcaster. The within named Jane Wilson having made oath before me Benjamin Brookbank Esquire, one of His Majesty's Justices of the Peace for the West Riding of Yorkshire that she has not been able on account of illness to perform her journey in the time limited in the Pass. I do hereby extend the time thereof to three weeks from this day.

Given under my hand and seal this 13th day of April 1796.

Benjamin Brookbank

18th April. Relieved Jane Wilson per Pass per Josh Stringer, Constable, Selby.[101]

Monday 25 April 1796. Committal of Hannah Cooper to Lincoln Castle for Shoplifting.

Monday 25 April 1796. Information and Complaint of Prosecutor.

The Information and Complaint of Thomas Cortis of Waltham in the said Parts, mercer and draper, taken on oath before me Thomas Dixon one of His Majesty's Justices of the Peace in and for the said Parts the twenty fifth day of April one thousand seven hundred and ninety six.

That on Friday night the 22nd instant April Hannah Cooper the wife of Christopher Cooper of Waltham in the said Parts, labourer, did steal take and carry away out of the shop of the said Thomas Cortis five silk hand-kerchiefs the property of him the said Thomas Cortis.

Taken before me, T. Dixon.

Signed, Thomas Cortis.

Thomas and George Cortis were linen and woollen drapers, grocers and haberdashers in Grimsby and Waltham.

---

[100] LAO, Dixon 8/1, Notebook 1, p.28.
[101] LAO, Dixon 8/3, Notebook 3, p.33, horizontal.

Friday 29 April 1796. Hannah Cooper Committed to Lincoln Castle.

April the 29th 1796. Committed Hannah Cooper the wife of Christopher Cooper of Waltham, labourer, to the gaol of the castle at Lincoln for felloniously stealing, taking and carrying away out of the shop of Messrs Thomas and George Cortes 5 silk handkerchiefs.

Expences of Joseph Wells, Constable of Waltham in apprehending and conveying to gaol Hannah Cooper the wife of Christopher Cooper for felony, April 29 1796.

Stamford Mercury, 6 May 1796.

On Friday last was committed to our county gaol, by T. Dixon esquire, Hannah Cooper, wife of Christopher Cooper, of Waltham, near Great Grimsby, charged with feloniously stealing and carrying away five silk handkerchiefs, out of the shop of Messrs Thomas and George Cortis, of Waltham aforesaid.

Thursday 14 July 1796. Hannah Cooper Tried at Lincoln Assizes.
Stamford Mercury, 15 July 1796.

Lincoln July 14. At the Assizes … Hannah Cooper, for shop-lifting, was sentenced to imprisonment for three months.[102]

Thursday 5 May 1796. Assault at East Halton.

Lincolnshire Lindsey. The Information and Complaint of Roger Anderson of Stallingborough in the said Parts, miller, taken on oath before me Thomas Dixon one of His Majesty's Justices of the Peace in and for the said Parts the fifth day of May 1796.

That on Friday the 29th April in the evening John Brown of Great Grimsby in the said Parts, baker, did violently assault and otherwise ill treat him the said Roger Anderson upon the High Road between Halton Skitter and East Halton.
Taken before me, T. Dixon.
Signed, Roger Anderson.[103]

---

[102]   LAO, Dixon 8/3, Notebook 3, pp.3–4; Dixon 8/1, Notebook 1, p.28; *The Lincoln, Rutland and Stamford Mercury*, 6 May 1796, 15 July 1796, 18 September 1796.
[103]   LAO, Dixon 8/3, Notebook 3, p.5.

Friday 26 August 1796. Absconding Harvest Workers at Great Limber.

Lincolnshire Lindsey. The Information and Complaint of William Mattison of Great Limber in the said Parts in behalf of Mr William Richardson of Little Limber in the Parts aforesaid who on his oath saith that on Monday the 22nd of this instant August he agreed with John Drakes and his son William Drakes and William Atkinson, all of Castor, labourers, to mow thirty eight acres of wheat the property of the aforesaid William Richardson at 5s 6d per acre and a quart of ale to each man and 2 quarts of malt beer, and on Tuesday morning the 23 instant they entered on the said work and on Wednesday evening they left the said work and are not willing to perform their agreement.

Taken before me, T. Dixon, the 26th day of August 1796.

Signed, William Mattison.[104]

Tuesday 4 October 1796. Disobedient Servant at Keelby.

This page is in a different hand, identified as that of Thomas Dixon's second son, Richard Dixon, Rector of Claxby and Normanby. It is signed by Thomas Dixon.

Lincolnshire Lindsey. The Information and Complaint of William Towle of Keelby in the said Parts taken on oath before me Thomas Dixon one of His Majesty's Justices of the Peace in and for the said Parts the fourth day of October 1796.

Who saith that Edward Trout of Keelby aforesaid servant in husbandry to him the said William Towle, hath in his said service been guilty of divers misdemeanours, miscarriages and ill behaviour towards him the said William Towle, and hath particularly disobey'd his lawful commands.

Taken before me, T. Dixon.

Signed, William Towle.[105]

Monday 13 February 1797. Theft of Posts at Aylesby.

Lincolnshire Lindsey. The Information and Complaint of David Phillipson of Aylesby in the said Parts, labourer, taken on his oath before me

---

[104] *Ibid.*, p.8.
[105] *Ibid.*, p.9.

Thomas Dixon one of His Majesty's Justices of the Peace in and for the said Parts the 13th day of February 1797.

Who on his oath saith that on Thursday night last the ninth instant he saw Michael Toft of Laceby, labourer, did steal, take and carry away out of ['the ground' deleted] close of Mr Philip Skipworth of Aylesby one oak post and one ash post the property of the said Mr Skipworth.
Taken before me, T. Dixon.
Signed, David Phillips.

On the blotting paper page opposite:
Mr Philip Skipworth, labourer, Complaint against Michael Toft for stealing taking and carrying away 2 posts of Mr Skipworths of Aylesby.[106]

May 1797. Servant Refusing to Begin Service at Great Limber.
Lincolnshire Lindsey. The Information and Complaint of Mr George Nelson junior of Great Limber in the said Parts taken on his oath before me Thomas Dixon one of His Majesty's Justices of the Peace in and for the said Parts.

That a few days before May Day last, at a meeting held at Keelby for the retaining of servants his mother Mrs Sara Nelson hired Maria Robinson now of Somerby for one year to May Day one thousand seven hundred and ninety eight and that she has refused coming to her said service according to the agreement made with her said mistress.
Taken before me, T. Dixon.
Signed, George Nelson.[107]

Monday 29 May 1797. Labourer Abandoning Work at Riby.
Lincolnshire Lindsey. The Information and Complaint of Mr Jonathan Winship of Riby, farmer, taken on his oath before me Thomas Dixon one of His Majesty's Justices of the Peace in and for the said Parts this 29th day of May 1797.

That on or about the eighth day of this instant May he agreed with Luke Lill of Ludborough, labourer, to assist him in thrashing a stack of wheat

106   *Ibid.*, pp.10,11.
107   *Ibid.*, p.13.

at 2s per quarter; if it did not yield so well as expected he was to have 3d per quarter more, and on Saturday the 20th instant he went home and has not since returned to his work according to the agreement made with his said master.

Taken before me, T. Dixon.

Signed, Jonathan Winship.[108]

May 1797. Absconding Servants at Irby.

Lincolnshire Lindsey. The Information and Complaint of Mr Josh Johnson of Irby in the said Parts, farmer, taken on his oath before me Thomas Dixon one of His Majesty's Justices of the Peace in and for the said Parts.

That on Monday the fifth day of this instant Mr Thomas Johnson in behalf of his brother Joseph Johnson hired George Procter late of Thoresby to serve him in husbandry business to May Day next and that yesterday morning he departed from his servis without his master's permission for so doing.

And also at a Statute Meeting held at Laceby for the retaining of servants a few days before May Day last he hired Thomas Brown to serve him for one year to May Day next and this morning he departed from his master's service without his permission for so doing.

Taken before me, T. Dixon.

Signed, Josh Johnson.[109]

[n.d.] May to July 1797. Servant Refusing to Begin Service at Riby.

Lincolnshire Lindsey. The Information and Complaint of William Cavill of Riby, servant to Mr Jonathan Winship of Riby aforesaid.

Who on behalf of his said master [*'Jonathan Winship' deleted*] he contracted and agreed with Mark Rowston of Laceby, labourer, to assist and work for him in husbandry from Monday the fifth day of this instant at twenty pence per day untill Mr Winship began to mow his seeds and that he has refused and still refuses to come to his work according to the agreement made with William Cavill on behalf of his said master.

Taken before me, T. Dixon.   Signed, William Cavill.[110]

---

[108] *Ibid.*, p.15.
[109] *Ibid.*, p.17.
[110] *Ibid.*, p.18.

June 1797. Absconding Servant at Nettleton.

Lincolnshire Lindsey. The Information and Complaint of Benjamin Barkworth of Nettleton in the said Parts, farmer, taken on his oath by me Thomas Dixon one of His Majesty's Justices of the Peace in and for the said Parts.

That a few days before May Day last he hired John Good for one year to May Day next and that on Wednesday night or early this morning he departed from his service without having his permission for so doing.
Taken before me, T. Dixon.
Signed, B. Barkworth.[111]

Wednesday 21 June 1797. Poor Child Bound Apprentice at Caistor.

This case is not in Dixon's notebooks, but the tradesman bound to receive the apprentice appealed against the decision at Quarter Sessions. The fact that the indenture was signed by two magistrates on a Wednesday suggests that it was completed at Petty Sessions in Caistor, and it is one of the few scraps of evidence that Dixon attended these Sessions.

Appeals: Roger Hiley, Appellant, and Caistor, Respondents.
At this Court an appeal was entered on behalf of Roger Hiley against an indenture under the hands and seals of Thomas Dixon esquire and Marmaduke Alington clerk, two of His Majesty's Justices of the Peace for the said Parts and one of them Quorum dated the twenty first day of June last past whereby Robert Jackson, a poor child, was bound apprentice to him 'till he attains twenty one, whereby the said Roger Hiley finds himself aggrieved.
Ordered (on the motion of Mr Ascough on the part of the appellant) that the hearing of the merits of the said appeal be respited to the next General Quarter Sessions of the Peace to be holden for and in the said Parts, no notice having been given to the Respondents.[112]

Wednesday 28 June 1797. Assault at Laceby.

Lincolnshire Lindsey. The Information and Complaint of William Hollingworth of Laceby in the said Parts, labourer, taken on his oath before me Thomas Dixon this 28th day of June 1797.

That on the evening of Saturday last the 24th day of this instant Nicholas

---

[111] *Ibid.*, p.16.
[112] LAO, LQSM A/2/22, Kirton, Midsummer, 15 July 1797.

Atkinson of Great Grimsby in the Parts aforesaid, carpenter, did violently strike beat and assault him the said William Hollingworth in the parish of Laceby aforesaid.
Taken before me, T. Dixon.
Signed, William Hollingworth.[113]

Friday 30 June 1797. Absconding Servant at Caistor.

Lincolnshire Lindsey. The Information and Complaint of Mr George Holgate of Hundon in the parish of Castor grazier taken on his oath before me Thomas Dixon one of His Majesty's Justices of the Peace in and for the said Parts this 30th day of June 1797.

That a few dayes before May Day last he hired Elizabeth Stephenson for one year to May next, and that on Thursday the 13th day of June instant in the morning she departed from her service without her said master's permission for so doing.

Taken before me, T. Dixon
Signed, George Holgate.[114]

Tuesday 18 July 1797. Warrant to Detain a Lunatic.

There is no record of the issuing of this warrant in Dixon's notebooks. It appears at Quarter Sessions because the overseer was indicted for failing to serve the warrant.

Epiphany Sessions 1798. Indictment.

The jurors … present that on the eighteenth day of July in the 37th year of the reign of … George Third … at Great Grimsby … Thomas Dixon esquire and William Thorold clerk then and there two of the justices in and for the said Parts in due form of law did then and there make a certain warrant under their hands and seals bearing the date eighteenth day of July 1797 directed to the Overseers of the Poor of the township of Cleethorpes … reciting that it had been proved before them on the oath of George Willerton of the parish of Waltham … farmer that Michael Bailey an inhabitant and whose legal settlement was in the said township of Cleethorpes was permitted to go at large and that the said Michael Bailey was by lunacy so far disordered in his senses that he was dangerous to be permitted to go abroad and authorizing and requiring him the said Overseer of

---

113   LAO, Dixon 8/3, Notebook 1, p.19.
114   *Ibid.*

the Township of Cleethorpes to cause the said Michael Bailey to be apprehended and kept safely locked up in some secure place within the township but only so long as such lunacy or disorder should continue and no longer.

Of which said warrant William Parker of Cleethorpes ... farmer, the Overseer of the Poor of the same township, afterwards ... on the 19th day of July in ... Cleethorpes unlawfully and contemptuously did neglect and refuse to execute the said warrant as he the said William Parker by virtue of his office according to law should have done.

A True Bill

Easter Sessions 1798. Punishment of the Overseer for Failing to Execute the Warrant.

Calendar of Sessions dated 28 April 1798 includes:

William Parker Overseer of the Poor for the township of Cleethorpes convicted of a contempt and misdemeanour – fined 20s and to be committed to the Bridewell at Kirton aforesaid there to remain one calendar month.[115]

July 1797. Absconding Servant at Riby.

Lincolnshire Lindsey. The Information and Complaint of Mr Jonathan Winship of Riby in the said Parts, farmer, taken on his oath before me Thomas Dixon one of His Majesty's Justices of the Peace in and for the said Parts.

That early on Tuesday morning on the 25th day of this instant July Thomas Good whom he hired for one year from May Day last to May Day 1798 absconded from his master's service without his permission for so doing. Taken before me, T. Dixon.

Signed, Jonathan Winship.[116]

Monday 4 August 1797. Assault at Killingholme.

This entry is signed by Dixon, but not in his hand. An archivist's note identifies the hand as that of Richard Dixon, Thomas Dixon's second son and Rector of Claxby and Normanby.

Lincolnshire Lindsey. The Information and Complaint of Richard Bywater of Brocklesby in the said Parts, bricklayer, taken the 4th day September

---

[115] LAO, LQS Files A/1/279, 280, Epiphany and Easter 1798.
[116] LAO, Dixon 8/3, Notebook 3, p.21.

1797 on his oath before me Thomas Dixon one of His Majesty's Justices of the Peace in and for the said Parts.

That on Sunday evening the 27th day of August last William Ellerby, servant in husbandry in North Killingholme, and John Barlow, servant, of South Killingholme did [*'obstruct, molest' deleted*] throw him into a hedge violently and assault the abovementioned Richard Bywater on the highway in the parish of South Killingholme.
Taken before me, T. Dixon.
Signed, Richard Bywater.[117]

Thursday 2 October 1797. Refusal to Pay Wages at Immingham.
Lincolnshire Lindsey. The Information and Complaint of Elizabeth Bullivant of Immingham, single woman, taken on oath before me Thomas Dixon one of His Majesty's Justices of the Peace in and for the said Parts this 2d day of October 1797.

Who saith that Robert Marshall of Immingham in the said Parts hired Ann Bullivant from about 6 weeks after May Day following for 3 guineas wages and that on Monday evening the 25th September last the said Robert Marshall forced her out of his house and locked both the out doors and refused and still refuses paying her wages which are due to her from the time of hiring and also detained her cloaths.
Taken before me, T. Dixon.
Ann Bullivant X her mark.[118]

Thursday 6 November 1797. Refusal to Relieve Pauper at Caistor.
Lincolnshire Lindsey. Ann Russell in the parish of Castor in the County of Lincoln and Parts of Lindsey maketh oath that she is very poor and impotent and not able to provide for her self and that on Thursday last she did apply for relief to the parishioners of the said parish at a vestry and was by them refused to be relieved.

Taken before me one of His Majesty's Justices of the Peace in and for the said Parts the sixth day of November 1797.
Ann Russell X her mark.[119]

---

[117] *Ibid.*, p.23.
[118] *Ibid.*, p.25.
[119] *Ibid.*, p.27. This entry is horizontal.

Thursday 13 November 1797. Bastardy at North Kelsey.
Recognizance. (Summary)
Taken before Thomas Dixon esq. 13 November 1798.
George Burkett and John Burkett both of North Kelsey, farmers, bound in £40 and £20 respectively; Ann Farr of Bullington singlewoman says George Burkett is father of child likely to be born bastard, therefore George Burkett is to appear at the next Quarter Sessions. Signed, Thomas Dixon.[120]

Thursday 27 November 1797. Absconding Servant at Roxton.
Lincolnshire Lindsey. The Information and Complaint of Ferdinand Drewry of Roxton in the said Parts, farmer, taken on his oath before me Thomas Dixon one of His Majesty's Justices of the Peace in and for the said Parts the 27th Day of the instant November.

That yesterday morning he hired John Morrison late of Roxton, serving man, to serve him in husbandry until May Day next and he asked his master's leave to acquaint his father that he had agreed with his said master Ferdinand Drewry to serve him to May Day next and he has since fetched his cloaths away and sayeth that his father would not let him return to his service.
Taken before me, T. Dixon.
Signed, Ferdinand Drewery.[121]

March 1798. Theft of Ferrets at Cuxwold.
Saturday 10 March 1798. Statement by Prosecutor.
The Examination of John Toft of Cuxwold in the said Parts and county, warrener, taken upon oath before me Thomas Dixon esquire one of His Majesty's Justices of the Peace for the said Parts, the tenth day of March in the year of our Lord 1798.

The said John Toft saith that he is warrener to Mr George Whitworth of Cuxwold, that on Friday the ninth day of March instant this examinant about six o'clock on the same morning missed three ferrets belonging to his master out of the tubs where they were usually kept upon which he went to his master's house and desired one of the female servants of Mr Whitworth to inform his master that the ferrets were gone and that he suspected that they were stolen,

---

[120] LAO, LQS File A/1/279, Epiphany 1798, Kirton.
[121] LAO, Dixon 8/3, Notebook 3, p.22.

further saith that his master got up and went to this examinant who both went to the tubs and found the ferrets gone. Upon further enquiry this examinant saith he was informed by two of his master's labourers that one Nicholas Wilkinson a ratcatcher had made enquiry for this examinant as he wanted to buy a ferret or ferrets or make an exchange.

This examinant saith that being informed that the said Nicholas Wilkinson had taken the road towards Rothwell this examinant by directions of his master followed the said Nicholas Wilkinson to Rothwell and from thence to Stainton le Vale near which place this examinant and one Joseph Kent overtook the said Nicholas Wilkinson in whose custody two ferrets were found one of which being a dog ferret this examinant saith is the property of his master the said George Whitworth.

John Toft

Taken before me, T. Dixon. [*This examination is not in Dixon's hand.*]

Saturday 10 March 1798. Statement by Witness.

The Information of George Whitworth.

The said George Whitworth deposeth that on Friday the ninth day of March instant at six o'clock in the morning one of his maid servants called to him and said all the ferrets are gone upon which this deponent immediately arose and went to his warrener John Toft who had care of the ferrets, then the said John Toft went with the said deponent to the tubs where they were usually kept and missed them.

This deponent then saw his shepherd who informed him that he conceived one Nicholas Wilkinson had very likely taken them away. In consequence of this information this deponent made enquiry which road the said Nicholas Wilkinson had taken and upon being informed he sent his warrener John Toft in pursuit of the said Nicholas Wilkinson who was as this deponent was informed found at Stainton le Vale.

G. Whitworth

Taken before me, T. Dixon. [*This information is not in Dixon's hand.*]

Saturday 10 March. Prosecutor and Witnesses Bound to Appear at Quarter Sessions.

Recognizance. 10 March 1798, before Thomas Dixon esq. George Whitworth of Cuxwold, grazier, bound in £20 to appear at Quarter Sessions and prosecute Nicholas Wilkinson, late of Great Grimsby, ratcatcher, for feloniously taking and carrying away one dog ferret the property of him the said George Wilkinson.

Recognizance. 10 March 1798, before Thomas Dixon esq. John Toft of Cuxwold, warrener, bound in £10 to appear at Quarter Sessions and give evidence on an indictment by George Whitworth of Cuxwold grazier of Nicholas Wilkinson late of Great Grimsby, rat chatcher, for feloniously taking and carrying away one dog ferret.

April 1798. Nicholas Wilkinson in the House of Correction at Kirton.

Calendar of Prisoners in House of Correction Kirton includes:
Nicholas Wilkinson, committed March 10th charged upon the oath of George Whitworth of Cuxwold, grazier, with feloniously taking and carrying away on dog ferrit. Committed by T. Dixon esq.

Tuesday 24 April 1798. Trial of Nicholas Wilkinson at Kirton Sessions.

Indictments.
Nicholas Wilkinson late of Great Grimsby Rat Catcher for petty larceny.
Plea Not Guilty, jury say Guilty.
To be recommitted to the said Bridewell and there confined one week.

Expenses of Prosecutor.

Kirton, Easter Wednesday 25 April 1798.
Ordered that the Treasurer do forthwith pay unto the several persons hereafter named the several sums set opposite their respective names being the amount of their bills for their trouble and expenses in prosecuting the following persons for felony and that the same be allowed to the said Treasurer in his accounts,

George Whitworth and Witness for prosecuting
Nicholas Wilkinson   £1   12s   6d[122]

Monday 16 April 1798. Absconding Servant at Caistor.

The Information and Complaint of Thomas Watmough of Castor in the said Parts, brickmaker, taken on oath before me Thomas Dixon one of His Majesty's Justices of the Peace in and for the said Parts the 16th day of April 1798.

That on Monday the 9th of this instant April he hired Samuel Varlow for one year at 14 guineas wage and 5s to his fastening penny and the same day he entered on his service and on Sunday morning the 15th instant he absconded and left his service without the permission of his said master. Taken before me, T. Dixon.
Signed, Thomas Watmough.[123]

---

[122]   LAO, LQS Files A/1/280, Easter 1798, Kirton; LQSM A/2/22, Easter 1798, Kirton.
[123]   LAO, Dixon 8/3, Notebook 3, p.29.

Friday 20 April 1798. Theft of Cloth at Aylesby.
Complaint of Prosecutor.
Lincolnshire Lindsey. The Information and Complaint of Philip Skipworth of Aylesby in the said Parts, grazier, taken on oath before me Thomas Dixon one of His Majesty's Justices of the Peace in and for the said Parts the 20th day of this instant April 1798.

That he has reason to suspect and doth suspect that Mary Metcalf did some time since felloniously steal take and carry away one yard and a half of printed cotton from one of the desk drawers of the said Philip Skipworth and gave it to Martha Blanchard to make a frock for her child whom she stood godmother for.
Taken before me, T. Dixon.
Signed, Philip Skipworth.

Examination of Witness, Martha Blanchard.
The information of Martha Blanchard the wife of John Blanchard of Ailsby in the said Parts, labourer, taken upon her oath this twentieth day of April … 1798 before us two of His Majesty's Justices of the Peace for the said Parts.

The abovenamed informant saith that about two months ago Mary Metcalf, servant to Mr Philip Skipworth of Ailsby aforesaid, came to her husband's house and gave her, this informant, a piece of printed cotton which she apprehends contains about one yard and a half, and that she desired the same might be accepted as a present to her child to whom she was godmother; and suspecting about ten days ago that the said piece of printed cotton had been stolen out of her master's house she sent for Mrs Skipworth who the next morning came to her and to whom she showed the said piece of cotton, who not being then able to identify it took it home and this informant followed her, when she showed her another piece containing about five yards and a half exactly of the same pattern and quality and from which the lesser piece appeared to have been separated Martha Blanchard X her mark.
Taken before us the day and year above written William Thorold, T. Dixon.

Mary Metcalf Committed to the House of Correction at Kirton.
Mary Metcalf committed April 20th charged for suspicion of feloniously stealing one printed piece of cotton about one yard and a half the property of Phillip Skipworth of Ailsby.
Committed by William Thorold, clerk, and T. Dixon esq.

Prosecutor and Witness Bound to Appear at the next Quarter Sessions.

Recognizance taken before William Thorold, 20 April 1798. (Summary)
Philip Skipworth of Ailsby, gentleman, bound in £20 for his appearance at the next Quarter Sessions sessions to prosecute and give evidence against Mary Metcalf, late servant, for stealing a quantity of printed cotton the property of him the said Philip Skipworth.

Recognizance taken before William Thorold, 20 April 1798. (Summary)
John Blanchard, Ailsby, labourer, bound in £10 that Martha his wife appear next Quarter Sessions and give evidence against Mary Metcalf, late servant to Philip Skipworth of Ailsby, now suspected of felony and committed to House of Correction Kirton

Tuesday 24 April 1798. Trial of Mary Metcalf at Kirton Quarter Sessions.

Indictment.
Jurors present that Mary Metcalf, late of the parish of Ailsby, spinster, on 20 April 1798, in Ailsby, one yard and a half of printed cotton, value 10d, good of Phillip Skipworth there being found, did feloniously steal take and carry away.
Endorsed Phillip Skipworth, Martha Blanchard sworn in court.
A True Bill.

Mary Metcalf late of Ailsby Spinster for petty larceny.
Submits.
To be recommitted to the said bridewell and there confined in a solitary cell one calendar month.

Expenses of Prosecutor.

Mr Philip Skipworth the Prosecution Expences on the Conviction of Mary Metcalf

Prosecutor's Loss of Time Two Days	3s	0d
Prosecutor's Expences two days	4s	8d
One Witness loss of Time Three Days @ 1s 6d a day	4s	6d
Horse hire for One Witness and the Prosecutor 20 Miles	13s	4d
Witness Expences Three Days @ 2s 4d per day	7s	0d
Prisoner's Expences One Day	1s	0d
For Guarding the Prisoner One Night and Expences and taking the Prisoner to Kirton and Horse hire	8s	8d
£2	2s	2d

Paid for the Indictment		2s	8d
	£2	4s	10d
Order		1s	6d
	£2	6s	4d

Kirton Easter Sessions 1798 allowed by the Court, R. Ellison.[124]

Monday 7 May 1798. Absconding Farm Servant at Irby.

Lincolnshire Lindsey. The Information and Complaint of Joseph Johnson of Irby in that said Parts, farmer, taken on oath before me Thomas Dixon one of His Majesty's Justices of the Peace in and for the said Parts the 7th day of the instant May 1798.

That on Tuesday the first instant John Plaskitt of Irby, labourer, whom he hired to serve him for one year did abscond from his service without his master's permission for so doing.

Taken before me, T. Dixon.

Signed, Josh Johnson.[125]

Tuesday 19 June 1798. Absconding Servant at Irby.

Lincolnshire Lindsey. The Information and Complaint of Joseph Johnson of Irby in the said Parts, farmer, taken on oath before me Thomas Dixon one of His Majesty's Justices of the Peace in and for the said Parts this 19th day of June 1798.

That William Reader whom he hired to serve him for one year to May Day next did on Friday morning the first of this instant June abscond and leave the service of the said Joseph Johnson without his permission for so doing.

Taken before me, T. Dixon.

Signed, Josh Johnson.[126]

Friday 13 July 1798. Bastardy Order at Riby.
Recognizances

Thos Dixon Esq.

William Green of Riby Servingman in £40

---

[124] LAO, Dixon 8/3, Notebook 3, p.24; LQS Files A/1/280, Easter 1798, Kirton; LQSM A/2/22, Easter 1798, Kirton.

[125] LAO, Dixon 8/3, Notebook 3, p.30.

[126] *Ibid.*, p.7.

William Marris of Keelby Labourer in £20

for the appearance of the said William Green at this sessions and to perform order of Bastardy for getting Mary Croft of Barnoldby le Beck Singlewoman with child.

Appears.[127]

---

[127] LAO, LQSM A/2/23, Midsummer 1798, Kirton.

1. Riby, Caistor and the surrouding area. Detail from C. and J. Greenwood, *Map of the County of Lincoln* (London, 1830). (Lincoln Cathedral Library.)

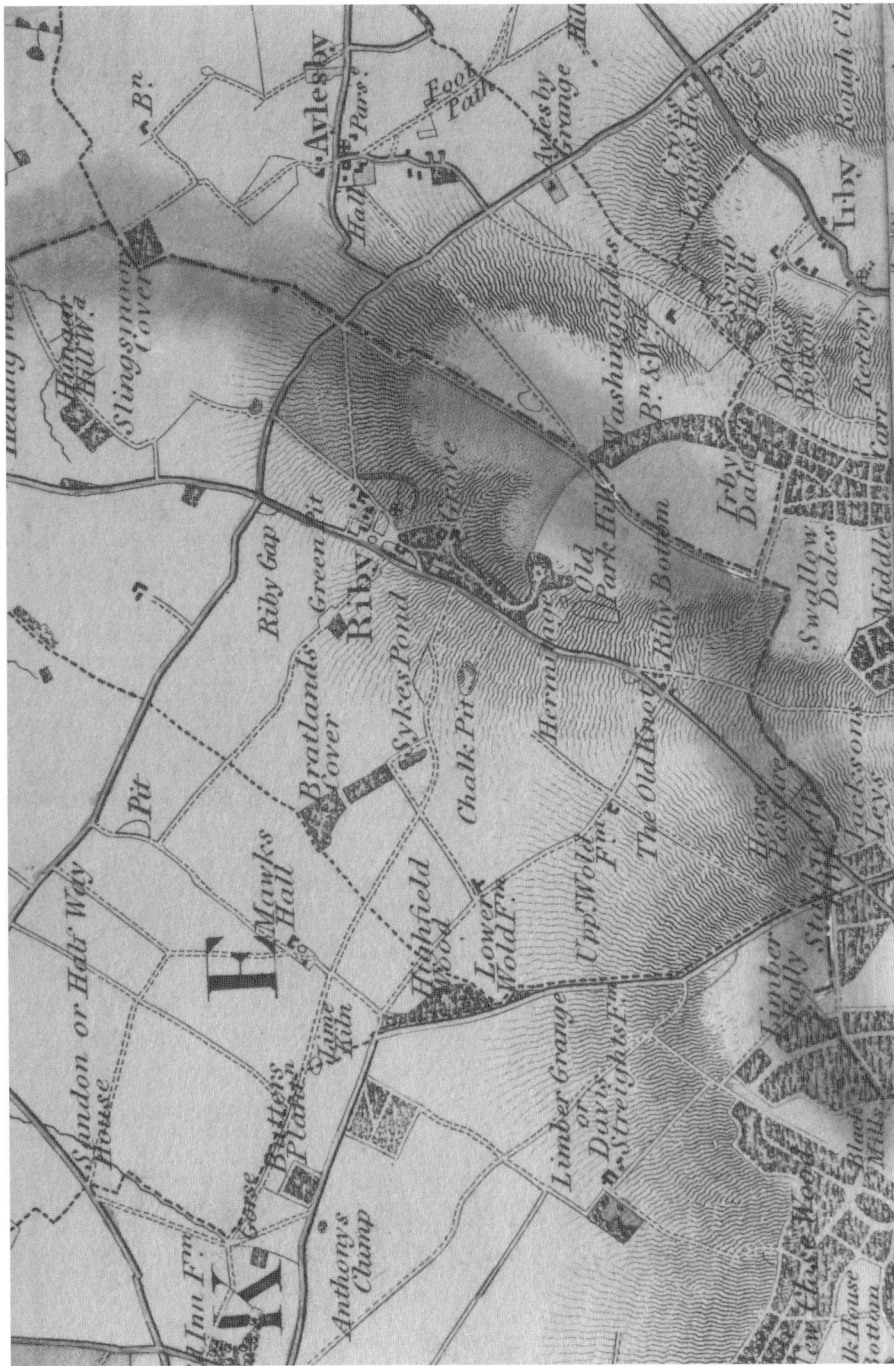

2. Riby: Thomas Dixon's house (Church Farm) was directly north of the church. Detail from A. Bryant, *Map of the County of Lincoln* (London, 1828). (Lincoln Cathedral Library.)

Lincolnshire } The Information
Lindsey } and Complaint of
Benjamen Barkworth of
Nettleton in ye said parts farmer
taken on Oath before me Thos.
Dixon One of his Majesty's Justices
of the Peace in & for ye sd. Parts
this twenty eight day of
Novr 1793 that as few Days
before old May Day he hired Wm
Mumby at a Meeting at Brigg,
for retaining of Servents for
One year. at 3..0..0. wages &
that on Monday last he
Absconded from his Service
without his Masters permission
for so doing

Taken before } Benj Barkworth
me. Dixon

3–4. Absconding servants: cases from Thomas Dixon's Justice Book.
(LAO, Dixon 8/2, pp.14, 17.)

Lincolnshire } The Information and
Lindsey } Complaint of John Bretton
of Kelkwith in ye S Ports Harbour taken
on his Oath before me Tho:s Dixon
One of his Maj:tys Justices of the
Peace in the S:d Ports this first day
of April 1794 ____ About three Weeks or
a Month since he agreed with Will:m
Stanley & John Stanam of Nettleton
in Ports aforesaid Labourers to ——
about four teen Acres of Land at 13/0
of Acre ____ to begin to work before old
Lady Day ——
Last ——
Coming —— Departed from their
work without the permission of their
Master said doing's
                        John Bratton

Taken before
me. Dixon

east view of the House of Correction at Kirton in Lindsey. 1793.

5. Kirton in Lindsey House of Correction: drawing by Claude Nattes, 1793. (Lincolnshire County Council: Lincoln Central Library, Local Studies Collection.)

Ground Floor of Kirton Bridwell.

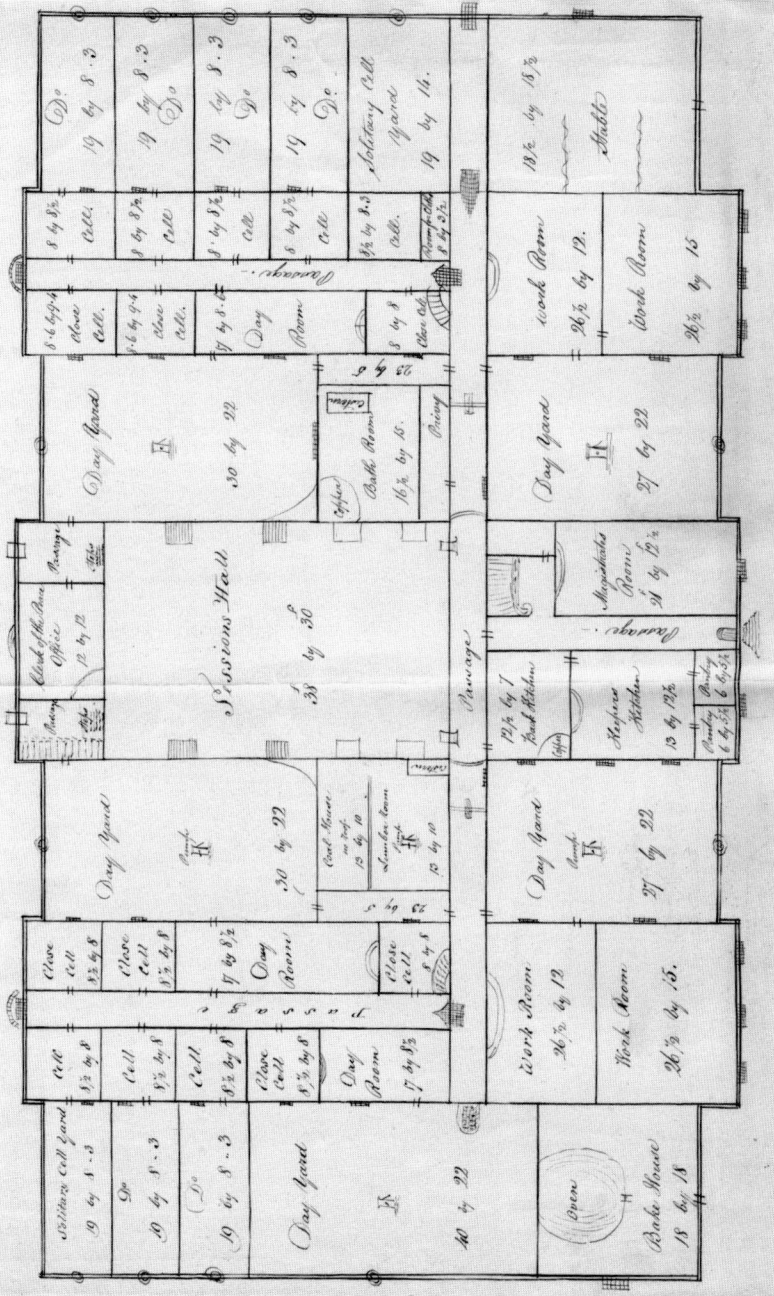

6. Kirton in Lindsey House of Correction: plan of ground floor. (LAO, LQS/B/5/266.)

7. Harmston: The old Manor House, showing the older rear wing. The front range was demolished about 1900. (Photograph: R. C. Wheeler.)

8. The Blackamoor's Head after it had ceased to be a beer house. (Photograph in possession of Mrs M. Mottram.)

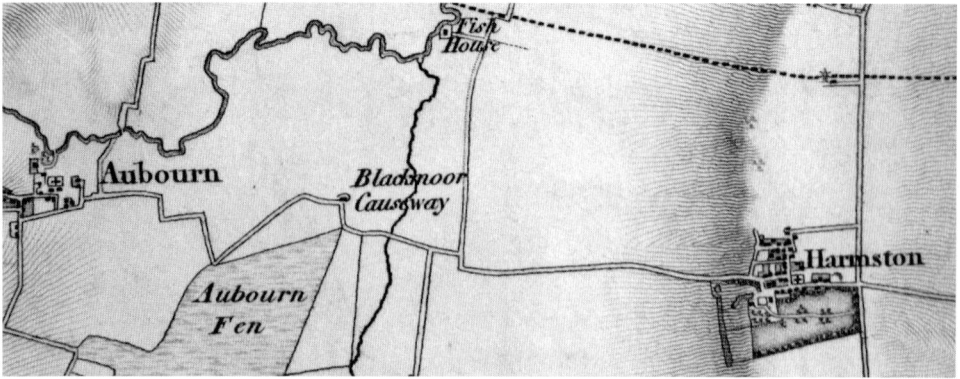

9. Aubourn, Harmston and the old Blackmoor Causeway.
(Ordnance Survey One-inch Sheet 83, surveyed 1820–21.)

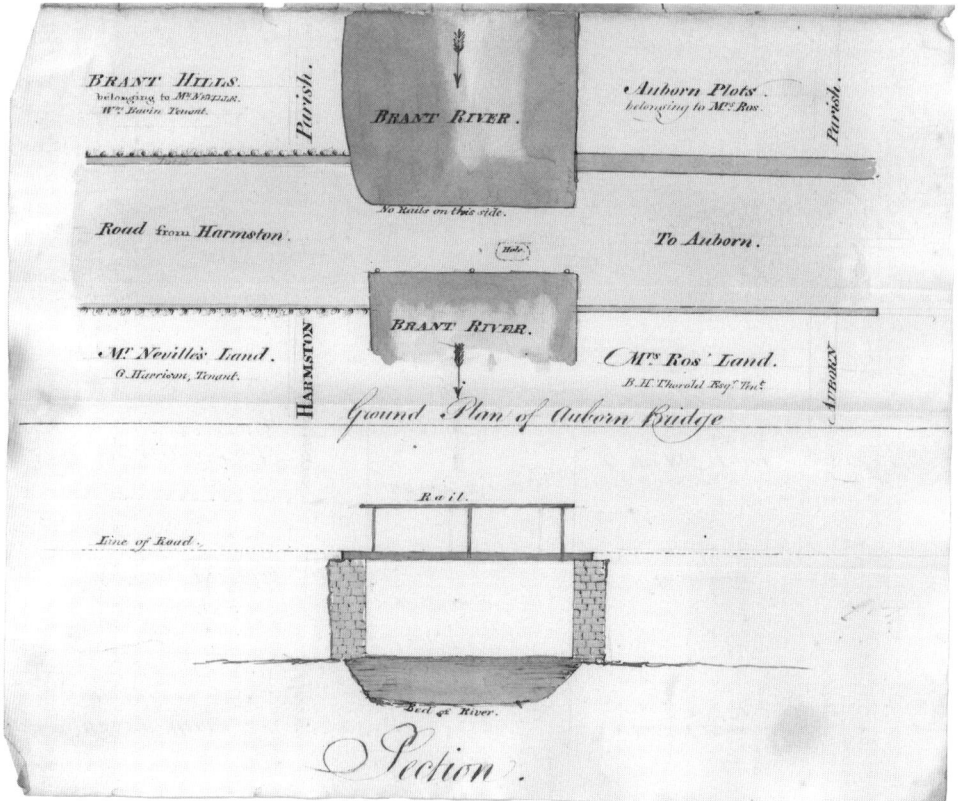

10. Plan and elevation of the old Harmston Bridge. Note the hole in carriageway
and the single hand-rail. (LAO, KQS/B/1.)

11. Blackmoor Causeway as rebuilt.
(Ordnance Survey Six-inch Sheet Lincolnshire 88 SW.)

		£	s	d
April 1	Lot of Cummicals Beast at gras	0	10	0
Do	80 Beast Do of Ditto		4	0
18	Lot of Ditto		10	0
Do	Lot of Sheep in the paddocks		5	0
May 6	3 Schore at 3 per schore		9	0
Do	100 of Sheep		2	6
7	Ducksworth 500 of sheep a 2 per hund		10	0
12	3 Schore Beast a 3/ per schore		9	0
18	Mr Morrinson 100 Beast		18	0
21	David Hairston 3 Schore a 3/		9	0
28	Mack Dornill 300 Sheep		9	6
June 7	Lot of Sheep		6	0
Do	4 Horses 1 night		2	0
16	Lot of Beast in the paddocks		5	0
22	6 Schore of Beast at 2/6 per schore		15	0
20	6 Schore of Beast at Ditto		16	0
Do	Received of Thomas Towars for Beast a turnips		10	0
Do	old nin died and souls to G Raby for		13	0
July	Mr Morrinson 6 schore a 3/		18	0
	Mr Millars Beast		16	0
	Lot of sheep in the sod closes	1	0	0
	Lot in the home paddocks		12	0
Sep 24	Lot in the paddocks		8	0
25	Lot of Beast in newing closes		10	0
Oct 8	James Scott 5 Schore in newing an 1 schore in sod	1	0	0
9	Mr John Walker 5 Schore a 2/6		12	6
10	Mr Hope 6 Schore a 3/		18	0
Do	James Millars 7 Schore a 3/	1	1	0
30	Sold 8 Ton of hay a 6/ per Ston		4	0
Do	6 Schore Sheep a 6 p s		3	0
Nov 2	Lot of Beast in newing		15	0
3	Lot in sod closes		10	0
10	Robinson 2 days with 4 Schore	1	0	0
20	10 Beast at Agist 4 weaks a 1/ per head	2	0	0
Do	50 Beast of John Walkers in newing 2 nights		5	0
22	Meggriar 4 Schore at 2/		8	0
Decbr	36 Beast hay and grass		10	0
		£ 21	10	6

1836.

12. Drove Account, 1836. (LAO, 4DEG/ Thorold of Harmston/ Box 6.)

PAPERS IN THE CASE *THOROLD* v. *CATTON*, 1830–1838

EDITED BY

R. C. WHEELER

INTRODUCTION

The Occasion

On 21–22 August 1838, an arbitration took place at the Green Man Inn in the parish of Blankney before James Hitchins, a Lincoln auctioneer.[1] The inn had been used in the past for Quarter Sessions, so was equipped for what appears to have been a formal hearing with evidence given on oath and witnesses subject to cross-examination.[2]

The defendant's solicitor was John William Danby. His papers for the case survive[3] and provide an unusually detailed picture of such an event.

The matter at issue was to settle the mutual indebtedness of plaintiff and defendant. In itself this is of little interest to the modern reader. However, the evidence casts unusual light on social relations between gentry and tradesmen; on the establishment of a beer house; on the improvements to the upper Witham seen through the eyes of the bankers working on it; and on the droving trade. For the last of these, it provides rare quantitative evidence.

The Defendant

Benjamin Hart Thorold (1799–1883) was the heir to an estate of some 3600 acres in and around Harmston. His mother, Ann Eliza Thorold (1772–1848), was the eldest daughter and heiress of Samuel Thorold, an eccentric of Italian birth and upbringing, who had died in 1820. His father was Benjamin Hart (1759–1836) who had abandoned a career as an Independent minister to become a barrister; he changed his name to Thorold in 1820 in order to inherit. Benjamin Hart Thorold had been born at 4 Brick Court in the Temple and might truly be said to have been bred to the law. Unfortunately he showed neither patience nor judgement. He was always keen to take advantage of new opportunities, but lost interest when difficulties arose. He could lapse into inactivity if that enabled him to defer some disagreeable action, logical argument notwithstanding. Under a family settlement made in 1822, he received an income of £400 per year, but he was unable to live within his

---

[1] Pigot's Directory (1841) lists him as of 24 Silver Street.
[2] The power to administer an oath only dated from 3 & 4 Wm IV c.42, xli. See Sir William Holdsworth, *A History of English Law* (London, 1972), xiv. 197.
[3] LAO, 4 DEG/Thorold of Harmston/Box 6.

means. He had married in 1820; his wife, who died in 1832, bore him two sons and six daughters.

Thorold had extended the old Manor House (**Figure 7**) to provide fitter accommodation, but not to any extent that should have stretched his finances. Yet the first court order against him for debt came as early as 1824, the first of an ever-increasing number. Perhaps he had been anticipating his parents' succession. Perhaps the later extravagance of a house near London, complete with mistress, went back to his early manhood. Whatever the cause, the effect was that he saw salvation in every new scheme for making money; and since he lacked the temperament of a businessman, he simply entangled himself in greater debts.

He was no doubt a cause of concern to his parents. His father had retired from the law and taken up religion again; he was held in high esteem in Lincoln as a Methodist lay preacher and as an advocate of Reform. But domestic matters and perhaps even the management of the estate he seems to have left to his wife Ann Eliza – she had, after all, grown up at Harmston Hall. Unfortunately, Benjamin Hart Thorold and his mother were scarcely on speaking terms.

The Plaintiff

John ('Jack') Catton was a stonemason by trade. The Catton family was widespread and mobile in and around Lincoln, some engaged in the building trades, others in farming. They were not noted for being religious – earlier in the century one of them achieved the distinction of being cited as the reputed father of a high proportion of the bastards that appear in the Harmston parish registers. John was getting on in years. He suffered from 'gout' – possibly arthritis – and walked with a stick. He was given to swearing to an extent that even rough men could find daunting.

Clearly he found that keeping a public house was an agreeable activity for his declining years. He moved from the Blackamoor's Head in 1836–1837 in order to take on the Bugle Horn at Bassingham, a couple of miles away, where he remained until his death in August 1847.

The Case

Benjamin Hart Thorold had tried his hand at farming in the later 1820s but had lost money and had been obliged to sell up: the accounts for a sale in March 1829 that raised some £500 are among the case papers. By this date, the Beerhouse Act[4] was under discussion. It was widely seen as an oppor-

---

[4]   11 Geo.IV & 1Wm.IV c.64.

tunity to break into the monopoly of the established brewers.[5] Others were about to make money, and Thorold did not want to miss out on the opportunity. He had the use of the old brewery at Harmston Hall and the estate included a former inn, still functioning illegally as such, as well as serving as a farm (**Figure 8**). This lay within a part of the estate that had been retained by Thorold's grandmother on her husband's death.[6] She died in 1830 and it is not clear whether Thorold arranged the lease with his grandmother or with her executors. His intention was to install Catton to keep a beerhouse and (perhaps) supervise the farming operations, which were probably intended to provide Thorold with a source of hay and oats for his carriage horses, though there was doubtless an element of commercial farming to it as well.

Catton's wife did not want to live in so remote a location. To persuade him to move, he was installed as manager rather than tenant, to sell ale that Thorold would brew at Harmston. Thorold underestimated the difficulties of brewing; his first brew was unsaleable and he gave up. Being imprisoned for debt certainly hindered him from giving much attention to the business, and he authorised Catton to buy beer from other sources. Catton claimed that his initial agreement only related to the sale of ale brewed by Thorold and that selling other people's ale was his wife's separate business and nothing to do with him. The reader may find this implausible, but there had never been a written agreement, and Thorold seems only to have demanded accounts after two years: his approach to business always was exceedingly casual. By this date, for quite separate reasons, Catton had become a tenant, no longer receiving any wages.

An attempt was made to settle up in 1832–1833, but it foundered on the absence of any accounts for sale of ale in those first two years. The matter remained unresolved until deteriorating relations caused Catton to take Thorold to court for various debts. Thorold counter-claimed, his claim including a sum of £500 for ale profits (implausibly large but no doubt intended to cover whatever the court might decide was reasonable) and a second blanket sum of £100 for hay sold off the farm. This stemmed from a separate dispute over whether Catton had permission from Thorold to sell hay from a close he rented from him.

The main point at issue was whether Catton had been selling the ale on Thorold's behalf in the first two years. He admitted receiving wages, but claimed these were for supervising the farming activities. In the absence of a written agreement, Thorold relied on hearsay evidence from a labourer called Slater, a dubious character now in Thorold's employment.

---

[5]   Sidney & Beatrice Webb, *The history of liquor licensing in England, principally from 1700 to 1830* (London, 1903).
[6]   This was Anne Thorold (1753–1830), daughter of Revd Sir William Anderson of Broughton, Bt. Shortly after the death in 1820 of Samuel Thorold, her first husband, she married Francois Joseph Ros.

The truth of the matter remains unclear to this day; indeed, it does not really matter. The value of the case is the vivid and often surprising picture it offers of a world in which the relations between the heir to the estate and a class of people who were not merely his social inferiors but were also pretty disreputable could nevertheless be surprisingly intimate. It also comes as a surprise to find a Lincoln auctioneer presiding over what was in most respects a formal court of law, with evidence mostly given under oath and subject to cross-examination.

Improving the Witham

The boundary between the parishes of Aubourn and Harmston is largely formed by the River Brant, which then joins the Witham before continuing north to Lincoln. Concerns about the inadequate drainage of the headwaters of these rivers had been voiced as early as 1818[7] but action was deferred until the river below Lincoln could be sufficiently improved to take the greater volume of floodwaters that would result. Those improvements were completed in 1826, and in 1827 the surveyor, J. S. Padley, was directed by the Court of Sewers to draw up proposals for widening, deepening and, to a small extent, straightening the upper Witham and Brant. Work started in 1828 under the direction of a committee that included Benjamin Thorold senior and continued until 1833. It was normal for such improvement work to progress upstream; it would appear from the papers produced in this case that Harmston was reached in 1832. Slater's evidence may be questionable in other respects but one cannot doubt his description of the main digging being contracted for by three gangs of bankers, while directly employed labourers were used for the easier surface work. Slater led one of those gangs and had the comfort of a bed at the Blackamoor's Head; where the rest of his gang slept we are not told.

The road from Aubourn towards Harmston followed a zigzag route as far as the Blackamoor's Head and thence to the bridge over the Brant; it was known as the Blackamoor (or Blackmoor) Causeway (**Figure 9**). The bridge was a timber structure reckoned to be at least sixty years old; a plan, seem- ingly of 1829 (**Figure 10**), shows a hole in the decking. The parish of Aubourn petitioned the Kesteven justices to rebuild it, the name of B. H. Thorold appearing at the head of the signatures. The parish intended to straighten the causeway: **Figure 11** shows its new route. The Kesteven justices were minded to rebuild the bridge but made do with repairs because it was too late in the season to start work. Tenders had been invited but nothing had been done when, on 13 February 1832, Charles Chaplin of Blankney crossed the

---

7   LAO, UWIDB/5/3/2, Lincoln Court of Sewers minutes.

bridge, saw that the river had been dammed for the Court of Sewers work, and realised that the County could save money by rebuilding the bridge while the river was empty. A decision to proceed was taken quickly. However, a temporary bridge was needed while the permanent one was being rebuilt. This seems to have been erected at Thorold's expense. (There was some discussion of reimbursing him, but it is unclear whether this happened.)[8]

The temporary bridge was built between 25 and 29 February[9] and lasted until the new (brick) bridge was complete on 3 April. During this period a night-watchman was provided at Thorold's expense, most of the turns being shared between Catton and George Raby (whom we shall encounter in due course). They were paid a normal day's wage for this and one suspects that they regarded dozing in a chair as an agreeable alternative to normal work. 'Paid' should really read 'credited': the amount was simply added to the overall settlement. This is perhaps key to the relationship between Catton and Thorold: the latter wanted to play his part but was always short of ready money; the former may have been a rogue but he was prepared to do things on credit – as long as there was sufficient profit for him in the deal – when others would baulk at it.

Droving

What made the Blackamoor's Head viable in so isolated a position was the droving trade. As late as the 1830s, vast numbers of cattle were bred in Scotland and walked down to the Home Counties for fattening up before slaughter.[10] The route followed was broadly that of the Great North Road, but wherever possible the drovers followed routes running parallel to it, both to avoid tolls and because the animals disliked the hard surfaces of the turn-pike. Typically they could cover ten to twelve miles in a day. The principal requirement for the night's stance was ample water for the animals – Blacka-moor was well suited in that respect. Accommodation for the drovers was welcome, but they were accustomed to sleeping in the open when necessary. The head drover was called a 'topsman'; such men might be uneducated, but they had a great deal of capital tied up in the animals and took care that they should arrive in the most saleable condition possible.

Catton had permission to accommodate droves on Thorold's land, passing on the sum received to Thorold. He also used the close he rented for this

---

[8]   LAO, KQS B/1/HARMSTON BRIDGE.

[9]   LAO, 4DEG/Thorold of Harmston/Box 6 – one of the ale accounts not presented here. The formal decision-making followed later: a new tender was submitted by John Preston on 3 March and was accepted by the justices at a meeting on 6 March.

[10]   A. R. B. Haldane, *The Drove Roads of Scotland* (Newton Abbot, 1973).

purpose, and sometimes put the beasts (with permission) on the land of other farmers. He actively sought out droves, principally, it was supposed, for the profit that accrued from accommodating the men. The droves diverged from the Great North Road and crossed the Trent at Littleborough; Catton would journey to Drinsey Nook or Torksey in the hope of meeting a topsman stopping the night there and of persuading him to spend the following night at Blackamoor. One learns from the evidence that it was usual for the drovers to take turns watching over the beasts at night. On the rare occasions when they did not depart the following morning, Catton himself would watch them by day.

To give an idea of numbers, 14,519 cattle passed through the Entercommon toll bar, just north of Northallerton, in 1828.[11] Estimating numbers of animals from the accounts Catton rendered for droves accommodated on Thorold's land is not easy: figures are not always given and the price per animal varied according to an overall assessment of how big the cattle were. Moreover, the bills are not always for whole years. But estimating as best one can, Catton seems to have accommodated some 2675 cattle in 1834 (plus any that passed through before mid-June). In 1836, there were 1760. The fall may be because an increasing proportion of the traffic was going by steamship. In contrast, sheep increased from 2873 in 1834 to 3140 in 1836. The sheep may not have been Scottish: only 4389 sheep had passed through the Entercommon toll bar in 1828, so many may have originated in Yorkshire. What is clear from these figures is that a significant proportion of the droving traffic stopped the night at Aubourn. Documentary evidence for the trade is generally poor so the evidence presented in these papers offers rare insights: we see the same topsmen making repeated visits, we know the size of individual droves, and we have testimony (not necessarily unbiased) on the abstemious habits of some of them.

Debt

Benjamin Hart Thorold was perpetually short of ready cash. Most tradesmen would provide goods and services on credit, though there are hints he found it increasingly difficult to find suppliers on such terms. When such creditors pressed for payment, they might be offered a promissory note, or 'note of hand', effectively a promise to pay the sum due after some specified period or simply on demand. Notes of hand carried interest at five per cent, as did outstanding bills generally. The difference was that if the creditor now applied for his money and was refused, he could obtain a court order with

[11] Janet Blackman, 'The cattle trade and agrarian change on the eve of the Railway Age', *Agricultural History Review* 23 (1975), 48–62.

little trouble or expense. Stamp duty was payable when notes of hand were drawn up; pre-stamped paper was normally used. This is referred to by witnesses as a 'note-stamp'.

Once a court order had been obtained, it was straightforward to obtain a writ allowing bailiffs to be sent in. A more serious writ was the *capias ad satisfaciendum*, or 'ca: sa:' as it was usually abbreviated. Technically it directed that the subject of the writ was to be held by the sheriff to ensure his appearance in court; in practice it was imprisonment for debt. It was not executed by the sheriff in person, of course, but by the sheriff's officer, who in this case was a certain John Harmston. The sheriff's officer would usually take the better sort of debtor to his own house in the first place and suggest that the individual might prefer to lodge there – for a consideration, of course – while any misunderstandings were sorted out, rather than face the debtors' prison. The house was normally made secure against escape and was commonly known as a 'sponging house'. Thorold appears to have stayed 'at Harmston's', as he liked to refer to it, for a significant period, settling his bill for lodging, it would seem, by a note of hand for £60.

Imprisoning a debtor was a form of coercion but still might not lead to payment. An alternative answer might be to turn the debt into a mortgage or some other form of secured loan like an annuity. Thorold was likely to resist such a move, chiefly because the income he was guaranteed under the family settlement was already pledged, but also because, since he was only a tenant-for-life under a strict settlement, on his death the estate would pass to his eldest son, who was under no obligation to honour his father's debts. An astute borrower was likely to demand a policy on Thorold's life to cover this eventuality, and the cost of premiums on such a policy actually made secured debt more expensive than unsecured debt for a man in Thorold's position. We know that at one point Thorold offered to convert his debt to Catton into an annuity. We are not told whether he offered security; we may suspect he hoped Catton in his ignorance would accept an unsecured annuity.

Farming

The *Lincolnshire Chronicle* in July 1842 described how, in the 1820s, Thorold had 'quit the study of law for agriculture, in which he became a wild and visionary speculator'. Perhaps this is merely a polite reference to some foolish deals, but in general the article is informed and carefully written. Had Thorold actually embraced radical notions of how farmer and labourer could work together more equitably? One of the witnesses refers to the use of a thrashing machine, but without any suggestion that this was novel or controversial.

It would be good to know more about how Thorold ran his farming. The witnesses provide some clues, but they were confused: was there a foreman, and if so, who was it? Certainly Thorold was disorganised, and his actions were often driven by a need for ready cash. Whether there was something more to his apparent waywardness is a question that must be left to readers more familiar with detailed practice in that era.

Outcome of the Arbitration

Hitchins published his award on 31 August: Thorold was to pay Catton £130 1s 2d on 1 November; he was to meet Hitchins' costs of £34 2s 7d, plus £40 of Catton's costs. He was, of course, to bear his own costs; we do not know what these amounted to.

We do not know Hitchins' reasoning. An arbitrator was not obliged to divulge the reasons for his award; indeed Stevens[12] advised that 'they should be for ever locked up in his own breast'. Clearly, Hitchins considered that Thorold had not proved his entitlement to the profits of the ale. Given that Thorold had waited so long before demanding accounts, and given that the only evidence he could produce in his favour was hearsay from a dubious character, this is unsurprising. On the other hand, Hitchins appears to have examined Catton's bills more carefully than Thorold ever did. He must have found many of them implausible. For example, the bill for masons' work submitted by Catton's brothers (not reproduced here) charges an implausible amount of time to some quite modest jobs. One gains the impression that for quite a period the brothers booked their time to Thorold whenever they had no other business to pursue. They may well have spent this time at Blacka-moor, but they were more likely to have been sitting idly with Jack Catton than pursuing their trade. Knowledge of what a reasonable cost might be and the ability to make a fair estimate when actual sums were uncertain were two of the advantages a well-chosen arbitrator offered over the normal courts.

If we assume that Thorold's own costs amounted to £50, he faced a total bill of £254 3s 9d. In contrast, Catton's net demands amounted to £329 7s 6d. So going to law had actually saved Thorold some £75. Arbitration had proved worthwhile.

The Documents

(1) The first document presented is the agreement to submit to arbitration. To the question of why Catton and Thorold should have agreed to such a course, a contemporary publication provides an answer: SPEEDY JUSTICE

---

[12] Robert Stevens, *An Essay on Arbitration: more particularly as it relates to commerce and marine insurance* (London, 1834), 69.

and DIMINUTION OF EXPENSE.[13] Arbitrators were not bound by the normal rules of evidence. This was particularly useful in a case like this one, where evidence that would satisfy the strict rules was scarcely to be expected. The respective solicitors had agreed that evidence would be taken under oath but that a formal written record was not required. The accepted view at the time was that where perjury was suspected – and in this case it certainly was – evidence should be taken down in the form of questions and answers, should be read back to the witnesses and signed by them.[14] Perhaps such a process might have induced in some of the witnesses a stricter regard for the truth. However, the evidence in conflict was generally about who had said what several years before. That certain witnesses made extensive use of statements of the form 'I do not remember such-and-such' suggests they were well aware that no case of perjury could rely on such statements, whether evidence were recorded in writing or not.

One advantage of having the draft of this agreement survive rather than the fair copy is that it becomes apparent that the procedures to be followed were settled before the name of the arbitrator was agreed. We know little about the man they selected. As an auctioneer, he was presumably conversant with normal commercial practice, and that, in Stevens' opinion, was one of the main considerations in the choice of an arbitrator.

(2.1) is Thorold's statement. The lengthy insertions suggest that it started as a draft of what Thorold intended to say. One of those insertions alleges a statement by Catton that he had 'no profit in the ale'. The phrasing of the expression does not quite ring true. One would like to how Thorold knew of this and (especially as this is an insertion) *when* he knew.

(2.2) consists of statements by Catton, his wife and his son-in-law. The document appears to have been written while the statements were being made: some of the words can only be made out with difficulty, and one section of Mrs Catton's statement has been condensed to a single terse phrase. There is no flow to their narrative; indeed, they read more like a record of cross-examination. One might suppose that the fuller record (such as survives for the other witnesses) has gone astray, except that this section was pinned together with **(2.1)**, although the two are separately paginated. There is a further problem: Catton's son-in-law appears as a witness in the account at **(4)**, although he expresses himself differently there. The other parties do not re-appear.

Statements by the parties to a dispute were quite separate from the evidence of witnesses. Only from 1851 could such statements be admitted as evidence

---

[13] Stevens, *Essay on Arbitration*, 3. The capitals are Stevens'.
[14] Stevens, *Essay on Arbitration*, 55.

in the normal way.[15] There was nothing to prevent Hitchins hearing these statements in his office in Lincoln a few days before the main hearing, if that was agreeable to the parties and their solicitors. Mrs Catton would technically be a party rather than a witness. Catton's brother-in-law had perhaps turned up with them – he may even have driven them – and perhaps his statement was taken before the solicitors agreed that he ought rather to be treated as an ordinary witness. In that case, it would follow that the insertions in Thorold's statement were made before the hearing proper opened on 21 August and thus before a certain banker named Slater claimed to have told anyone about his recollection of a statement being made about 'no profit in the ale'. Such a hypothesis would also explain why the notes of the parties' statements come in a different form to those of the witnesses' evidence.

(3) is Danby's copy of a brief prepared by him for the arbitrator. The document provides verbatim copies of the judge's order which was the basis for the arbitration, and follows this with verbatim copies of the submissions by the parties' solicitors. (Most of this is summarised here rather than being reproduced in full.) It concludes with outlines of what the witnesses to be called on Thorold's behalf would state. Interpolations have been added to these at an uncertain date; some of the latest entries, on unnumbered folios, may also have been added to this copy without being on the original brief to the arbitrator.

The reverse of some of the pages carry a hastily written account of witnesses' testimony. The pages have not necessarily been used in order, and there is no record of the examination of Catton's witnesses or the cross-examination of Thorold's. Clearly these are Danby's own notes: he was only in a position to take notes when Andrew (Catton's solicitor) had the ear of the court.

(4) is a fair copy of a summary of the evidence. It was made by a clerk who clearly was not present at the hearing, copying a rough transcript which does not survive. This is evident because 'Blackamoor' is usually changed to 'Bassingham', presumably because the place was unfamiliar to the writer; it has then been corrected back to 'Blackamoor' in a different hand.

With such summaries, it is always useful to know how close we are to the original words of the witness. In this case, we also have the partial transcript, taken down by Danby, on the verso of **(3)**. This is not the source for **(4)**, because the wording sometimes differs. On the other hand, when the wording appears to reflect the witness's own words, the two sources usually agree. When the fair copy uses words unlikely to have been chosen by the witness, **(3)** sometimes gives a version closer to the witness's words. For example,

---

[15] 14/15 Vict. c.99.

(4) has George Catton say 'From the first of my father going to Blackamoor to the time he left I made his house my home'; the main clause seems very artificial. **(3)** has 'Has lived with his father (being out a night or two) ...'; one can see why the shorter form was adopted.

The biggest deficiency is that the questions are not given. We do not even know whether a witness is continuing to answer an earlier question or is responding to a new one. On the other hand, we do know the general line of questioning being adopted by the two attorneys. Both normally start by asking what the witness knows about the terms under which Catton went to Blackamoor. Witnesses usually know about the cows – the rate for keeping cows was presumably a matter of wide interest; in contrast, the arrangement over the beer is something Catton seems not to have talked about. Questioning then turns to what agricultural work Catton performed for Thorold; his case is more plausible if he is shown to have been doing something for his wages in the first two years. Andrew appears not to have interviewed his witnesses beforehand: some of the answers he receives are distinctly unhelpful to Catton's case. A question to Elizabeth Catton about whether Catton smoked appears to come under this heading: from her reply, Danby would appear to have suggested that he sat around smoking. Idleness was his concern, not carcinogens.

Edward Slater is Thorold's key witness, because of a remark he claims that George Catton made to him. Andrew is no doubt keen to imply that he has been coached in what to say, but Slater declares that he was only asked about it that very morning. Andrew is keen to show him a liar, but, notwithstanding an ambiguous remark he makes on leaving court at the end of the first day, Slater sticks to his story. The evidence concludes with Slater and George Catton re-examined, both denying the truth of the other's account.

At the end of the paper are Danby's notes for his summing-up – or rather a few fragments he must have intended to weave in. His opening is given here. He then turned to points about particular items in the bills; these are not very legible, nor do they amount to more than building blocks for a speech which is not preserved, so they have been omitted.

The fact that these notes were added to a fair copy of the evidence seems to suggest that the closing speeches by the attorneys were made subsequent to the second day of the hearing. There was no requirement for witnesses to be present, so this stage probably took place in Hitchins' office in Lincoln.

The documents hitherto have been generated by Danby's office; their hand is often difficult but their orthography is fairly standard. The bills that follow seem to have been drawn up by George Catton. He writes very clearly but his spelling is largely phonetic. It is sometimes necessary to read his words aloud (and to remember his Lincolnshire accent) in order to understand the sense.

(5) is the bill presented by Catton for ale in connection with work on the Brant. Every weekday, between 31 January and 22 February 1832, a quantity varying from twenty-eight to forty-three quarts is charged. It looks as though this was one quart per banker, and the evidence of Edward Slater does indeed confirm that there were about forty men employed on the work. Nothing was charged on Sundays, presumably because no work was going on. The most likely explanation of the bill is that Thorold made a point of visiting the work every day and ordered Catton to provide a quart for each of the men. Certainly he was in the habit of calling by to see what his own labourers were up to and ordering drinks for them: there is an 'account of the men's bills to Mr Thorold as he stopped' and an item in another account for 'Muir ale as you stoped'. A variant on this is an entry from 28 September 1833: 'Sovering you gave the bankers' (presumably they were back again briefly). So while it is possible that the amounts in this bill merely represent an allowance distributed via Catton, it seems more likely, especially in view of Thorold's need for activity, that he rode down each day and exchanged at least a few words with these men, notwithstanding the fearsome reputation that bankers generally had.

(6) has been reproduced in order to set (5) in context: this bill appears as the last item. (It seems not to have been charged until May.) There is at least one other bill of comparable size for supplying bankers; the bankers' bill of £8 15s 0d is described in the evidence as a 'Private' bill. This category appears to cover ale bought by Thorold for his own labourers. He did drink there himself sometimes but such entries are clearly distinguished, not least because he usually drank porter, which was a stronger bottled beer costing 8d per pint, and was reserved for him alone (plus, occasionally, his eldest son) – unless others sometimes bought it at their own expense. So despite the enormous size of this ale bill – by way of comparison, recall that his allowance was £400 per year – there is actually no evidence that he himself drank to excess.

As for the other items in this bill, 'grass pints' appear to have been a customary allowance to drovers, more than offset by what they paid for their animals' feeding overnight. The brickmakers appear to have been there in connection with extensions to and rebuilding of Thorold's farm at Black-amoor. Finally, Spalding and Hodgson were two of Thorold's labourers accommodated at Blackamoor and given an allowance which, in the case of Spalding, included bread and tobacco.

(7) to (9) constitute the evidence on which any quantitative basis for the droving traffic must be based. (7) shows Catton just starting to gain business in 1830–1831. The crude form of the account seems to suggest the novelty of it all. The fact that just four droves were remembered – as the first, the second, etc. – seems to confirm this. The 'grass pints' in the deductions we have already encountered; the others I am unable to explain.

(8) shows business in full swing in 1834, though for some reason the account starts in June. Was there a separate account, long since settled, for the earlier part of the year, or had a late spring delayed the arrival of the first animals from Scotland? Some at least of the drovers are now old acquaintances rather than strangers and the accounting suggests an established routine.

(9) gives a full year's receipts for 1836, with a couple of miscellaneous items thrown in. Some names – Walker, Millars, Morrinson – recur after a gap of about six weeks. If one allows ten miles a day for the southbound journey, thirty miles a day for the return, and a few days for haggling at each end, that would give enough time for a journey from the great cattle fair at Falkirk to the Home Counties: these are lowland drovers. Jolley recurs in 1834 after a gap of three months, but perhaps this represents two such cycles. Carmichael appears almost at the start, both in 1834 and 1836, reappearing once after a gap of almost four months. The accounts offer tempting glimpses suggesting a trade more complex than is sometimes envisaged.

Editorial Conventions

Larger type has been used for verbatim transcriptions, distinct from the smaller type used for other text and for summary listings. Verbatim transcriptions have punctuation modernised (including apostrophes) and abbreviations may be expanded where appropriate. Capitalisation is adapted to accord more closely with modern usage. Italics are likewise the editor's. There are places where words appear to have been omitted by the writer; in such cases suggested interpolations are in square brackets accompanied, where there is doubt, by a question mark; square brackets are also used for occasional editorial notes within the text. Where text has been inserted later, this is placed in curly brackets – {}; but insertions which appear to be merely the rectification of clerical carelessness or the resolution of a doubtful word in a rough copy are not usually indicated. Monetary amounts are normally presented in the form £9 16s 8d. Asterisks indicate missing or illegible words.

PAPERS IN THE CASE *THOROLD* V. *CATTON*, 1830–1838

1. Draft agreement about arbitration
In the Queen's Bench
Catton v Thorold & Thorold v Catton

Both actions to be referred to the sole arbitration of {James Hitchins of the City of Lincoln, Auctioneer} by a Judge's Order,[1] the arbitration to extend to all matters whatever in dispute between the parties up to this time. Each party up to this time to pay their own costs, and all expenses attending the arbitration on both sides, as well of witnesses as otherwise to be {paid in such manner as the Arbitrator may direct such expenses to be taxed.}[2] The parties and witnesses to be examined upon oath.[3] Each party to produce any papers, accounts, books or writings in their possession or in the possession of any person over whom they have a control. The solicitor for each party mutually to deliver to each other 8 clear days previously to the time appointed by the arbitrator for entering upon the reference a full statement of the particulars of their respective clients' demands & also an admission of such claims, facts, and matters that they do not intend to dispute before the arbitrator …

2.1. Statement by Benjamin Hart Thorold
I did upon the passing of the Beer Act commence brewing as a wholesale brewer. I was asked to supply two persons in Harmston.[4] I thought that

---

[1]   By seeking a judge's order, the parties ensured that the arbitrator's award would be enforceable. The arrangement also enabled evidence to be taken under oath and witnesses to be compelled to attend.

[2]   This replaces the clause: 'Mr Thorold in case he fails to prove himself entitled to the profits of the ale sold by Catton during his residence in Mr Thorold's house at Blackamoor & also in case in addition to this that Catton proves himself to have been the yearly hired servant of Mr Thorold but that in default of Catton proving himself to have been the yearly hired servant of Mr Thorold or Mr Thorold proves that he was entitled to the profits of the ale sold by Catton at Blackamoor then all expenses attending the arbitration as well of witnesses as otherwise to be paid by Catton.'

[3]   'and their evidence to be taken down in writing and signed by them' – deleted.

[4]   William Thistlewood stated in evidence that these were James Bee and H. Catton, who

the house I held at Blackamoor was well situated for taking droves and, knowing that Mr Dalton had often been threatened with informations for selling spirituous liquors and ale,[5] I thought this house well situated for a beer licence. Mr John Catton did at that time, and formerly had, worked for me as a stonemason. He had given up that business in favour of his sons and said that he did not wish to do much so work as he had been in the habit of doing but wished to lead a rather more easy life, and, upon my giving up farming in 1829 I had at his request let him have more land in order to enable him to keep cows and other stock purchased by him at my sale.[6] I, wanting some person to live at Blackamoor, asked Mr Catton whether he would take that house and keep his cows at Blacka-moor instead of keeping them at Harmston, a man of the name of Moore being about to open a house at Waddington.[7] Catton objected to take this house stating that he should never be able to sell any ale there, it being a beer house, and he mentioned the circumstance to his wife in my pres-ence; and they were of opinion it would not answer their purpose. I then observed to them 'Why, you pay me £10 a year for your house rent here and supposing you only made £2 a year at Blackamoor by selling ale you would be that sum better than you are here, because you could work at your trade as you do now;[8] as your son Henry (who was about to open another beer house) now does, and it was my intention to have work done at Blackamoor such as building a new barn & stables and making additions to the house,[9] and I said 'It will save you the labour of walking from Harmston to Blackamoor, which you would have to do, as most of your time will be occupied at Blackamoor in making those buildings these next 12 months'. I stated I had no doubt he would make as much money by the sale of beer at Blackamoor as would pay his rent, it then of course being my intention to supply him with ale at a wholesale price. To this, he and his wife replied 'No, we never shall. There is nobody to drink any there, Sir, and as to cattle we shall never get any to agist[10] as Mr Dalton

(in view of Thorold's remark a few lines on) is presumably Henry, John's son. James Bee was a carpenter, whose beerhouse became the Joiners' Arms in what is now School Lane.

5   In other words, the previous tenant had kept it as an inn, without having a licence.

6   At Thorold's sale in March 1829, Catton bought eleven ewes with lambs, one cow, a dun heifer and calf, items of harness, 36 trays [hurdles], a tumbrel and a pig cratch, spending a total of £66 11s 6d.

7   John Moore of Waddington paid rates for a beer shop and garden there in 1832.

8   There seems some confusion as to whether Catton was still working as a stonemason. Perhaps he was semi-retired.

9   He was about to start farming again and would use Blackamoor as a remote farmstead.

10   This is the normal term for taking in strangers' cattle.

is too well established with the topsmen' and at length they proposed if I would give him a guinea a week and pay his wages winter & summer he would go; but he would pay no rent but his wife should sell the ale & pay me 2 shillings per gallon for it.[11]

The next question then arose as to the cows. 'Well', I said, 'if you will not take the house, I will not let you any land.' 'But', he said, 'I must keep my cows.' 'Yes, but I will keep them for you at Blackamoor in the same manner that I have done for you and for others – I will agist them at 3s 6d per week each.' He then said 'I must have my mare kept' and he would allow her to work for me for her keep; that he would find her corn and should very seldom want to use her. These terms I agreed to and that he should go to Blackamoor, which he distinctly understood, although not reduced into writing.

So, in consequence of the Act of Parliament, I entered in the books of the Excise my intention to brew in pursuance of that act and did brew several hogsheads of ale during this time. I was taken in execution under a [writ of] *capias ad satisfaciendum*, taken to Lincoln and in consequence of there being no person to attend to the beer in my absence I was informed that most of it was spoiled. Mr Catton came to me at Harmston's[12] and stated 'Now this has happened, am I to go to Blackamoor?' I told him that I had paid the debt on which the [writ] was issued, that it was a mistake and that I should be discharged in a day or two. I believe Catton had been given to understand by other people I should be longer detained than I appeared to think but I told him he could take from the brewhouse such ale as he wanted and that if he went to Carley, who had the key,[13] he would let him have it. He then left me. He again called on me and stated he had got some ale but that it was spoiled and not fit to sell and that he had examined all the barrels which were all alike. He said that Mr Edwards[14] would sell him some good beer at a wholesale price and he would buy and pay for a barrel if I would give him leave and that he

11 2s per gallon was the full retail price. Under such an arrangement, the Cattons would have no profit in the ale.

12 John Harmston was Sheriff's Officer for the County.

13 Carley lived at the lodge to Harmston Hall, so it was probably the hall brewhouse that Thorold was using.

14 William Edwards kept the Crown on High Street in the parish of St Mary, according to Pigot's 1828–1829 Directory.

could account for it afterwards, he stating that it would be a pity now he had begun that he should not be able to supply people.

He said he was supplying my own men with their allowance and told me that he would let me have what ale they wanted and keep an account. I said 'Do so, and in making out the account against me charge me 6 pence a quart for it.' He said 'Why so, when I only give 4?' I said because then I should have nothing else to do but to look at Mr Edwards's books and see the quantity of ale he [Catton] had had and know the amount he had to account to me for, the same as I had told him I should have done had the ale come from my cellar, and he continued so to do.

I saw him several times after, he stating he and his wife had come to Lincoln for more ale and that they were selling more than he expected. I then stated I thought I should have to go to London. 'It being winter', I said, 'you cannot do anything at your trade except pulling down the old buildings. Keep things as well together as you can and get on till I get at liberty at a future time.' He lent me £60. He was to take the money for droves and pay any demands on me for rates, etc. I went to London and did not return home till the latter part of the summer. I told Catton to make certain tunnels[15] and had given the carpenter directions to make such wood work as he required. He did not work at them, I suppose, his sons afterwards sending me a bill for the same works.

I pulled down a barn which I intended him to rebuild and gave him directions to do the same. Nothing was done, and then the bankers came. I urged him to go on with the building but he stated the whole of his time was occupied in attending upon the bankers who came to his house, and his wife and daughter said it was not safe for two beer women to be left with such a set of men as the bankers were, having the money, ale, and other things to look after. I told him 'Certainly you are doing so much business here and the profits of the ale will amply pay me for your wages; and whilst you are earning money for me I do not mind what it is at.' Consequently he abandoned all other work to wait on those men. I often was there and particularly when John Catton went down the banks with the ale to the men, which he frequently did. {There were generally some bankers at the house. Once Catton said he wished I would allow him something for fire and candle as the bankers had him there all the last

---

[15] i.e., culverts.

night and had burnt more than a pound of candles and had kept up two fires. I told him I would [not] as I gave him 1 guinea a week and had let him off working. He then told the bankers 'Now boys, drink what you want and go home, for I shall not keep my house later than 10 o'clock for I haven't fire and candle and have no profit in the ale. I have often heard him say the same thing.}[16]

In the year 1832, after they [the bankers] left, I again urged him to work at his trade. He then said he would be d_d if he would, for he was getting an old man and his boys were getting up and they might work as he had done before them, and he said 'I have money enough in your hands to maintain me as long as I live in the way I wish to live, and if it should run out I do not think you would let the poor old man that has worked so long for you ever to want'. I said 'No, I would not, and, to prevent that, if you like to sink the money due to you on your notes I will grant you an annuity as long as you live equal to the value. But if you refuse to work I will not go on giving you wages'.

This was in the early part of 1832. He did not work in 1832 and I said 'I shall stop your wages but your cows shall be kept as usual'. No final arrangement was then made but in the beginning of 1833[17] Mr Catton, to the best of my belief George Catton too, came up to me and brought their bills and their books to be settled and at that time they brought their notes and a stamp for their receipt of rent and there as I set down each item of their demand against me I endorsed on the back of their bills that their interest was then settled to a certain day, as appears by the endorsement, and requested them to be put to one side. I took all the items on his credit side, some of which had become due previous to his going to Blackamoor. I added the same together. I then charged him with the cow keeping for one year, all things making together £37 16s 4½d and showed it to Catton. He said 'Take off another year's cow keeping and it will be my wages.' I did so and took the sum remaining (£10 12s 4½d)[18] from the amount demanded by Catton, leaving £115 10s 11d. I then said to him 'Now let me look at the accounts of the ale sold, because I have to place

---

[16] This is a key piece of evidence because it corroborates Slater's statement. However, Thorold does not say that he was present when the words were uttered. It would be useful to know whether the words were added before the morning of 21 August 1838 because that is the earliest Thorold should have been aware of Slater's evidence.

[17] George Catton says about June 1833.

[18] If 52 weeks × 10s 6d is to be deducted, the result is too large by 2s.

the profits of that to my credit.' He said 'I have not got any accounts: that was between Alice [his wife] and you'. I said 'You must get such account before we can settle and then come again. He then said he had got a note stamp with him and I might as well give him a note for £115 10s 9d and we could settle the ale profits another time. Mr Harmston then just arrived. I said to Catton 'I shall certainly give you no note at present because the profits of the ale would amount to more than that demand but when I got the account I would pay off the £60 note that was given at Harmston's by him and myself and would give a fresh note for the balance under my own hand. At that time, he left his ale bills, took his books, and left my house.

Some time after, I asked Alice for the account and she replied she had not kept any. I said 'It does not signify: I can get it from Mr Edwards and Mr Winn.' I applied to Edwards who said he kept no such account. I went to Mr Winn who said he knew nothing about it but I have now discovered that I applied to the wrong person.[19] At this stage the matter rested till 1836.

Mr Catton acquainted me that his licence would not be renewed because he did not rent his house as it was necessary that his rent should be £10 per year and to pay the rates to entitle him to a licence. I told him I would go down to him, look at the house and premises, and settle which I would let him and which I would retain: 'This will bring you to the position in which I first proposed you should be placed.' I went down accordingly and agreed that he was to have the house and a paddock at the back, the use of (but not the whole) stable as I kept my own horses there,[20] the yard. He said 'This will be dear at £10 per annum' and a piece of land was added for him to grow potatoes on (in the half-moon)[21] and he said 'I have set potatoes in two pieces of ground in the nursery where the trees which came from Newark have died. Let me keep these [too] in the bargain.' I afterwards went with him to Mr Fieldsend[22] believing him to be parish

---

[19]   Pigot's 1830 Directory lists two Lincoln brewers of that name: John Winn on Waterside, and Frederick & Charles Winn in Broadgate. Catton got his beer from the former; Thorold presumably went to the latter.

[20]   Other witnesses explained that Thorold kept two horses and a labourer (Codd) there for farm work, or did Thorold mean he kept his coach horses there at this date?

[21]   A marginal sketch indicates that the land between the old line of Blackamoor causeway and the new road is meant.

[22]   Lucius Fieldsend of Aubourn, farmer.

officer. He referred us to Mr Houghton,[23] to both of whom I stated I had so let the land to Catton in his presence, which he [Catton] did not deny, at £10, and that I had also let certain lands to Raby and Ward.[24] I afterwards attended the magistrates at Lincoln on a summons for the payment of the rate and there stated the same thing and appeared to take my oath of the correctness of the fact but I do not remember whether it was done or not. Catton's name was inserted in the rate, which he paid.

It was expressly stated at the time of making this bargain that the cows were to be kept as usual and that the heifer beasts and horses which Mr Catton had should also be paid for and that he was to have the privilege of agisting droves of cattle on my land and he had also leave to sell the hay grown in Sandgate Field to droves of cattle to be consumed on any of my premises. I afterwards directed my servants to plough up some of the lands at Blackamoor and sow them with corn. Mr Catton hindered them from so doing stating he had a right to put the beasts upon the ground. I had several times threatened to discharge Codd[25] for not obeying my orders, he having horses of mine that were to be so employed; but I never instructed him to employ Catton's horse for cultivating my land, for when I had wanted to use Catton's horse he told me it should not work for me as it had enough to do to fetch his ale and carry George and himself to meet the droves (she being kept by Catton to feed).

In consequence of this conduct, his not allowing me to plough, I sent him a notice to quit,[26] telling him I would put up with it no longer. He directed Mr Wilkinson[27] to write to me demanding payment of his notes, which he did, and in consequence of my telling Mr Wilkinson that I had larger sets off, it was agreed that Mr Moore[28] should make the accounts and ascertain what the balance was and to whom due. Mr Moore proceeded to make out such accounts and put all subtractions to Mr Catton after several sums due to him which he showed to me and asked whether they were correct, together with the statements Mr Catton had made. I told him I would look at them and he left them with me. I then discovered in looking over

---

23 Richard Houghton of Aubourn, farmer.
24 George Rabey, labourer, and Joseph Ward of Harmston, carrier.
25 James Codd, a labourer employed by Thorold.
26 Catton's own evidence suggests he left in November 1836, but Thorold says Lady Day 1837. A bill for ale in 1837 is marked 'supplied from Bassingham'.
27 Presumably John Wilkinson of Lincoln, attorney.
28 R. C. Moore of Harmston, schoolmaster (see below).

them that £54 12s was charged in Thistlewood's account[29] and, finding it impossible to obtain the account of the ale sold by Catton, which he did not attempt to deny I was entitled to in the presence of Mr Moore, I furnished him with the particulars amended to enable Mr Moore equitably to strike a balance; but which he never did and Mr Wilkinson had instructions to issue a writ, which he did, and sent to me, and showed me the writ at his house, and said he had not served it.[30] I told him to send it to Mr Williams[31] as I should give him instructions to resist it, but if he and Mr Williams could settle it without the expense of an action they were to do so. These gentlemen met and Mr Wilkinson, seeing no prospect of success, abandoned the proceedings, generally, to speak as to accounts.

John Catton
Various potential questions, including:
What took place at Harmston's?[32]

Alice Catton
As to fire, candle, etc.
Warn her as to the solemnity of the oath.

2.2. Statements by John Catton and family

Mr Wm Thistlewood[33]
Has been married 10 yrs last 5th September. Have lived at Harmston ever since and, although we were intimately connected I never heard Catton say he was selling ale for Mr Thorold. George Catton has fetched in ale from Mr Winn's, sent the money and he paid for it: Mr Winn would not

---

[29] This refers to a bill headed 'Account of things in Thistlewood's House' and is the sum due to him for fixtures and fittings and for farming stock left for the succeeding tenant. The largest item is £15 for hay.

[30] Obtaining a writ in order to get a recalcitrant person to act by the threat of legal proceedings was common practice.

[31] Mr Williams collected Thorold's rents.

[32] Catton's statement below gives a reasonably detailed account of what took place at Harmston's. The question is unlikely to have been formulated in response to Catton's statement and must therefore have been written down in advance. The same point could be made of some of the other questions for Catton. Likewise, the 'fire & candle' question to Alice reflects Thorold's statement, not Alice's.

[33] William Thistlewood married Susanna Catton (who appears to have been Catton's daughter) at Harmston on 5 September 1826. From 1833 he was licensee of the Thorold Arms there.

sell it to him.[34] Was in Mr Thorold's service when he commenced brewing. Mr Thorold said he was going to send the ale he brewed to James Bee's, J. Catton's & H. Catton, and a deal further, made no distinction between the statements of the sending the ale to Bee, H. Catton & John Catton. Newing was mowed(?) twice.

Alice Catton

Remembers going to Blackamoor. Began to sell ale 2 months after we went; sold it in my husband's name; got the ale of Mr Winn. I went more there [than] anyone else; I made no terms with Mr Thorold for the sale of the ale. I never made any afterwards with him. He never asked me about the profits of the ale; never asked the quantity I had from Lincoln. He did not object to my charging him 6d for what he had himself. I remember Mr Thorold often coming to my house when the bankers were there. I have seen him in every room. I remember nothing taking place in any of the rooms nor yet any conversation. I never heard my husband ask Mr T. for money in our own house. I never said & heard my husband say 'Will you help me to a little money?' I never heard him ask for a particular sum. I do not remember any conversation taking place in a bedroom with Mr T. I do not remember my husband pressing Mr Thorold for any balance. My husband once told me he was going to Mr Thorold for a note for an addment that Mr T. had promised to pay him before. Mr Thorold never promised my husband to pay it. I never heard my husband say or yet Mr Thorold say that I was selling ale for Mr T's profit. I never said so, & I never thought so. I never had such a thing in my head. I always considered I was selling beer for my own profit. I had the trouble of it; my husband never asked me for a halfpenny of the ale money. If my husband wanted money I gave it to him.

I had cows.[35]

John Catton

I remember going to Blackamoor in 1830. Mr T. came to my house at Harmston. I had worked for Mr Thorold ever since he has been in the town. He asked me whether I would be his servant and go & live at Blackamoor. He came several times and wanted me to attend the droves. When we made the bargain after he had been 4 or 5 times he said 'I have

---

34 Has 'on credit' perhaps been omitted?
35 Presumably whoever was recording this considered Mrs Catton's recollections of her cows not worth noting down.

made up my mind now as to what I shall give you'. He said he should give me a guinea a week and he should charge me half a guinea a week for cows keeping & the mare he said would addle[36] her living. Nothing was said about the rent. I thought I was to live rent free and I agreed to those terms. He said he would sell me ale at 1s a gallon & he said I was to make what I could of it. Mr T. had these beasts; I was to look after the beasts and do masoning work when I was set on. I did so; and when I was not fully employed I helped to shear and get hay. I did other farming(?) work: I mowed 16 acres of rubbish;[37] in twitching time I helped to gather twitch and clean it for turnips. I never ploughed; I have harrowed. She was always [p.5] at their work same as their own.[38] They could fetch her & do as they liked with her. When my year was up I went to Mr Thorold who was at Mr Harmston's. I knocked at the door and saw Mr T; he said 'Well, Jack, what do you want me for?' I said 'My year is out'. Mr Thorold then said 'You may stop on as usual another year' and I did so & worked as usual. The profits of ale were never mentioned at any time, I will positively swear. The whole trouble of the ale rested with her. I went to Mr Thorold at the end of the first 2 years. I went to have a settlement. The profits of the ale were never mentioned. Mr Thorold never mentioned the profits of ale to me till at Mr Williams's office. Mr Thorold promised to pay me the balance in 1833. My son George made the account and Mr T. then admitted there [p.6] was a balance of £115 10s 5d and Mr T. then never claimed the ale. Mr T. promised to pay the balance the 20th April after the balance had been struck. He did not pay it then. I applied to him and he put me off till the 25th. I went up and he, Mr T., said the lawyers were such d__d engines;[39] that he was going to take up £3 or £4000 and he had only got £400, therefore he could not pay me but would allow me use[40] for the money till it was settled. I think we once called him upstairs and he promised again to pay use. I only lent Mr T. £60 in cash. At the end of 2nd year in November 1832 I went again to Mr Thorold & he pulled my 10s 6d standing wages off & he was to keep me 3 cows for nothing & my house rent free. I was to meet the Scotch droves [p.7] and take them in and look after his stock both winter & summer. The mare was to earn her own living. I had only two agreements from the 1st year to my leaving there.

---

36 *earn.*
37 Weeds grown (or allowed to grow) for pasture or hay.
38 'She' presumably refers to Catton's mare rather than his wife.
39 i.e., *snare* or *wile.*
40 *interest.*

I lost my licence because I was not rated. To enable me to get my house again I did not take my house for £10/year.[41] Mr T. said I must be rated in Mr Houghton's book and pay 4s a year. During the last four years I made no agreement. There has been no subsequent agreement as to the cows or mare. The bankers were there about 3 months having ale at Blackamoor. Mr Thorold paid me the money.[42] I never received any money of anyone. I have never refused to work for Mr Thorold. I considered myself Mr Thorold's servant 6 years. I never received the agistment money. I often paid it to Mr Thorold.[43] I took it up as I got it. The [p.8] price varied. I always looked after the beasts in the day time. I believe the sum admitted to be due for agistment is all I owe. The time I first pressed Mr Thorold was when Mr Moore was engaged to make out accounts.

I went to him a many times. I went three or four days together. I saw him on the 4th day and watched him into the privy and I waited till he came out & he said he could advance me no money. I might get what I could of Mr Moore and he would pay me the remainder. I asked for leave to sell the hay. I have laid money down for Mr Thorold before I have had it in hand. I never repaid myself.

3. Brief
In the Queen's Bench
Between John Catton, Plaintiff, and Benj: Hart Thorold Esq, Defendant, and
Between Benj: Hart Thorold Esq, Plaintiff, and John Catton, Defendant.

In the matter of an Arbitration by the order of Lord Denman.

Brief for Benjamin Hart Thorold Esq

---

[41] Has a spurious 'not' crept in, or was Catton claiming that he was to pay rates but not rent?

[42] Was the question 'How were your wages paid?'

[43] This is unclear. He certainly *received* agistment money due to Thorold; he did not always pay it to Thorold immediately, which is the reason for accounts **7**, **8** and **9**. Perhaps he meant that he often paid Thorold immediately rather than adding it to the account.

For Mr Hitchins the Arbitrator

Danby, Lincoln.

Recto
ff.1–3.
Marginal note: Tuesday, Old Crown, 10 o'clock.
Copy of order by Lord Denman referring action to arbitration by James Hitchins of Lincoln, auctioneer on or before 20 August, *inst.* Witnesses to be examined upon oath if Arbitrator shall think fit. Costs since 14 July last to be apportioned by Arbitrator. Solicitors to each party to deliver to each other eight days prior to hearing particulars of their clients' demands, an admission of matters they do not intend to dispute, and a statement of matters they do intend to dispute. Neither party to bring proceedings in Equity against arbitrator or each other concerning matters referred. Dated 10 August 1836.[44]

ff.3–4. Copy of Notice delivered by Mr [William] Andrew, solicitor for John Catton. He will dispute all monetary claims by Thorold except those in the accompanying admissions. Dated 8 August 1838.

ff.4–5. Admissions by Mr Andrew:

For 5½[45] years' rent of a Close at £16 per year up to Lady Day 1838	£88
(from this must be deducted any levy under a distress entered by Thorold 2 June last)	
Money received by Catton for agistment and not paid or accounted for	£23 5s 10d
For a parcel of oats	£5
For some pigs	£2 12s 0d
Total	**£118 17s 10d**

Dated 8 August 1838.

ff.5–7. Copy of Notice by Mr Andrew of Catton's demands against Thorold:

1829, Feb 1. Promissory Note of Hand		£80
Interest at 5%, 1 Feb 1833 to 21 August 1838		£22 4s 3d
1830, Dec 24. Promissory Note of Hand	£60	
Interest at 5%, 24 Dec 1832 to 21 Aug 1838[46]	£16 19s 5d	
1837, 27 Dec. less sum received on account	£44	
		£32 19s 5d

---

[44] The year should have read 1838, and a second order was issued to correct it.
[45] The ½ is an addition and the monetary amount has been altered accordingly.
[46] Danby queries the charging of full interest when a partial repayment is admitted.

Balance of account due to Catton, agreed 10 Jan 1833	£115	10s	9d
Interest at 5%, 10 Jan 1833 to 21 Aug 1838	£22	8s	0d
1832. 4 tons hay at £3 per ton[47]	£12		
1833. 1 ton hay	£4		
1834. 4 quarters oats	£4	10s	0d
Sep 19. Brickmakers Bill (Londoners)	£1	7s	1d
59 Quarts of ale when lean-to was building at Blackamoor	£1	4s	7d
Laths and tiles	£2	12s	6d
Pantile laths		9s	6d
No. 1 Ale Bill	£8	13s	2½d
No. 2 Ale Bill	£6	1s	4½d
No. 3 Ale Bill	£3	17s	11d
Ale Bill for 1835	£12	10s	8d
Ale Bill since April 1836 to this time	£24	11s	9½d

For cash paid on Mr Thorold's account

To different people for work	£28	10s	4½d			
Paid Thomas Edwards		3s	2d			
Paid Richard Sutton	£1	2s	7½d			
For harrows purchased at Newby's sale	£2	7s	0d			
Paid John Longmate		4s	4d			
Paid different people as per acct	£41	2s	3½d			
Sub-total				£73	9s	9½d
Interest on this sum at 5%, 6 Apr 1836 to 21 August 1838				£8	14s	6d
Total				**£447**	**5s**	**4d**

Dated 8 August 1838.

f.7. Copy of Notice by Danby that he will dispute all these items, dated 11 August 1838.

ff.8–9. Copy of Notice by Danby of sums claimed by Thorold:

Mich 1830 to Mich 1837, rent of House, Field, and keep of cows, horses etc	£443	2s	0d
Lady Day 1837 to LD 1838, rent of a field[48]	£16		
Ditto, LD 1838 to 6 August 1838	£3	6s	8d
Cash for agistment received by Catton and not accounted for	£60	6s	0d
Pigs, oats, etc, sold by Thorold to Catton	£50	4s	0d[49]
Profits from sale of ale which, by agreement, was to be accounted for and paid	£500		
Total	**£1074**	**18s**	**8d**

---

[47] Marginal note indicates this and the following items are contested.
[48] This and the following item are struck through.
[49] Struck through and altered to £7 12s 0d.

Dated 11 August 1838.

f.9. Copy of notice of further claim by Thorold of £100 as compensation for Catton not managing a certain close in a husbandlike manner and contrary to the custom of the Country by disposing of the hay grown thereon and not consuming the same on the premises. Dated 13 August 1838.[50]

Case

Mr Catton on the 11th November 1830 went to live at a house in the parish of Aubourn called Blackamoor's Head, the property of Mr Thorold. The original agreement between the parties up to the 10th January 1833 (when a fresh agreement was entered into) was that Mr Catton should receive 1 guinea a week wages, should pay Mr Thorold 10s 6d per week for three cows' keeping and that he should also pay for the keep of a horse and that Mr Catton should pay Mr Thorold the profits of the ale sold at Blackamoor.

The next agreement which was entered into between the [f. 10] parties in January 1833 was that Mr Catton should no longer be servant to Mr Thorold, consequently have no wages, that he was to pay Mr Thorold 10s 6d per week for three cows' keeping, £16 per year for the occupation of a close; and that a horse was to be kept by Mr Catton on Mr Thorold's land without his paying for the same on condition of Mr Catton allowing it to be occasionally used by Mr Thorold when he required it. And Mr Catton was also to pay £10 a year for the rent of the house. Mr Catton was also allowed the privilege of taking in droves of cattle and agisting the same in a field of Mr Thorold adjoining the inn, he promising to render an account to Mr Thorold of the sums so received by him; this was a great benefit to Mr Catton as it was an inducement for the men attending such droves to go to Mr Catton's house. The terms of this agreement remained unaltered up to the time of Mr Catton leaving Blackamoor's Head at Lady Day 1837.

In the month of May last, Mr Catton caused an action to be brought against Mr Thorold for a large sum of money which as stated by his attorney consisted [? not only] of money but accounts stated and several other items (amongst which was a sum for compound interest).

---

[50] Note that this is later than specified by the order, but that Mr Andrews is not objecting on this ground.

Mr Thorold caused a cross-action to be brought for the several sums due to him under the agreements hereinafter set forth.

At this stage of the proceedings, Mr Thorold's attorney proposed to Mr Catton's that both actions be referred to arbitration, which was ultimately agreed to, and that object was ultimately accomplished by the order of Lord Denman as hereinabove shown.

Observations

The objections raised to Mr Thorold's demands on behalf of Mr Catton I understand originate from the case which Mr Andrew wishes to establish of Mr Catton [f. 11] always acting as the hired servant of Mr Thorold; which he contends was a sufficient return to that gentleman for the rent etc. now demanded by him; the witnesses that will be produced on behalf of Mr Thorold will not only swear that Mr Catton never worked; but also that they have heard him admit that he paid 10s 6d per week for the keep of his cows and also that he was tenant at Mr Thorold of the house; and their testimony is of such a nature as to entirely defeat all the demands and claims now produced by Mr Catton.

Proofs

John Ruston of Harmston, carpenter

Remembers Mr Catton going to Blackamoor in 1830 and his leaving at Lady Day 1837, was frequently in the habit of calling at Mr Catton's house and has heard him often state that during the first two years of his residence there he was to have wages of 1 guinea a week and was to pay 10s 6d per week for his cows' keeping; after the expiration of the first two years he has heard Mr Catton also state that he was to pay the same price for his cows' keeping and that his horse was to be kept by Mr Thorold on condition that it worked for him occasionally (but which Mr Catton refused to allow it to do) {& Catton to have no wages. Remembers Mr Thorold requiring him to build tunnels but he declined so doing. During the first two years remembers Catton's time being entirely employed in serving the Bankers with ale; and never knew him work at anything else.} During the last four years of Mr Catton's residence at Blackamoor he never worked except to assist a few times during the summer to unload a waggon of hay, which other idle people are frequently in the habit of doing merely for a quart of ale; but never saw him do anything during the winter season; he was sometimes in the habit of riding to meet drivers of cattle travelling on that road, which were adgisted on Mr Thorold's land, but any person keeping a public house would act exactly the same, although the profits of the adgistment were paid to another, in order to insure the custom at his house of the men attending such cattle. Has never had the circumstances of the dispute between the parties mentioned to him by Mr Thorold or any one on his behalf previous to my attending him on Tuesday last. {Never knew Mr Catton to act as foreman.}

[f.12]

George Puttergill of Harmston, labourer
Will prove the same facts. And also that he has heard heard Mr Catton during the last 4 years of his residence at Blackamoor state that he paid rent for the house to Mr Thorold.

Richard Sibsey of Harmston, labourer
Will prove the same facts as Mr Puttergill {and that a person was sent to attend Mr T's cattle when any was sent to Blackamoor}.

George Raby of Aubourn, farmer
Will prove the same. {Has heard him state he paid his wife for the ale he drank.}

Richard Houghton of Aubourn, farmer
In 1833 he was Overseer of the Poor of that parish and summoned Mr Thorold before the Magistrates for not paying the rates for the Blackamoor's Head Inn and other premises adjoining as he had been in the habit of doing during the first two years of Mr Catton's residence there (which was the time he acted as servant) to which Mr Thorold replied that he had let the premises to tenenants[51], consequently they were the persons that must be looked to for payment of the rates; this [the] witness communicated to Mr Catton [and] assessed the Blackamoor's Head Inn in his name, to which he made no objection, and paid the rate. Once witness asked Mr Catton to pay Mr Thorold's (in order to save witness the trouble of going to Harmston) which he refused, saying he would only pay his own.
Witness was also Collector of Taxes for that parish & states that, the Land Tax chargeable on Mr Thorold's lands being in arrear, he distrained for the same and took under his levy some cows which happened to be those of Mr Catton's adgisted on Mr Thorold's land, on which Mr Catton went to witness and stated that he ought not to have levied the tax on his cattle

---

51   *Sic.* The clerk perhaps started writing 'tenements' and changed it to 'tenants'.

for they were adgisted with Mr Thorold and he (Mr Catton) paid 10s 6d per week for them. Witness never knew Catton work for Mr Thorold.

Joseph Dalton of Auborn, farmer
Remembers Mr Catton going to the Blackamoor's Head. Never knew him work the latter part of the time of his tenancy and must have seen him had he been in the habit of so doing. [f.13] Also remembers Mr Catton taking in cattle to adgist on Mr Thorold's land. Once heard a topsman say that Mr Catton took in a large number of beast for him to adgist on Mr Thorold's lands on condition of the topsman drinking 2 bottles of Gin at the house; and also heard people say he would take them almost at any price; which he supposes was done without any regard to Mr Thorold's interest (viz the profits of the adgistment) and only with an intention to get the men to spend an additional sum in drink of which Mr Catton reaped the profits the last four years.
If Blackamoor were to let, witness would consider £10 a year a low rent. Remembers Mr Catton keeping cows – from 3 to 5.

Mr John Harrison of Harmston, farmer
Was in the habit of visiting the Blackamoor's Head Inn during Mr Catton's residence there, and he never knew him work. Has heard him state that during the last 4 years of his residence that he paid Mr Thorold 3s 6d apiece for the adgistment of his cows and also that he had taken the house of Mr Thorold. Has often bought ale there on credit at 5d per quart and other people did the same. {[Catton] has adgisted the cattle of drivers in Mr Harrison's land & paid the sum him as he obtained from the drivers.} It is quite contrary to the custom of the country to sell hay off the premises which he remembers Mr Catton doing without the consent of his Landlord.

Mr R. C. Moore of Harmston, schoolmaster
Was employed as agent to make out the accounts between Mr Thorold and Mr Catton and on that occasion had some conversation with Mr Thorold on the subject of the agreement between the parties during the first two years' residence of Mr Catton at Blackamoor when Mr Thorold stated it was the agreement that he should have the profits of the ale sold by Mr Catton. This, witness communicated to Mr Catton and it was not denied. Mr Catton has also stated to Mr Moore that Mr Thorold kept[52] his

---

[52] Meaning he provided its 'keeping' or grazing.

horse for the occasional use of it. Mr Moore never remembers the horse being used by Mr Thorold. On the Blackamoor being first opened as an Inn, Mr Moore remembers Mr Thorold instructing him to get him cards printed advertising that circumstance. This [f.14] Mr Moore did, and paid for them, and was afterwards repaid by Mr Thorold.

If the house at Blackamoor were to let, Mr Moore would consider £10 per annum a low rent.

Mr Joseph Emmerson of Harmston, servant
Once, on going to Blackamoor, heard Mr Catton state that he was Mr Thorold's master.[53]

Mr Lucius Fieldsend of Aubourn, farmer
Remembers Mr Catton living at Blackamoor and never during his residence there knew him to work.

Was frequently in the habit of buying ale and never paid more than 5d per quart and has known other persons pay the same price.

Sometimes has known Mr Catton go to meet droves of cattle which were agisted on Mr Thorold's land but which was no more than other people keeping a public house would have done, in order to insure the custom of the drivers at his Inn. And Mr Fieldsend has had people apply to him for the same privilege as allowed by Mr Thorold to Mr Catton for the benefit they might reap in entertaining the men attending the cattle.[54]

{What horses has Mr Catton kept? Prove when Brant cut & whether Slater there.}

William Elkington of Harmston, labourer
Worked for Mr Thorold at Blackamoor's Head & never considered Mr Catton foreman to Mr Thorold nor yet his servant. Has known Catton agist droves of cattle on his own land.

Joseph Ward of Harmston, carrier
Remembers Catton living at Blackamoor in 1832. Was frequently in the habit of visiting his house. Has taken droves into his field for Mr Catton

---

[53] This is an odd statement and quite different from Emerson's actual testimony. There, Emerson uses the word 'master' so much that one can only assume Danby gained quite the wrong impression from his initial interview.
[54] From this it would appear that the droves accommodated by Catton were only a proportion of those stopping in Aubourn.

at the same price that Catton charged the drivers. Has given him the privilege of gaing(?) to name the money himself. Never charged any thing for providing him with the droves. Mr Thorold had a man there for the purpose of looking after the appurtinences(?) and doing any thing that was necessary. Mr Catton once [f.15, unnumbered] refused to give possession of a field to witness from an idea that it was depriving him of part of the land that he found so accommodating to the droves. Remembers Mr Catton {in 1835} having 2 horses (one a brown one and one a gray one) which Mr C. lent to witness; the gray one was afterwards sold to witness by Mr Thistlewood; the bargain on the horses being lent to witness was that Mr Catton should have half of his earnings. Remembers his having a colt which was afterwards sold by him to Mr L. Fieldsend.

Edward Slater of Harmston, labourer
Worked as a banker at the Brant & Witham Drainage. Catton was in the habit of bringing the ale. Has heard Catton state in the house before many persons that the ale was no profit to him for he was selling for Mr Thorold. Has also heard George & William C. say the same.

Mr Moore would believe Slater on oath & believe him as soon as he would George Catton. …

4. Summary of evidence
f.1
Robert Coddington Moore
A Bill[55] of £80 bearing date February 1st 1829 admitted by Mr Thorold, also a Bill for £60 bearing date December 24th 1830 endorsed with a receipt of £44 on the 27th December 1837 – 'J. Catton'.
Admits the account produced to have been made out by him in the Spring of 1836, a copy I delivered to Mr Thorold.[56] I recollect reading the same over to Mr Thorold at Harmston at his own house. John Catton was present and also George Catton. Mr Thorold asked me if I had examined the bills which I said were ready for him. He disputed the £115 10s, the balance and the interest upon the balance, the ground of his objection being that the statement was only on one side. The book from which I made the account is that now produced, and the figures

---

[55] i.e., a bill of hand or promissory note.
[56] A second copy was for Catton, according to the summary on the reverse of Document 3.

Amount	£126 2s 1½d
[less]	£10 12s 4½d
Remains	£115 10s 9d

'January 10th 1833' are the words and figures of Mr Thorold. Mr Thorold had stated his objection to be that he had a set-off to the balance. The interest he objected to because he was entitled to interest upon his set-off. The items stated in the account I gathered from some papers. To some [of] these were receipts. These items I believe to be correct and Mr Thorold asked me whether I had examined the bills. I stated I had, and he was satisfied. I believe Mr Catton was authorised by Mr Thorold to pay laborers' wages and I believe he did so. I am not aware at the time of reading over the account that Mr Thorold made any objection to the items 1, 2, 3 so stated in the account for ale. Afterwards he objected to the period being charged 6d[57] unless he was allowed the profit, which he was entitled to from his original contract, which, he contended, was that John Catton should sell the ale and he was to have the profits. What I understood by the *original contract* was when John Catton went to live at Blackamoor, which was 1830. The time Mr Thorold raised his objection to the ale account was at the second interview with him in company with John Catton. Catton said that was the original contract that Mr Thorold was to supply him with ale but he only supposed [supplied?] one barrel and that was small beer. I began to make out an account of monies due to Mr Thorold by Catton but did not finish it in 1836. I got as far as the rent of Sandgate Close at about £17 – receipt produced, £16. Another account [f.2] was for monies received by Catton for agistment for droves, amounting to something more than £20. Mr Catton furnished me with the items. These were the only two items. The bill was then produced is £21 10s 6d. I stopped making out the account as Mr Thorold said Catton must furnish him with the quantity of ale sold. I, a few days afterwards, stated this to Catton. Catton stated that he kept no account nor was he required to do as Catton had to buy ale at other places.

I paid over to Catton in December 1837 £300 but Mr Thorold did not know, as I believe, that I had paid it; it was Mrs Thorold's[58] money. I was instructed by her to pay the money as I had informed her there were notes out. These I was to pay but not meddle with other accounts as I told [her]

---

[57] i.e., at 6d a quart. 5d was the usual price of beer in the later bills.
[58] Thorold's mother, Ann Eliza.

they were in dispute. I believe Mrs Thorold had never any conversation with Mr Thorold. Mr Williams was Mr Thorold's attorney. He had stated to Mrs Thorold that he could not get the rents from Catton. I do not recollect any claim for £60 for agistment, but I do recollect a scrap of paper in George Catton's handwriting which was something about agistment, but there were no figures. There was no such sum as £60 – nearer to £6 than £60. My impression is that the money received for agistment from Mr Catton would be nearly expended in the payment for rates and other things for Mr Thorold. The sum of £21 10s 6d is all I recollect that was due for the agistment.[59] This was up to the Spring of 1836.

Cross-examined

I believe the remarks and figures proved to [be] in Mr Thorold's handwriting were merely a statement and not an admission of the correctness. My reason for so believing – the 1st item was in 1832 for the hay, was in the account & if correct it could not have been again brought to the 1836 settlement as the balance would have been £127 10s instead of £115 10s 9d. As far as Mr Catton's account went, I believed I had got all, but when I began with Mr Thorold's I put [it] down for the reasons before stated. I also intended to make Annual Rest.[60] Mr Thorold blew me up for paying the £300 because the money was not due and it might compel him to sue Catton to recover moneys that were due to Thorold for rent and other things. The rent was due to Mr Thorold but paid to Mr Williams. The time I was to get the ale account *from* and *up to* was not stated. One of my reasons was that the getting the rent was very simple.

[f.3]

George Catton

[Examined] by Mr Andrew[61]

I am the son of the plaintiff, am 25 years of age, have always lived with my father. I kept his books. I have furnished Mr Thorold with a copy of this bill for £24 11s 9½d and the ale has all been delivered. I recollect my father pressing Mr Thorold for the payment of £115 10s 9d, or a sum above £100, in April 1833 in the bed chamber. Bankers being below, my father and mother called Thorold up into bed room. I was present. Mr Thorold admitted the debt to be due and promised before this to pay it

---

59   This is **(9)**, which is the agistment account for the whole of 1836.
60   i.e., balance.
61   Marginal note in rough copy: 'Observe the manner in which he took the oath.'

on the 20th April, and father said it was not giving him a fair chance to get a place on the 6th April. Mr Thorold then promised to give my father a Note for the money, viz. £115 10s 9d. I know the amount by the book (before produced).[62] Mr Thorold never said anything about profits of ale at that time. Father got a Note stamp out of his desk and took it up to Mr Thorold's to get [it] signed; this was about two months afterwards. I do not think that it was ever given.

I recollect Elkington delivering the 4 tons of hay.[63] Charged £12 in 1832; it was for Mr Thorold's coach horses. I kept my father's account to 1833, & that charge for 4 tons of hay was not in the account then made out. I gave the amount to Mr Moore when he made the account out in 1836. Mr Moore did not make any remark. I have always kept an account of all the money received for agistment. There are two bills due by father: one for £19 10s, another for £21 {odd};[64] these are for moneys received by my father for agistment of beast. The £19 10s was reckoned in the £602[65] before Mr Williams but not the £21 {odd}, therefore the £21 10s 6d is still due to Mr Thorold. The £19 was taken off when Mr Moore made out the general account, and Mr Williams in my presence read over the account to Mr Thorold and he admitted it then to be correct. This was in 1836 and according to this statement Mr Williams said Mr Thorold would owe about £600. {Mr Thorold here claimed a set off of £400 & odd. See f.19.} This was said before Mr Thorold. Mr Thorold did not deny it. Mr Catton was to have some land of Mr Thorold. Mr Williams took down the names of the closes. Mr Thorold staid all night and on going the next Friday[66] Mr Williams said 'Your father has pitched upon all corn land & therefore he could not have it but the best way would be to pay it off, & [be] done with it.' Father stamped his stick and said 'Today, if you like'. Mr Williams said a sum of money like that could not be raised all at once, but if Mr Thorold has not the money I've get[67] it and it shall be paid off.

---

62   Rough copy: 'appears doubtful as to the balance'.
63   Having dealt with the £115 10s 9d, the witness must have been asked about the next substantive item on Catton's demand presented in (3), namely the 1832 bill for hay.
64   Reproduced at (8) and (9).
65   This is the £602 14s 6d which appears among the case papers consolidating Catton's bills to Thorold from 1832 to 1835 and which includes set-offs to the amount of £68 0s 6d.
66   'day' has been written and then deleted. This should probably be understood as 'next day (Friday)'. Rough copy qualifies Mr Williams's remark 'on calling again' and records that in the morning Thorold 'disclaimed so doing' in respect of the land, so it was only Thorold who stopped the night. One suspects that the offer may have been made when he was not entirely sober.
67   'got' must be intended. Rough copy: 'Mr W stating that he had the money if Mr

[f.4]

Cross-examined

I staid at home to keep my father's books. I sometimes worked for Mr Thorold in the Nursery.[68] At other times I worked at my trade, of stone mason. I delivered the account for ale to Mr Thorold; my father was with me, and he asked Mr Thorold to let him have some pigs. He said he might have some: he had two. Father asked him for some money – he asked for some upon the bill. Father had also 5 quarters of oats at 21s a quarter of Mr Thorold, the pigs each 20s. When father pressed him for payment of the £115 9s 10d, Mr Thorold did not say that he had a set off. Father did not produce the stamp at the time. The whole conversation took place in the bed room in allusion to the £115. The items in Mr Thorold's hand-writing in the book were furnished by Mr May.

Father was about to leave: that made him say it was not giving him a fair chance. Father took the stamp; I did not go with him. When my father returned, he said he had not got the Bill because Mr Harmston the Sher-iff's Officer had gone to the Farm House. Mr Thorold always received the money[69] as we got it, except the two bills, and that was the reason I did not add the books up.

I never knew a topsman being taken into my father's house & by[70] that two bottles of gin were given by the topsman, and no charge made for agistment. I will swear there never was a glass of gin sold in my father's house. I was never paid for 2 bottles of gin.

Mr Thorold did not say at the time the accounts were read over that he had any account against my father. We were short of money was the reason the two bills were not paid and had no money for ale.[71]

Re-examined

Mr Thorold, when the accounts were read, claimed for part of the profits for ale but did not say what amount.[72] The books produced are those

---

Thorold had not.'

[68] Some of the land at Blackamoor was devoted to growing trees. Whether these were to improve the plantations around the hall or for resale is never made clear.

[69] i.e., the money for agistment of droves.

[70] Word is unclear, but the meaning is 'on condition that'. This is anticipating Dalton's evidence.

[71] i.e., the reason that the receipts for agistment summarised in the two bills mentioned above were not paid directly to Thorold is that they needed the money to buy in more ale.

[72] A distinction is being made between the occasion of the accounts being read over (before Mr Williams?) and the earlier occasions when the witness asserted that Thorold did not claim the profits of the ale.

which contained the accounts of the agistment. There is nothing more owing to Mr Thorold.

[f.5]
John Ruston, Harmston, carpenter

I recollect Catton going to Blackamoor, 7 years since. I have heard him say that he was to have 1 guinea a week and pay 10s 6d a week for 3 cows – said nothing about a mare. I never heard him say what alteration in the agreement was made. The first two years Catton helped me to shear corn and to make hay – about 40 acres of hay, about 30 acres of corn. I made two centres to throw arches over a tunnell. I expected as Mr Thorold had Catton as his man that he was to do it. He did not do it. At that time the bankers were there and he attended them with beer. During the last 4 years he came and helped us to do what he liked – worked while he chose and then he went. He would come and help us a bit – he helped occasionally with stacking. I never saw him plough. If I kept a public house I should be satisfied with the droves coming to my house. I do not know how the payment is made. I have known Catton have 3 cows, 2 and 1 – these do not include steers and heifers. Thistlewood I have known to take them in for the advantage of his house.[73]

Cross-examined
I never asked Catton to come up to do work.

[f.6]
George Puttergill

I have heard Catton say that his first agreement was a guinea a week and to keep 3 cows and pay Mr Thorold 3s 6d a head. I never have heard him say that there was any alteration. I never heard him say that he paid rent.

Cross-examined
Catton has helped to shear and get hay. His mare has helped me to lead hay. I have helped Catton to do Mr Thorold's Statute Work;[74] it was about 5 years ago.

---

[73] 'Them' refers to droves. Thistlewood kept the Thorold Arms in Harmston.
[74] i.e., road maintenance.

[f.7]

Richard Houghton

I live at Auborn, am a small farmer. I occupy my own land.[75] In 1833 I was overseer of the poor. I recollect Mr Thorold's rates being in arrear for that year – I summoned him to pay – he had paid the rates before Mr Catton resided there – that he had told me to assess fresh tenants & therefore he objected to pay them. He mentioned Mr Catton as tenant. Catton was at the Magistrates' room when Mr Thorold attended to my summons & I told the magistrates that he objected to pay. Catton never told me he had taken the Blackamoor of Mr Thorold. Catton paid the rates. I asked him to pay Mr Thorold's but he refused: he should pay his own but not Mr Thorold's. I was Tax Collector for 4 years. Mr Thorold's taxes were in arrear in 1834. That was what I distrained for. I distrained 1 cow for £2 16s 7d for taxes. Mr Catton came and said he objected that I should take the cow as it was his. He swore loudly and that he paid joist[76] for it. There were one or two more cows.

I was accustomed occasionally to go by the Blackamoor's Head; I never saw Catton work. I have no land near to Mr Catton. James Codd was a laborer; he had two horses which did Mr Thorold's work. I did not consider Mr Catton as Mr Thorold's foreman. Catton had one mare. I heard him say it was his own. He lent me her once or twice. I never heard Catton say [on] what terms he kept his horse.

I have never seen the mare plough Mr Thorold's land. I have seen it fetch ale.

Cross-examined

Catton hardly ever missed Lincoln market. I never saw the mare work for Mr Thorold. I have seen Mr Catton attending on horse back riding to meet droves.

The fences were not very good and in some places there were no fences. Beasts were likely to be out. The men who bring the droves tent[77] the beast day and night – I have observed they are tented by the drover. Drovers are paid by the topsman. If any get out, the drovers will follow them. I never knew Catton go after the beast. At hay time I never saw Catton at work nor at seed time.

---

75 Grange Farm, Malborough.
76 i.e., agistment.
77 i.e., attend. 'Tent' was the normal term used for looking after beasts.

Re-examined
If it was profit, it might be for the ale, if not for the beast.

[f.8]
Joseph Dalton, farmer, Auborn
Cannot say what year John Catton went to Blackamoor.[78] I live within a mile. I was not very often passing – perhaps once or twice in the week just as my business called me. I never took any notice whether Catton was working or playing – it was no business of mine. I have several times seen him, sometimes about his business, sometimes not. I have seen him in the stack yard. I have seen him plough – I can't say within the last 2 or 3 years. I think I have seen him in the potato ground most, by the road side. I have never hear[d] him state the terms that he lived there.

He was in the habit of taking in cattle – the terms he did not know. I have heard many topsmen say that he took cattle reasonable – that is, low and cheap. I would not have taken them in at that price. I have heard some say that he has taken them in for 2s a score. I should have charged them from 5s to 7s per score. Can't say that droves ever went into anyone's ground but Mr Thorold's. I know Catton kept three cows and sometimes a heifer. Sometimes he might have had some left for agistment.[79] Catton kept one horse to ride about on. I should think I have seen Catton's horse plough. There is a good bit of difference in the charge for large beast and small beast because they want a better keep. I know the land is very good – I have none so good. If I had New Ings, for large cattle I should charge 8s and for small 3s or 3s 6d for the night. There are as ma[n]y large as small travel. I mean I should charge for large Scotch cattle 8s per score.

[f.9]
John Harrison
I reside at Harmston. I know Catton lived there some time. I very often went to the Blackamoor Head. I used never to see Catton work at all at any time. I knew that he kept cows. I heard him say he paid 3s 6d each for his cows to Mr Thorold. I heard him say he took the house and paid

---

[78] If Dalton had previously occupied the place it is odd that he should not know when he was supplanted. Perhaps the Mr Dalton that Thorold refers to as having been at Blackamoor is another member of the family. 'Blackamoor' has been inserted in place of 'Bassingham', but that has happened in numerous places in this document, as if a clerk making a fair copy did not recognise the former word and guessed at an appropriate place name.

[79] He uses *agistment* here in the strict sense of keeping animals not one's own.

rent for it – not what amount. I know him to have lived there 4 or 5 years: it was 5 years back he told me he paid 3s 6d; it was three or 4 years that he told me he paid rent for the house. I was accustomed to buy ale: he used to charge 5d per quart.

It is not customary to sell hay off the premises without the consent of the landlord. I know that Catton has sold some off. I know that Catton kept a horse – it was on Mr Thorold's land. I think I have seen it work for Mr Thorold. I cannot say I have seen it work ½ score times during the last 2 years. I have known he'd ride out to meet droves – he has put them on my land occasionally at the latter end of the year. I have known him to put them on his own land. I used to receive the money [sometimes] from the topsman and sometimes from Catton. Catton's remuneration was the profits of the ale. The house is worth £10 a year. Catton had two horses sometimes, but not long.

Cross-examined

I am a tenant of Mr Thorold. He is in the habit of coming to my house. I know Samuel Lamb of Auborn. I recollect Mr Thorold and Mr Lamb being at my house. I never heard the terms that Catton went to Blackamoor's. It was in his own house that he told me that he paid rent. I never heard from Mr Thorold or anyone else anything connected with the contract or agreement. The mare used to draw ale, coals, and occasionally do harvest work. Catton might count them out or see them so. I never heard Thorold say what Catton went to the Blackamoor Head for. I have heard Thorold call Catton 'Jack'. I never asked Mr Thorold what the bargain was between him and Catton, nor did he ever tell me, neither did Catton tell me. Lamb was at the Asylum – about 6 years since he went in – he has been out for 4 years.

[f.10]

R. C. Moore, examined by Mr Danby

I met Mr Williams in London 10 days ago. I had some conversation upon the subject of the arbitration. He said Mr Andrews had seen him and asked him to attend but he should not, for he knew nothing about it.

In 1836 when I made out the account the subject of the original agreement was introduced by me to John Catton. I took down the conversation in writing.

John says that the 1st 2 years had wages at the rate of 1 guinea per week but paid Mr Thorold 10s 6d per week for 3 cows' keeping. This was the original agreement when he first went to Blackamoor to look after the grounds[80] generally. January 10th 1833, Mr T. said 'I cannot stand the wages but I will give you the cows' and mare's keeping but not wages and your house rent-free'. When the Excise Officer refused to grant the licence,[81] Mr T. said 'Catton, you must pay the poor rates on the house' which was fixed in the parish books at £4 in Auborn and, a shilling rate being 4s, was paid to Mr Houghton.

I read this to Catton and he said it was right. I then took it to Mr Thorold and *he* said the original agreement was as follows:

House rent-free, 3 cows' keeping to be paid for and a mare, with a guinea a week wages, to work at his trade and to render an account of all ale sold and to ____ [82]

Catton entered 1830. After Mr Thorold had told me this, I saw Catton and he said that was their original agreement: he was to have the ale to sell from Mr Thorold but he only had [small?] beer. Catton also told me he went to Harmston's house when Thorold was in custody in the month of November – can't say what year – I believe it was 1830 – I believe he was there from November 1830 to January 1831– cannot positively state that the conversation took place at Harmston's. Catton said he lent Thorold £60 at Harmston's. I never knew the mare to be at work for Mr Thorold. I recollect Mr C. having a black mare which he exchanged for a bay. He had a black colt. The gray mare was at Blackamoor and also the bay mare – he had her in October 1835. I remember Mr Thorold giving him orders to get some cards printed and I asked Mr T. who was to pay for them. Mr T. said he should pay for them; it was for his benefit. I got them and charged them. George Catton fetched some and the rest were taken to Mr Thorold's. Blackamoor is worth £10 a year. Mr Catton sold ale. I remember Catton keeping 3 cows and that he was to pay 3s 6d each the first 2 years – never heard after the first 2 years what the terms were. Catton said he was paid his wages. I really cannot say whether, during the first 2 years, I ever saw him work. While he was [f.11] at the Blackamoor I never saw him work at his trade. While Catton resided there the Blacka-moor underwent repair by having a lean-to. Catton's son built it and I measured it up for him. Other property of Mr Thorold did undergo repair during the few years. Stone mason work was required. I never saw Mr Catton working at them – his son Henry worked at them and charged his labor to Mr Thorold. I made out the account – Henry Catton instructed me

---

80 The word has been changed from 'proceedings'.
81 The Beerhouse Act required that the applicant for a licence must be a householder.
82 It appears that the clerk was unable to keep up with Moore's reading of his notes and regarded the final condition as unimportant.

to make them out – the bills were so made out. I never saw him working. Mr Thorold had a laborer and two horses at the Blackamoor to plough the land and do his work.

Cross-examined
I never saw him work at his trade.
I go always once a month to the Blackamoor.

[f.12]
Joseph Emerson, groom to Mr Thorold 4 years
I went to Bassingham[83] to take some horses – Master was in London, they were by[84] Master's horses – to turn them out to grass. I saw Catton. He swore they should not go in the close but I don't know why. That was my Master and my Master's Master.[85] My master was often going out and he was very often out three months at a time.

Cross-examined
It was about 2 years ago. The horses had been diseased.

[f.13]
Lucius Fieldsend of Auborn, farmer[86]
I do remember Catton living at the Blackamoor Causeway. I was in the habit of passing by sometimes 5 or 6 times a week, & repeatedly went into the house in the forepart of the time. I have seen Mr Catton work for the first year or so. John was, like me, rather particular. During the latter part I have seen him work at twitching (never ploughing, stacking, hay making, statute work) not very often. There was a great deal of twitch in the ground. I have seen him in Mr Thorold's field.
I have bought ale frequently – have paid 5d per quart – have known other people pay the price. That was the usual price. I have bought it frequently. It made no difference: ready money or credit. I attended the Witham and Brant drainage – it is about 5 or 6 years ago. I have seen Catton on the bank. I have seen a man of the name of Edward Slater there. I have

---

[83] Probably 'Blackamoor' is meant, although 'about 2 years ago' is the time that Catton moved to Bassingham.
[84] 'my' is presumably intended.
[85] The second 'Master' has been substituted for 'father'. Thorold's father died in January 1836. So is this a reference to his *mother*?
[86] Aged about forty-six, and of farming stock, he had established a brickworks in Harmston Lowfields. He died in 1840.

known Catton go to meet droves of cattle. He used to agist them, sometimes on his own land, sometimes on Mr Thorold's. I have known them
at Harrison's and George Raby or Samuel Lamb's land. If the topsman
is not satisfied with the pasture he will get another – it lays with him. I
have seen other cattle agisted by Catton on other people's land when that
of Mr Thorold was equally good. I agisted cattle for a man of the name
of Porter who resides at Auborn & keeps a public house:[87] he paid me so
much a score, the rate that he received, his benefit being what he got from
them at the public house. I should think it answers his purpose because
he has asked me a second time. I did it as a kindness to him. Woolhouse,
the former publican,[88] did so apply. Dalton has also applied. I cannot
say positively that I ever heard Catton say on what terms he lived with
Mr Thorold. Sometimes Catton had 3 cows and a heifer and at times 2
horses and a foal – slouch-eared one I bought. I know Catton's mare to
have worked for Mr Thorold when I was bringing trees from Newark.[89]
I assisted Mr Thorold by the loan of my team. At the same time, John
Harrison did {value of} summer keep £3 10s, winter £5 10s, the year
worth £15 as Mr Catton kept.[90] I considered Mr Catton as Mr Thorold's
foreman the first year or two. The other part not so, because I heard there
was a different agreement, and after two years he did not trouble himself
much with work. Therefore I thought he was not the servant. He used to
shew the different fields. One of the drovers tent the beast night and day
where the fences are not sufficient. The custom of paying is half. I never
saw Mr Catton watch. [f.14] The drovers would not allow anyone else to
watch them. The parish objected to Mr Catton keeping the House because
he was not assessed.[91] I recollect hearing that he had ceased to sell ale; he
was afterwards assessed; he admitted his tenancy.

Cross-examined

I never saw him do statute work. Edward Slater is now in my employment. Tunnerdine[92] is the foreman. I have known Slater 5 or 6 years. I

---

[87] John Porter was licensee of the village's public house from 1837 to 1843.

[88] John Woolhouse was licensee 1827 to 1836.

[89] This will have been for the nursery that Thorold established at Blackamoor.

[90] If this means £3 10s etc. *per cow*, it adds to £9, which is almost exactly what Catton
was paying annually. So the sentence is comprehensible if '9' is substituted for '15',
though this is a curious error to have crept in.

[91] i.e., was not assessed for parish rates, because he was not the householder.

[92] Probably William Tunnadine, who by the time of the 1841 census, lived at Thorpe on
the Hill.

know nothing against the character of Slater.[93] I have heard of his being in Lincoln gaol.[94]

The land was not in high condition when Catton went there. I think it has not much improved. There was not much merit due to Catton. The slouch-eared colt was 3 years old,[95] it was in Hovel Fen and not on Mr Thorold's land, but had been on Mr Thorold's land before put on the Hovel Fen. This was since the first 2 years. I recollect Catton attending Mr Thorold's plots.[96] I knew the cattle to be rather troublesome to that land. I have seen him send a dog and bring them up. The fences in the boundry were not very good throughout, but some were very fair. Cattle would require more tenting when the fences are bad. There were two beasts went where the fences are deficient and I have known them 20 years – about 20 or 30 acres of arable, perhaps not quite so much. The farm where Catton lived was about 150 acres. That which was not arable was grass. Part was apportioned for mowing.[97] The New Ing was mown by Mr Thorold, about 38 acres – the fences are fair.

I considered Catton as foreman because he looked after the stock and other things that were on the farm. During Catton's time I have known Mr Thorold to have a good deal of stock there. I have seen a similar card to the one produced. I did consider John Catton going there was to attend to the droves.

Re-examined

Thorold's plot was occupied by Harrison, but not at the first period of Catton's going there. John Harrison has had it 4 or 5 years. Catton was attending in that plot. I have frequently seen Catton attending cattle the same as on Mr Thorold's land.[98] I never heard Mr Thorold say what was the agreement. Mrs Thorold[99] died four or five years ago, at which time

---

93 Rough copy: 'He does his work well and never heard anything against him.'

94 Rough copy add: 'for poaching [I] think. There was a gathering to get Slater out.'

95 Inserted in lieu of 'The foal I bought.'

96 Rough copy: 'Remembers Catton watching cattle in fields – Mr Thorold's plots.'

97 It had long been customary for a large part of the meadows here to be let annually. The lots were generally taken by those wanting hay for their own use. This is probably what is being referred to.

98 Marginal note: 'Attending Cattle for Harrison.'

99 This is presumably a reference to Thorold's grandmother, who, having remarried, was actually Mrs Ros, and died in 1830 at Cheltenham. What the witness was presumably recalling was the winding up of her estate, which might well have been delayed until 1833.

there was a sale, and then I[100] let the ground called Thorold's Plot to Mr Harrison.

[f.15]
Joseph Ward, Harmston, carrier

I was in the habit of going to Blackamoor – it is 5 or 6 years since, Catton has put in droves on my land – he let the Eddish for [me]. It is about 3 or 4 years ago. He never offered that anyone else should pay me. I recollect his saying I might go to the drovers. I don't know how he was paid. The men put up at his house and I expect he thought that would pay him. Mr Thorold let me a field. Mr Catton said I should not have it. It was four acres meadow. I remember Catton having 2 horses, 1 black, 1 brown. There was a grey one on the premises – it may be 3 or 4 years ago. I do not know how long he kept them. He lent me the brown horse to go and lead some planks. I said if he lent me him I would give him half what he addled.[101]

Cross-examined

I did not give him half. The bay mare he had a good long while. I bought the gray mare. I do not know how much a score.

[f.16]
Edward Slater

Laborer in the employment of Mr Tunnadine, brickmaker, of Harmston, have been employed by him 5 weeks. Before that, I worked upon the roads. Was originally a banker. I remember the Witham and Brant being opened. I worked at both. I remember Catton being at Blackamoor. I went every day between 11 and 12 o'clock. I don't exactly know the time when it[102] was cut. I worked there 5 months altogether and that was during two years. I think I have worked two months without going to another job.
There were three gangs when they first started, 1 [of] 5, 1 [of] 7, & one had 8 or 9. There were other men working who were not in gangs, employed in taking off the surface – in the whole, when the work was going on, 40. I have seen Mr Catton in the house and on the banks. He used to bring us some beer. I have been in his house and had heard Catton

---

100 This must be an error. Mrs Ros's portion would have reverted to Thorold's parents, and *they* presumably insisted on letting it to a tenant, who would pay rent, rather than to their son.
101 Dialect, meaning earned.
102 i.e., the new course of the river.

say he had no profit in the beer, was selling it for Mr Thorold. I have heard George Catton say so and the plaintiff's wife also. Catton brought us ale whenever we ordered it. I have heard him say many times the beer was no profit to him. He said so in the house when many were present, a vast [number?] of bankers.

Cross-examined

I was first asked this morning about coming here. Richard Sibsey asked me if I had heard John Catton say any thing about selling beer at Blackamoor. I said I had heard him say (what was reported). He said Mr Thorold sent him. He is one of Mr Thorold's laborers. It was four or five years back. I repeat: I heard several times. I have heard Catton let go and swear that he had no business with the beer, it was Mr Thorold's beer. I slept with George Catton and I said 'George, this is a rare job, being at Blackamoor selling beer and taking in beast'. George said it would be no good to his father, because if he did not get his wages of Mr Thorold he had no profit on the beer. I have also heard Mr Catton say so. It was when we wanted to beg the beer that Catton used to swear in this way. Catton would not give us the beer when we begged it. I used to swear when he refused it. I never took an oath before. I was not frequent in wanting to beg it. I have been before magistrates, for assault. I have slept with George several times and have always recollected what George told me. I have never mentioned the conversation to any one.

[f.17] I have been working out on the roads for Mr Moore.[103] When I left the Witham and Brant, I went to work for Mr Day,[104] a farmer at Harmston. I worked for a month. I then went to Mr Thorold's. I worked six months for him. I have lived 5½ years with Mr Thorold. I have, since I left the banking business, often been to the Blackamoor. I have never heard Mr Catton say any thing about the beer since. I have begged an odd pint[105] since. He did not swear at me but gave me it and did not charge me any thing. I have never slept with Geo Catton since. I have never heard him say anything about it since, nor Mrs Catton. I worked in a gang. I was gangsman. Robert Slater was one, Joseph Priestley, John Staple, Michael Cambers. The gangs used to go to the house together. I can't say I heard it was the gangsman's place to beg for others. Sometimes begged for

---

[103] R. C. Moore filled most of the Harmston parish offices, including that of Surveyor of the Highways.

[104] Samuel Day farmed 262 acres from what is now called Old School House in the High Street.

[105] Inserted in place of 'pot'. A pot was half a pint, so the correction may be erroneous.

them when at work. Have begged for them when they have been at the house as well as when they have been at work. He has said that he had no profits before them.

Re-examined
What I understood by Catton Junior's remark was that he had his wages for selling the beer and doing the work.

[f.18]
Richard Sibsey, laborer in the employment of Thorold
I remember Catton. Know nothing of the agreement when he first went down. I have heard Catton say that he had to pay 3s 6d each for his cows being kept – to Mr Thorold. It was four or five years ago. It was at his own house. I heard him after he had been there for some time. I never heard him make any other statement. Have heard him say that he was to have wages a guinea a week and he was to pay 3s 6d for each cow per week. That was making half a guinea a week. I have heard Catton say that he was not going to have any more wages. Mr Catton's cows were to be kept on the same terms as when he had wages. I have heard Catton say this two or three years since. I have seen Mr Catton work: he has worked along with us a piece of a day or so. He did not work as one of us. Catton was no foreman of mine: he never set me a day's work in his life. Seen Catton's horse plough for Mr Thorold a bit – two or three times. Was often in the habit of going down to Blackamoor. Have seen Thorold plough Catton's land near the house, about 1½ acre. My boy went to tent the cows that week to Blackamoor – from Mr Thorold's – a whole summer. I have heard Catton say that he was to pay rent for that house or that he could not get a licence. I heard him say he was going to pay £4, but whether for rent or taxes I don't know. I never heard any thing of this business except on Tuesday last.

Cross-examined
I know Edward Slater just when he came here. I saw him this morning at Harmston about 7 o'clock. He lives at Harmston. I asked him about this concern, whether he knew any thing about it. He said he did. He told me he heard John Catton and his wife say that they had no profit upon the beer.[106] He said this before I had 4 words with him. Slater and I did not meet; I went to him on my own head. My master told me to find out all

---

[106]   Rough copy has 'ale'. The two words appear to be regarded as synonyms.

I could. I have lived with him 7 or 8 years. I have during the time seen Catton at the Blackmoor many a time. Sometimes[107] he was helping hay making. Helped to get in a few beans.

Slater was working at the brick yard – Mr Fieldsend. I and Slater have frequently talked this matter about Catton's concerns & about selling ale. He never told me before this morning that Catton and his wife said they had no profit upon the beer. I went to him because he had been banking there.

[f.19 – headed *Catton's defense*]
George Catton
I have been present when a conversation between Mr Thorold and my father respecting taking the hay off Sandgate Close has taken place. The conversation was at Blackamoor in 1834. Father asked Mr Thorold for some money. Mr T. st[at]ed he had none at present but he should have some after a bit. Father said he had a chance to sell some hay if he would give him leave. Mr T. said if he had a chance to make a shilling he was quite welcome off his own place. He sold some hay to Thomas Towers at Lincoln. John Harrison's team took it, about 1½ ton. We have sold some to Scotch beast in our closes. The last year my father was at the Blackamoor he had but one cow [the last year],[108] the next but 2, the next before 3. He never has had more than three cows. He had a yearling heifer three months. He had a steer 6 months. He had a slouch eared colt: it was not quite 2 years old when sold. It was pastured about 6 months [on Mr T's land].[109] Father swapped the black mare for a bay one. Afterwards he had a gray one. These were both in the ground together for about 2 months.[110] From the first of my father going to Blackamoor to the time he left I made his house my home.[111] I have never heard either my father or mother or sister say at any time that Mr Thorold was entitled to the profits of the ale, but that Mr Thorold was to supply him with ale and he was to give the same as he would to other brewers. It was not till 1835[112] that I heard Mr Thorold claimed the profits of the ale. That was at Mr Williams's. I have myself presented bills to Mr Thorold several times. They were ale

---

107   Rough copy precedes this with: 'I never knew him work a whole day.'
108   From rough copy.
109   From rough copy.
110   Rough copy is more explicit: 'bay one and the gray one together 6 or 7 weeks'.
111   Rough copy has: 'Has lived with his father (being out a night or two) …'.
112   Marginal note: 'It was in 1836 & in previous examination he states Mr T made no objection.'

bills. 5d a quart was charged the last, sixpence for the first. Mr T. never objected to these bills. He has promised to pay them several times, both at Blackamoor and at his own house. We got our ale chiefly from Mr John Winn's[113] and some little from Edwards at the Crown.[114] We have given Mr Edwards 1s 9d [a] gallon, Mr John Winn 1s per gallon. My father and myself used to fetch it. My mother took the money and drew ale and so did my sister. I think my father never took 2½d in his life for ale. I made out the account in 1833[115] in which there were charges for ale: Brant £14 11s 3d, Private £17 10s 3d. When my father went to Mr Thorold's with the account he never said Mr Thorold objected to them. I was present at Mr Williams's office in 1836 when Mr Williams, my father and the squire were there. I recollect at this time Mr Thorold asked for part of the profits of the ale. My father said it was [f.20] never likely as he had nothing to do with it for he was to get the ale of Mr Thorold like other brewers. My father asked Mr Thorold whether he had ever agreed with him for the profits of the ale. Mr Thorold said 'I believe not, for it was with Ellse or Allis'.[116] I knew that my father's mare had led muck, hay, has ploughed, and harrowed. I have ridden to Drinsey Nook to fetch beast. My father can write his name.[117] I kept his books. Every farthing paid for adgistment except 2 bills.[118] We never kept any money but the two bills. It was father's duty to tend the beasts of Mr Thorold.[119] The drovers tented the drove beasts at night & barring some odd times they went the next morning. When they stopped, father did keep them off the corn. {He has had to keep other beast off Mr Thorold's corn.} I mean the beasts that trespassed. He has pinned[120] some – locked them up in a crew yard of Mr Thorold's. They were Mr[121] Houghton's that was there; we let them at liberty again. Richard Challans's were also pinned. I don't recollect any one [else?]. I know my father had paid money for Mr Thorold.

113 Marginal note: 'In page 5 Winn's acct shows it to have been got in 1837.' Pigot's Directory of 1828–1829 lists John Winn as a brewer and maltster of Waterside, Lincoln.
114 William Edwards kept the Crown on High Street in the parish of St Mary, according to Pigot's 1828–1829 Directory.
115 This is a bill for £142 10s 6d headed 'Account of Ale sold by Mr Catton to Mr Thorold'. In this bill, both the sums referred to are described as 'bankers'.
116 Presumably Catton's daughter Elizabeth or wife Alice. Rough copy has 'he believed it was with Alice (Catton's wife) from all bills to Mr Moore to make out accounts'.
117 Rough copy: 'Father cannot write, never kept books.'
118 From rough copy. Fair copy has: 'Everything has been paid but the bills.'
119 Inserted from rough copy.
120 Rough copy has 'pinded'.
121 Rough copy. Fair copy calls him *Parson* Houghton.

It was my[122] father's money and not the agistment money that he paid. He has paid some of the agistment money for mowing and other things. I never heard my father state he was to pay rent for the house but I have heard him say he was to live rent free. I have heard him say he was not to pay for the cows. I knew of a fresh agreement. I recollect our licence being discontinued because we were not assessed. I recollect Mr Thorold assisting my father to get the licence again. I recollect my father going in a gig with Mr Thorold.[123]

Cross-examined

I kept my father's books. I put down what my father told me was right. It was in 1836 at Blackamoor where Mr Thorold and my father talked about the hay taken off Sandbeck Close. I think it was there[124]– I can't swear it – off his own close. I understand what he rented. Mr Thorold had allowed my father to fodder the Scotch beast before that time. We had full authority to take down hay to any ground of Mr Thorold's and the first year the keep of four[125] cows was from hay grown upon Sandbeck Close. We had permission in 1834 to sell the hay to Scotch beasts and to take it off the premises. In 1836 was the first time we sold the hay and that was to Towers – except what Mr Thorold had. In 1830 or 1831 my father had not permission to take the hay from Sandbeck Close to Blackamoor. When we first went down my father had permission to agist beast in the Sandgate Close.

[f.21] The next spring after 1834 Scotch beast were fed by the hay from Sandbeck Close. My father's reason for asking Mr Thorold for the privilege was that he had not money to buy stock. I don't know that my father pressed him for money at that time. We ate by the Scotch beasts the rest of the hay. We mow every year and have about 8 tons. I never sold any hay to Mr Cook. I will not swear there was only 1½ ton. I did sell some to an innkeeper at Lincoln, George Rumble – Magpies[126] – one ton, the same year. I do not recollect selling more. Our bay mare & Mr Thorold's and one of Mr Fieldsend took the ton. James Codd went with us: he was Mr Thorold's man. It was my brother Henry's cart, Harrison's shelvings; the price was £4 or £4 4s 0d. Mr Thorold gave my father leave to take

---

122 Original has 'by'.
123 This was perhaps in response to the summons of 1833 that Richard Houghton mentions in his evidence, when Catton was also in the magistrates' room.
124 MS has 'the'.
125 Did he actually say 'of *our* cows'?
126 Waterside, Lincoln, according to Pigot, 1828–1829.

any horse where they were not engaged, and also a man if he pleased. He had the heifer 6 months. He had the steer 2 or 3 months. He had no more than one horse at a time. My father bought the gray mare at Newby's sale; it was a ploughing mare and it was then about 2 months. It was sold to Joseph Ward and Mrs Thorold[127] now has it. I have never been out a week. If I was out my sister put down [items in accounts?]. I never in this world knew my father to pay mother for ale when he drank it, and I never knew my mother to ask for it. Sometimes we went once a week at Lincoln for ale. Sometimes twice when the bankers were there. Never brought more than four: Catton's cellar will not hold more than 4 barrels. Mr Winn always entered the purchase of the ale in Mr Catton's name. I have seen the name of Catton written in the books; I cannot swear it was Mrs Catton. The first two years we set down the ale that was not paid for.[128] My mother took the money for the ale because she had the management of the house and the profits were applied to our living. I will swear I did not know that my mother was selling the ale for Mr Thorold and was to account to him for it. I have never heard my mother and Mr Thorold talk upon the subject. What I understood by my father's saying he had nothing to do with it because Mr Thorold was to supply him with ale. While the bankers were there my father never sold ale to the profit of £100. It was part of the profit not the price. Mr Thorold always took the mare when he wanted it.

[f.22] I have seen her plough days and days, and harrow. I have harrowed with her and James Codd has ploughed with her. Father used Mr Thorold's horses for his potato close and he blowed Codd up for letting us have them & was going to settle with him there about it: he was in one of his Rigs[129] and after that they were allright again. Mr Thorold could claim the mare when he chose. The last agisted money ever received was paid to Mr Thorold in my presence. It amounted to £2 0s 11d, being the balance of the agistment account.

Matters of Account

I will swear that this money amounting in separate items to £34 19s 0d was paid to Mr Thorold and whenever there were ale bills for laborers Mr Thorold allowed me to deduct them.

---

[127] Ward's evidence said it was sold to Thistlewood; there is possibly a transcription error here.
[128] i.e., supplied to customers on credit?
[129] Dialect for storm or tempest.

Bills for agistment	£34	19s	0d	Sibsey	£2	19s	11d
small do.	£1	19s	4d		£1	2s	10d
	£36	18s	4d	Raby		8s	6½d
(less)	£4	11s	3d		£4	11s	3d
	£32	7s	1d				

I have seen money paid to Mr Thorold between the years 1833 and 1836. I have been both with my father and mother to pay him. I never put down any beast but in that book. The drovers have paid Mr Thorold some money. I never made a statement of account without my father's sanction containing the item of 21s per week.[130]

Re-examination Geo Catton
I recollect Slater coming out of the room yesterday after he was examined. He had some conversation with me. He said the gentleman asked him things he very little though[t] on, but he might easily be got off if I said he was put in the News for a Common Liar. I replied 'That was the very thing I was going to say if you had not.' He said he did not want to speak either for one side or the other.

[f.23]
Samuel Lambe, farmer, Bassingham[131]
In 1830 or 31, I occupied a farm at Harmston. I recollect Catton leaving Harmston and going to Blackamoor. I do recollect having a conversation with Mr Thorold at Mr Gervis Harrison's at Harmston – father to Mr John Harrison [and] since dead – in the house.[132] Mr Thorold said he had bargained with Catton to go to Blackamoor; he was to give him half a guinea a week and keep 3 cows, & live rent free; & Catton was to work, I suppose, at anything there was to do at his trade, or anything else. I have heard Mr Thorold talk about this more than once. The conversation was the night after the agreement was made. He always stated the same thing. Was frequently in the habit of meeting Mr Thorold.

---

130 This item would be Catton's wages.
131 Rough copy: 'Mr Samuel Lamb, gentleman'.
132 Gervis Harrison died November 1834. The house, in Chapel Lane, is now called Longridge.

Cross-examined

From 1826 to 1831, [and] I occupied it [a]while [in] '32.[133] It was my own farm. I do not occupy it now. Thinks he heard Mr Thorold make the last statement in 1831.

I never saw Catton work at his trade: he was a stone mason. I never employed him in my life. About 3s 6d a day, stone masons are paid.

Re-examined

Never at that time Mr T. said anything about ale. I heard Mr T. afterwards talk about John going to keep the Jerry.[134] I understood Mr T. was going to supply John with ale: he was going to be a wholesale brewer. The Excise man came to Mr T's brewery. Mr T. never said anything about the profits of ale. He did not say John was going to sell ale for him.

[f.24]

William Thistlewood, publican,[135] living at Harmston

I don't know any thing of the agreement. I lived 11 years as foreman to Mr Thorold. It is 6 years since I left him. I was in his employ till 1833. I know that Catton took beast in for Mr Thorold. I have known him mason when the bankers were there, make hay, fill manure. I thought Catton was servant. I have, by Mr T's orders, told him to do some work. He has refused because Mr Thorold, he said, had told him not to do any thing. The fences were very bad. I have seen him tent the beast in the day to keep them out of the corn. It is not the usual way to put cattle near the corn. He had a black, a brown and a gray horse, a slouch eared colt, but not all at a time. He has had two at a time. I've seen Catton's horse leading hay. I never took an account of Catton's time because he received and paid the money. If a drove were to come I would take them in on consideration of the drovers' expenses, but at Blackamoor I would not. I never knew Catton to work for any one else. When droves came up, Catton engaged with them when Mr Thorold has been there and Mr T. told them to go to old Jack and agree with him. I have received the money from Catton and given it to Mrs Thorold and Mr Thorold as he sent me. Many times Catton has paid me for the cattle in advance and was to take it out of the next. When Mr Thorold has been from home I fetched the

---

133 Samuel Lambe succeeded his father at Hill Top Farm in 1826. He is still listed as owner and occupier in the 1832 Land Tax return. The land was subsequently leased to a tenant of one of the larger Thorold farms.
134 Term for a low beerhouse.
135 Licensee of The Thorold Arms, 1833–1855.

money. I got £9 one time to pay the Irishmen.[136] If Catton had not watched them[137] they would have been in Bavin's corn – and I have seen them in. The money for the agistment was applied to support Mr Thorold's family.

Cross-examined

I am son-in-law to C. I left Mr T. in 1832. Towers was not foreman. I succeeded him. I was in ¾ qtrs of a year. I was married before Catton went to Blackamoor. I left a good bit before Lady Day 1832. I paid to Mr Thorold what money I received for cattle, deducting the allowances and Grass money.[138] I never went to seek them. I did not sit up all night. I have not known him to buy nor sell horses. I don't know how long he was masoning. I have never seen him down with ale to the bankers, but I have seen him in the house. I have set men at work at Blackamoor: it was not my duty to give orders there without Mr Thorold's orders. I considered Catton was to be with the women but the hay was lead[139] by Mr Thorold. Mr Catton let the mowing. Mr T. has given me orders to let the mowing; he has ordered me twice. I brought the men to Mr Thorold [f.25] and he let the mowing. It was during the time I lived with Mr Thorold that I let it, not in the two years that Catton was there. I left Mr Thorold once and occupied land under him for 3 years,[140] and when Towers left I again went for 3 qtrs of a year, which was about May 1831. During the time I left I was one year overlooker & then Mr Catton let the mowing. Catton, as well as droves, has taken other stock in, has taken in sheep at nights. I have seen Catton's horse employed in leading and, Mr Thorold having told me that the horse was to work for his meat, I had him several times to do Mr Thorold's work. I am speaking of '32 when they were leading hay and when I left his service. I never went back. I have seen Catton's horse harrow: there were not sufficient horses to work the land; they were very mean,[141] they could not work. We were not often fixed that way. Two good horses would work it. The fences are better than they were. I have seen Catton in Lincoln. He was not often in the habit of going. I never took up the money when I left. Catton has advanced me money.

---

[136] Gangs of Irish were regularly engaged on harvesting.

[137] The cattle, presumably, rather than the Irishmen.

[138] 'Grass money' seems to have been a payment, normally taken in drink, when the drove was put out to grass.

[139] Written by mistake for 'let'?

[140] He is listed as such in the 1829 Land Tax returns. He was rated at £16 10s so the land must have been about 25 acres.

[141] 'In low spirits or health', listed by *OED* as US colloquial usage.

My wife and I lived with Mr Thorold. After Mrs Thorold's death[142] the land at Harmston was let; before that he had it in his own occupation. I was not engaged solely to look after the land at Blackamoor but to drive a carriage and look after the men and carriage horses. I will swear when I went down Catton had the management and Mr Thorold told me to go down to tell Catton to do work. Mr Thorold said to me: 'I have told Catton to stock when he likes. I have sent men down to work there and they are under my orders.'

[f.26]
Thomas Towers[143]

Lives at Barrow. I was formerly a shepherd and foreman to Mr Thorold fourteen years. I was with him [when] Catton was at Blackamoor.[144] I left the service '32, in May. I have worked with him in several little[145] jobs: helped to clear the manure out of the yard, that fronting the barn, at May day.[146] He has assisted at the thrashing machine and he has also shorne[147] with me. I do not know who attended to the cattle at Blackamoor. Catton managed them himself. I considered him a yearly man. We had no words about my taking Catton away from the beasts. I've heard him say 'Mind the cattle, Jack'. I don't know whether Catton went out for droves or knew that they were coming. I have worked with Catton at the statute work on the New Road. I never heard from Mr Thorold what the agreement was between him and Catton.

Cross-examined

Catton could not work like other men because he attended to the beast. I have often heard Mr Thorold say 'Jack, attend to the bankers'.

[f.27]
Elizabeth Catton

I recollect being on the road between Harmston & Blackamoor in company with Mr Thorold and Jas Catton; it was in the April after father and Mr

---

[142] Thorold's grandmother died 1832, but winding up her estate seems to have taken time.

[143] Rough copy adds 'coachman'.

[144] Rough copy: 'was there a part of the time Catton was at Blackamoor, one year'.

[145] From rough copy. Fair copy has 'different'.

[146] From rough copy. Fair copy has 'helped to clean manure out, fronting the barn, made hay'.

[147] Rough copy is more explicit: 'has cut corn also'.

Thorold had made the second bargain. He (father) had been at Blacka-moor more than 2 years, not 3. Mr Thorold said to father: 'Now, Catton, remember you have your cows kept as usual, your house rent free, but you must pay the taxes. As to your mare, Jack, it will always addle its living, but remember, Jack, no wages.' It was not his wish for him to work or do any thing else except attend to the droves & looking after the men. My father did ride many miles to meet the droves.

I have always lived with father, but for ¾ of a year before he left Blacka-moor. Father used to look after the droves always. I never knew my father to work, except for Mr Thorold. I have known my father to make hay, to twitch, and likewise his own work. He helped to lay some tunnells.

Thistlewood has fetched father up to the Hall.[148] I have seen Mr Thorold take the money for the droves of my father and mother many times. Mr Thorold has taken it very often when father had not had the money ½ an hour.

Cross-examined

I am 25 years old. I was fourteen years old when I left school, 11 years ago. I have always lived at home[149] except the 3 quarters when I went to Cambridge. I never was more than once at Mr Andrew's office. I have seen my father do all sorts of work, all that he was required to do. Mr Thorold in our house said he wished him to act as his foreman. Up to the time when I left he acted as foreman to Mr Thorold. Father did smoke, but not whole afternoons, nor not except when necessity called him out. Father has gone to Torksey Swan and Drinsey Nook. We had more than a drove a week. We have been up for 8 nights at a time, mother and I, to let the drovers go to bed. My father was in the house sitting up, as we had no more beds. We had 7 beds; they slept 2, making 14. We have sat up before. The drovers generally bring their own tobacco. There are ma[n]y drovers that don't drink. I have given them a glass of gin. I have known my father to put droves on other peoples' ground – on Mr Harrison's plot – I do not recollect any body else – and this was by Mr T's wish. According to where the cattle is, so is tenting required. We used to charge for dinner 8d & some dinners only 3d. Many would come who did not drink ale. Some nights when we have been up, father has gone up to see whether the men on duty were watching. My father paid [f.28] the half

---

148   After the death of Thorold's father in 1836, his mother moved to London and Thorold moved into Harmston Hall; the exact date is uncertain. Possibly the witness is referring to very recent events, or possibly she means the Manor House.

149   Rough copy has, implausibly, 'Has worked for Mr Thorold ever since, except …'.

for Mr Thorold. My mother used to take the money for ale. We got ale from Mr Winn's. I think the cellar will hold 4 barrels. We don't always get 4 barrels in. I don't know what quantity was consumed. Sometimes my brother fetched the ale with the mare and cart, but we always sent for it. Mother has been for it. I can't say how often. When the bankers were there we had it more frequently. I do not know how much they drank; they have gone. My father did not go every Friday; he went to sell a cow. I know he was helping in the tunnell. Thistlewood is my brother-in-law. I knew they were going sometimes with the money (sometimes they met Benjamin)[150] if Mr Thorold or some one else did not come.

Re-examined

John Harrison was at Blackamoor this year. Mr Hales, a farmer, and him began to talk about this dispute. He actually said he knew nothing about it and would not know any thing. I heard him repeat the same thing last week at Thistlewood's house. Mr Lamb told Mr Harrison that he had heard the same words as Lamb had himself. He made no reply. I can't remember.

Re-examined

I mean by 'usual way' that Mr Thorold intended my father was not to pay for the cows. I have heard father and Mr Thorold talk and have heard Mr Thorold say that Father was to have a guinea a week & his cows kept and his mare, in our house. Mother did not want to go to Blackamoor. Thorold said to father: 'You are as bad as Thistlewood, you are tied to your wife's apron strings'. He often came to my father's house to get him to go to Blackamoor. My brother Henry, I believe, was in the house when Mr Thorold spoke about the first agreement. The bill produced is George's handwriting.

[f.29]

Slater re-examined

I have heard what Catton has said & I can't deny the truth of it. I was put in for saying a man was a poacher. I do not wish to contradict any word I said yesterday: it is all true.

Geo Catton

Slater has slept with me more than once. I never told him any thing about

---

[150] Thorold's eldest son.

the agreement between my father and Mr Thorold. I never heard him say to me any thing that I recollect. We never had any conversation about the good situation my father was in by being at the Blackamoor. He never said it was a good job. I never said so to Slater, but I have said it would not be a good job for my father if he did not get the money for the beer that the bankers were drinking. Mr Mills was the person who paid me for the beer.

Slater

repeated what he had before stated. I will positively swear that Catton did not say so more than once. I never talked to Sibsey about this affair. I never had any conversation about this business – not about the beer. Sibsey asked me if I had heard Catton say any thing about the beer, and before that period I never had any conversation with Sibsey upon any other matter connected with Catton and Thorold.

Henry Catton

I have had some conversation with Slater this morning & he told me he knew nothing of Catton and Thorold's agreement.

Slater

I did say so. I did not think he was asking about the beer.

L. Fieldsend re-examined

Mr Thorold came to me with Catton & said he had let the house to Catton for £10 a year. Before that the parish had disputed the right to grant him a licence. Catton told me he had taken the house but did not say the rent.

[f.30 – sheets of a different paper fixed by a pin to a blank folio]
[Danby's Summing-up]
Never in the course of any proceedings to which I have been witness – and I trust I shall never again in my professional career – meet with a case more involved in intricacy than the present, nor yet one where the testimony and evidence of the witnesses is more conflicting & opposed and from which it is very evident, notwithstanding the notice of the nature and solemnity of an oath which you were pleased fully to explain to certain of the parties, yet its sacred bonds appear to have been broken. Doubtless the parties were actuated by anxious wishes for success but by your ingenuity I rest satisfied of your being capable of sifting the truth from the falsehood.

5. Ale bill, February 1832

Mr B. H. Thorold Junr To John Catton 1832

January 30	Left to pay in the old bill	£4	12s	0d
do	To 29 quarts at 6d per qt	£0	14s	6d
31	To 30 quarts at do	£0	15s	0d
Feb 1	To 29 quarts at do	£0	14s	6d
2	To 28 quarts at do	£0	14s	0d
3	To 30 quarts at do	£0	15s	0d
4	To 27 quarts at do	£0	13s	6d
Item	4 quarts to cod and raby for daming	£0	2s	0d
6	To 29 quarts the men at the brant	£0	14s	6d
do	To 2 quarts to baker and hadkin	£0	1s	0d
7	To 28 quarts at the brant	£0	14s	0d
8	To 36 quarts at do	£0	18s	0d
9	To 43 quarts at do	£1	1s	6d
10	To 43 quarts at do	£1	1s	6d
11	To 43 quarts at do	£1	1s	6d
Item	Item 2 quarts to cod for minding the dam	£0	1s	0d
13	To 42 quarts at the brant	£1	1s	0d
14	To 40 quarts at do	£1	0s	0d
15	To 41 quarts at do	£1	0s	6d
16	To 43 quarts at do	£1	1s	6d
do	To 6 quarts for watching the dam	£0	3s	0d
17	To 37 quarts the men at the brant	£0	18s	6d
18	To 42 quarts at do	£1	1s	0d
do	To 2 quarts to cod for watching the dam	£0	1s	0d
20	To 36 quarts the men at the brant	£0	18s	0d
21	To 39 quarts at do	£0	19s	6d
22	To 40 quarts at do	£1	0s	0d
	carried forward	£23	17s	6d

[verso]

	brought over	£23	17s	6d
23	To 10½ quarts at the brant	£0	5s	3d
do	To 2 quart for Crembling the pump	£0	1s	0d
24	To 6 quarts at the brant	£0	3s	0d
25	To 9 quarts at do	£0	4s	6d
		£24	11s	3d
	Received in part	£10	0s	0d
	Remainds due to J Catton	£14	11s	3d

6. Fuller ale bill

Account of Ale sold by Mr Catton to Mr Thorold

1832	Ale on Bridge building		11s	6d
1832	Bankers	£29	11s	3d
1832	J Spalding	£2	11s	8d
	Bankers	£11	11s	6d
	Private Bill	£17	2s	0d
	William Hodgson		10s	0d
1830 Aug	Grass pints		5s	0d
	Bankers	£14	15s	0d
Feb 1832	Spalding	£2	3s	2d
	Shueing Ale	£1	2s	6d
May 1832	Bankers	£8	15s	0d
May 1832	Bankers	£17	10s	3d
	Brickmakers	£21	10s	5d
	Bankers	£17	[deleted]	
	Bankers	£14	11s	3d
		£142	10s	1d

7. 1830 Drove Account

[laid paper, w/mk CLARKE]

[Recto]

Mr David Haston Drove, Agust 23rd 1830

1 Drove 7 Score at 4s per Score	£1	8s	0d

Mr Lambert Stubs drove Agust 23, 1831

2 Drove 7 Score	£1	0s	0d
Mr Johnson 6 Score @ 3s per score	£0	18s	0d
Sheep men 600 @ 6d per Score	£0	15s	0d

	1 Drove	£1	8s	0d
	2 Drove	£1	0s	0d
	3 Droves	£0	18s	0d
	4 [Dro]ves	£0	15s	0d
		£4	1s	0d
	Laeft	£0	3s	6d
	Gres pints	£0	2s	6d
	Water	£0	2s	0d
	Gres pints	£0	2s	6d
			10s	6d

	£4	1s	0d
	£0	10s	6d
Remains due	£3	10s	6d

[*verso*]

7 Score Beast	£1	8s	0d
6 Score Beast	£1	0s	0d
6 Score Beast	£0	18s	0d
600 Hundread Sheep		15s	0d
	£4	1s	0d
	£0	10s	6d
Remainds due	£3	10s	6d

[*Verso (turned round, different hand)*]

Mr Smith	5 score –	15s 0d	
__ Robinson	10 score	£1 10s 0d	
			£2 5s 0d
Grass pints	10 men	2s 6d	
			£2 2s 6d

8. 1834 Drove Account

Account of droves from June 18 to December 9, 1834

June 18	Mr Pagin, 9 Schore	£1	4s	0d
19	3 Horses 2 nights		3s	0d
21	40 of Cimmicals[151] Beast		7s	0d
24	35 of James Nichols		5s	6d
28	8 Schore of Mr Hopes	£1	4s	0d
July 3	11 Horses 1 Night		8s	0d
16	Lot of Sheep in the cows close		8s	6d
do	40 Beast of Jolleys		9s	0d
do	6 Schore of do	£1	1s	0d
do	10 Schore of do	£1	10s	0d
[Aug?] 15	Sheep in the rod[152] closes		10s	0d
20	3 Schore of Beast		7s	6d
21	40 Beast in the home paddock		7s	0d
do	6 Schore of Mr Parks		18s	0d

---

151 Carmichael's.
152 road.

24	Lot of sheep in the rod closes		12s	0d
26	Lot of Beast in the home close	£1	1s	0d
Sep 3	38 sheep in paddock		1s	0d
4	14 Schor of Mack Ginn's	£1	10s	0d
9	400 Sheep in the paddock		10s	0d
22	Sheep about the house		17s	6d
24	Lot of Beast		10s	0d
Oct 7	Rob's Beast in newing	£1	0s	0d
10	James Farginson 11 Schor	£1	13s	0d
12	Cimmicals Beast		12s	0d
13	11 Schore of Jolleys in newing	£1	13s	0d
do	Sheep about the house		6s	0d
16	Lot of sheep in the paddock		3s	4d
20	James Scott 4 Schore		16s	0d
Nov 4	11 Schore of Mr Frenches	£2	0s	0d
11	5 Schore in newing		15s	0d
23	3 Schore Beast in the rod closes		5s	0d
Dec 6	Sheep in ditto		3s	6d
9	Mack Bain 4 Schore		6s	0d
do	6 Schore @ ditto		9s	0d
		£24	5s	10d
	Received in par of money	£5	0s	0d
	Remainds due to B. H. Thorold	£19	5s	10d

9. 1836 Drove Account (Figure 12)

B.H. Thorold's Bill

April 1	Lot of Cimmicals Beast at gras	10s	0d
do	30 Beast at ditto	4s	0d
18	Lot of ditto	10s	0d
do	Lot of sheep in the paddocks	5s	0d
May 6	3 Schore at 3s per schore	9s	0d
do	100 of sheep	2s	6d
7	Duckworth 500 sheep @ 2s per hundred	10s	0d
12	3 Schore beast @ 3s per Schore	9s	0d
18	Mr Morrinson 100 Beast	18s	0d
21	David Harston 3 Schore @ 3s	9s	0d
28	Mack donnil[153] 300 sheep	9s	6d

[153] Macdonald.

June 7	Lot of sheep		6s	0d
do	4 horses 1 night		2s	0d
16	Lot of Beast in the paddocks		5s	0d
22	6 Schore of Beast at 2s6d per schore		15s	0d
23	6 Schore of Beast at ditto		15s	0d
do	Received of Thomas Towers for Beast @ turnips		10s	0d
do	old nim died and sould to G Raby for		13s	0d
July *	Mr Morrinson 6 score @	3s	18s	0d
*	Mr Millars beast		16s	0d
*	Lot of sheep in the rod closes	£1	0s	0d
	Lot in the home paddocks		12s	0d
Sep 24	Lot in the paddocks		8s	0d
28	Lot of beast in the newing[154]		10s	0d
Oct 8	James Scott 5 Schore in newing			
	an 3 Schore in rod closes	£1	0s	0d
9	Mr John Walker 5 Schore @ 2s6d		12s	6d
10	Mr Hope 6 Schore @ 3s		18s	0d
do	James Millars 7 Schore @ 3s	£1	1s	0d
30	Sold 8 ston of hay @ 6d[155] per ston		4s	0d
do	6 Schore sheep @ 6d		3s	0d
Nov 2	Lot of beast in newing		15s	0d
3	Lot in rod closes		10s	0d
10	Robinson 2 days with 4 Schore	£1	0s	0d
20	10 Beast at Agist, 4 weaks @ 1s per head	£2	0s	0d
do	50 beast of John Walkers in newing 2 nights		5s	0d
22	Meg griar[156] 4 Schore at 2s		8s	0d
Dec 5, '36	Beast hay & grass		10s	0d
	[Total]	£21	10s	6d

1836[157]

<hr>

154 New Ing.
155 Original reads '6s'.
156 McGregor?
157 Pencil note in a different hand.

INDEX OF PERSONS AND PLACES

References to illustrations are in bold.

INDEX OF SUBJECTS